Literary Theory and Criticism

by Steven J. Venturino, PhD

ALPHA

A member of Penguin Group (USA) Inc.

ALPHA BOOKS

Published by the Penguin Group

Penguin Group (USA) Inc., 375 Hudson Street, New York, New York 10014, USA • Penguin Group (Canada), 90 Eglinton Avenue East, Suite 700, Toronto, Ontario M4P 2Y3, Canada (a division of Pearson Penguin Canada Inc.) • Penguin Books Ltd., 80 Strand, London WC2R 0RL, England • Penguin Ireland, 25 St. Stephen's Green, Dublin 2, Ireland (a division of Penguin Books Ltd.) • Penguin Group (Australia), 250 Camberwell Road, Camberwell, Victoria 3124, Australia (a division of Pearson Australia Group Pty. Ltd.) • Penguin Books India Pvt. Ltd., 11 Community Centre, Panchsheel Park, New Delhi—110 017, India • Penguin Group (NZ), 67 Apollo Drive, Rosedale, North Shore, Auckland 1311, New Zealand (a division of Pearson New Zealand Ltd.) • Penguin Books (South Africa) (Pty.) Ltd., 24 Sturdee Avenue, Rosebank, Johannesburg 2196, South Africa • Penguin Books Ltd., Registered Offices: 80 Strand, London WC2R 0RL, England

Copyright © 2013 by Alpha Books

International Standard Book Number: 978-1-61564-241-0

Library of Congress Catalog Card Number: 2012949208

15   14   13   8   7   6   5   4   3   2   1

Interpretation of the printing code: The rightmost number of the first series of numbers is the year of the book's printing; the rightmost number of the second series of numbers is the number of the book's printing. For example, a printing code of 13-1 shows that the first printing occurred in 2013.

Printed in the United States of America

Note: This publication contains the opinions and ideas of its author. It is intended to provide helpful and informative material on the subject matter covered. It is sold with the understanding that the author and publisher are not engaged in rendering professional services in the book. If the reader requires personal assistance or advice, a competent professional should be consulted.

The author and publisher specifically disclaim any responsibility for any liability, loss, or risk, personal or otherwise, which is incurred as a consequence, directly or indirectly, of the use and application of any of the contents of this book.

Most Alpha books are available at special quantity discounts for bulk purchases for sales promotions, premiums, fund-raising, or educational use. Special books, or book excerpts, can also be created to fit specific needs.

For details, write: Special Markets, Alpha Books, 375 Hudson Street, New York, NY 10014.

Publisher: *Mike Sanders*

Executive Managing Editor: *Billy Fields*

Senior Acquisitions Editor: *Tom Stevens*

Senior Development Editor: *Megan Douglass*

Senior Production Editor: *Kayla Dugger*

Copy Editor: *Amy Borrelli*

Cover Designer: *William Thomas*

Book Designers: *William Thomas, Rebecca Batchelor*

Indexer: *Brad Herriman*

Layout: *Ayanna Lacey*

Proofreader: *Virginia Vought*

Contents

Introduction

Learning about literary theory and criticism opens doors to dozens of topics, from pop culture and psychology to philosophy, history, and science. And each discussion begins with the books you already love—or have yet to discover. *This* book is designed to help you make the most out of the literature you read and even the movies you watch.

The Complete Idiot's Guide to Literary Theory and Criticism will also introduce you to a fascinating range of approaches to literary interpretation, from Plato's cranky (but thoughtful) complaint that literature is bad for you, to the most recent trends in understanding literature as a part of our cultural and even environmental interactions. Along the way, you'll find step-by-step, conversational explanations of each perspective.

This book has been prepared with several types of readers in mind. Book club and reading group members will find that each chapter offers accessible, thought-provoking insights for discussing any literary work you choose. Throughout this book, I'll suggest some specific examples and questions for your consideration, but the real value is bringing your own interests into dialogue with any of the literary critics and approaches you'll read about. For students of literature, film, philosophy, and sociology (as well as their teachers), this book is intended as an authoritative and lively summary of issues important to your studies.

I had two other types of readers in mind as I wrote this book as well. One is the reader who is also a writer (or would-be writer)—one of the best-kept secrets of literary theory is that by reading about it, you are also being let in on many of the "tricks of the trade" that writers have used successfully for generations.

And then there's the "ordinary" reader. How are you? Here's a book that requires no previous training in literary studies. If you're an active reader, you've already experienced many of the concepts covered in this book, but without the technical terms. This book is designed to help you explore some of these issues in more depth. I hope you'll also find that recent literature can charge older theories with new relevance and that newer theories shed fresh light on classic works.

No matter what your interests, you can read this book straight through, or start at any point that interests you and design your own path through the chapters. I've included plenty of cross-references to indicate how some key concepts and questions are debated within the book by various critics.

How This Book Is Organized

The Complete Idiot's Guide to Literary Theory and Criticism is divided into six parts:

Part 1, Basic Ingredients and Useful Terms, sets out the central issues and concepts that you'll find running through this book, followed by a quick review of the most relevant literary terms for anyone learning about theory and criticism.

Part 2, In Theory, How Do You Read?, explores what "reading" has meant to some of the most important literary critics, from Aristotle to the present. And we consider how their methods of reading can add to your own literary experiences.

Part 3, What Is Literature, Anyway?, dives into theories of literature's very nature. What's it made of? How does it work? What's at stake when you read? These chapters explore how literature has been defined, and how literature has been linked to the other arts and to human nature itself.

Part 4, Hey, Whose Book Is This?, examines the importance of community perspective when it comes to interpreting literature. These chapters survey the theories and critical methods developed in opposition to a one-size-fits-all perspective.

Part 5, Try to Watch Your Language, considers the complex intersection between literature, language, and thought. The chapters in this part explore cultural, psychological, and philosophical dimensions of interpretation.

Part 6, In the World and Of the World, considers the central importance that history and society have always played in literary appreciation and interpretation. These chapters remind us of the importance of what literature does, as well as what it means.

Extras

As you read, you'll see helpful boxes, or sidebars, appearing in each chapter. Each sidebar contributes to what is being discussed on that particular page in any of the following ways:

DEFINITION

These sidebars provide concise definitions of terms important to literary theory and criticism.

IN THEORY

These sidebars offer direct quotations from the critics themselves, as well as occasional bits of background information on them.

RELATIONS

These sidebars include cross-references alerting you to interesting connections between theories, critics, and other topics.

APPLY IT

These sidebars suggest hands-on ways of applying the literary theory you're reading about.

Acknowledgments

This book would not have appeared without the help and professionalism of Tom Stevens and Megan Douglass at Alpha Books. I would also like to thank Micael M. Clarke, Thomas Kaminski, and Timothy Wager for early support and advice. Last and most, thanks to KMZ.

For readers interested in the single best anthology of Plato-to-present literary theory, seek out David H. Richter's *The Critical Tradition*, with its miraculous headnotes. And for lively in-depth discussions of theory in general, I recommend anything written by Raman Selden.

A note on the quotations placed throughout this book: I've included many brief quotations from a variety of theorists themselves in an effort to give you a real sense of the voices of literary theory and criticism, and to show you how engaging it can be to read the original texts. In the case of quotations not originally appearing in English, the work of the following translators has been used: B. Brewster (Althusser); Leon Golden (Aristotle); Caryl Emerson and Michael Holquist (Bakhtin); Stephen Heath and Annette Lavers (Barthes); Harry Zohn (Benjamin); H. M. Parshley (Beauvoir); Richard Macksey, Eugenio Donato, and Gayatri Chakravorty Spivak (Derrida); I. R. Titunk (Eichenbaum); Constance Farrington (Fanon); Josué Harari,

Robert Hurley, and A. M. Sheridan Smith (Foucault); A. A. Brill, I. F. Grant-Duff, and James Strachey (Freud); John Cumming (Horkheimer and Adorno); R. F. C. Hull (Jung); Alan Sheridan (Lacan); Claire Jacobson and Brooke Grundfest Schoepf (Lévi-Strauss); J. and N. Mander (Lukács); Robert C. Tucker and Foreign Language Publishing of Moscow (Marx); Lane Cooper and Benjamin Jowett (Plato); Wade Baskin (Saussure); and Lee T. Lemon and Marion J. Reis (Shklovsky).

Special Thanks to the Technical Reviewer

The Complete Idiot's Guide to Literary Theory and Criticism was reviewed by an expert who double-checked the accuracy of what you'll learn here, to help us ensure that this book gives you everything you need to know about literary theory. Special thanks are extended to Jonathan K. Cohen, MA.

Trademarks

All terms mentioned in this book that are known to be or are suspected of being trademarks or service marks have been appropriately capitalized. Alpha Books and Penguin Group (USA) Inc. cannot attest to the accuracy of this information. Use of a term in this book should not be regarded as affecting the validity of any trademark or service mark.

Basic Ingredients and Useful Terms

The two chapters in this part introduce all the basic issues and terms you'll need to start getting the most out of this book.

You'll first learn what theory and criticism are, how to tell them apart, and then how to put them together again. You'll also read about the essential questions that critics have been asking and answering for centuries. After that, we'll run through eight literary terms that are indispensable for bringing theory and criticism to life in your own reading experiences.

It's Just a Theory

In This Chapter

- Making sense of things
- Theory meets criticism
- Writers and their sneaky ways
- The words on the page
- Critics and the world

What does "meaning" mean? Is it given, found, or made? What's the difference between what a literary work *means* and what it *does?* Will I ever finish *The Brothers Karamazov?* Literature has always raised questions like these. And many, many more.

In fact, people have responded so differently to literature that the phrase "literary theory and criticism" has become a handy way of grouping together in one place a lot of different things that might not look like they belong together. Like a salad bar. Sure, you'll find things you expect, like lettuce and tomatoes, but then right next to the carrot sticks you'll see ham, lentils, and chicken tenders. It doesn't matter what's there; if it's on the salad bar, it's salad, so grab a plate and load up.

Compare that to literature. You take a novel, for example, and load it up with all kinds of thoughts, questions, expectations, and judgments. Some of these seem to fit as naturally into a literary discussion as lettuce does in a salad, while others seem to come from a completely different, well, course.

Still, whatever comes to your mind and all of your reactions to the novel end up being part of theory and criticism. You're creating theory and criticism as you read—and so are other people. And just as often as you look at someone else's plate and think "How can you eat that?!," you also glance around and think, "Maybe I'll try that next time."

This book lets you explore all the options, from lettuce to lentils, so you can decide what works best.

You Can't Help It

People are meaning-making machines. We can't seem to help it; when we see (or hear, touch, taste, smell, or sense) something we *read* it, we try to make sense of it. So while some of the theories and critical approaches discussed in this book may seem wildly complicated or strangely imaginative, keep mind that they all spring from the same urge to find meaning in what we experience.

Even the activity of "just reading" or "just watching a movie" provokes theory and criticism, since you're always, at some level, organizing and explaining what you read and see, and you always have an approach—even if it just seems natural. One of the goals of this book is to help make your own response to literature more critical and to help you become more aware of the meaning-making processes that literature inspires.

IN THEORY

"We are always talking theory whether we know it or not." —Gerald Graff

So how many of you out there are architects or botanists? Okay, got it. Now how many of you have seen buildings or flowers? Okay, now those in the first group, you go ahead and explain that your specialized knowledge doesn't keep you from appreciating a beautiful building or stopping to smell the roses. In fact, knowing something about the structural and design principles of a building or the life process of a flower probably makes you more appreciative of what you see.

This will be the case with any set of experiences and skills. Plumbers, doctors, lawyers, knitters—everyone has a critical approach to bring to their reading. Anyone can spot some detail or aspect of a story that others might miss or think unimportant. One consequence of learning about literary theory and criticism is developing a heightened sense of how literature works and what it does.

So will this take all the fun out of reading? No, I say! And why do I say that? Because you picked up this book, which suggests you're the type of person who doesn't mind raising your consciousness about your meaning-making self.

Or take Mark Twain as another case in point. In his autobiographical book *Life on the Mississippi* (1883), Twain describes the complex process of learning how to be a riverboat pilot. After months of training that transformed what he used to see as a beautiful but mysterious river into a working, technical sense of what goes on below the surface, Twain bids farewell to his innocence, sighing, "All the grace, the beauty, the poetry, had gone out of the majestic river!" What then follows is one of the most beautiful descriptions of the Mississippi ever written, followed by another sigh, "No, the romance and the beauty were all gone from the river." Twain then wraps up the whole ironic lesson by humbly suggesting that it takes a trained riverboat pilot to truly describe the beauty and mystery of a river. The river became more beautiful because of what he had learned, and Twain discovered that his knowledge would even help him share his experiences with others.

So Which Is It, Theory or Criticism?

Theory organizes and explains, while criticism does all the analysis, interpretation, and evaluation. And yet …

… And yet, theory and criticism are often referred to at the same time because of the way they always interact. Theories lead to critical approaches and critical approaches are needed to create new theories. So while it's generally okay to think of theory as an abstract plan or prediction, and criticism as the resulting practice, you'll find throughout this book many examples that illustrate how theory and criticism are both actively connected in your experience of literature.

Getting Some Perspective

Theory comes from the Greek word for a mental conception that gives you a particular view of something. The word *theater* is related to the same Greek word, which suggests how theories position you as a spectator; they give you a way of seeing things, of taking everything in. In literary theory, this generally happens in two ways. One is by describing a scheme or plan that suggests how literature should be produced; another is by setting out the principles underlying literature itself.

These two aspects—prescription and description—are often mingled as well, since it's tough to separate what we think of as artistically proper from what we think of as objectively true. As we'll see throughout this book, however, theory in any form describes the assumptions that get you from one logical point to another when you think about literature. Theory *informs* your reading behavior; that is, it influences your view of what counts as literature and guides your interpretations. Theory provides a way of accounting for the details of what you read—it tries to explain why they're there and what they do.

Consider the definition of theory as a description of the underlying principles at work in literature. As we'll see in the chapters to come, critics have been fascinated not only by what literature means, but why it *acts* the way it does. What is it about literature, for example, that makes some plots, character types, and images endlessly repeatable? Does literature follow rules, and if so, where do they come from?

Some critics take a very deep look, suggesting that literary theory isn't exclusively about literature at all, but about all of human nature. Literature, according to these critics, reflects or participates in a bigger picture. As we'll see in Chapters 9 and 10, for example, Marxism and Freudian psychology are examples of theories developed to systematically account for all of history and the nature of the human mind. From these perspectives, literature and art inevitably reflect the underlying principles that are also at work in every other aspect of life.

Suspicious Minds

Criticism is related to the Greek term for judge, and this association is clear when you describe criticism as fault-finding, negative judgment, and the evaluation or even ranking of literary works. But literary criticism actually emphasizes analysis, comparison, and interpretation rather than strict judgment. Criticism, as we'll see throughout this book, works through critical approaches, which are the perspectives or methods for addressing literature.

Critical approaches can help illustrate a particular literary theory by showing how a theory adequately accounts for details of a literary work. On the other hand, criticism often challenges theories by calling attention to features that can't be accounted for by an existing perspective.

The term *critique* is useful in emphasizing the distance, or thoughtful space, you can put between any theory and your own experience. Taking a critical stance—that is, not taking things for granted—means looking at things closely, and recognizing that literary works may have meanings and effects that demand correction and even condemnation. As we'll see in Chapter 12, for example, feminist critics have long recognized the oppressive character of traditional male-centered perspectives, including those in literature. In such cases as this, and in many others, critique leads to new theories.

Do Writers Know All This Stuff?

It's a good question. Do writers know about literary theory when they write, and do they intend for you to pick up on certain features or even "hidden messages"? You probably won't be surprised that the answer is "yes and no."

The "yes" part comes from that aspect of writing and reading that Twain mentioned. That is, the more you know about something the more sensitively you can appreciate and describe it. Writers, with or without formal training, recognize literary styles and techniques as elements they can copy, manipulate, improve upon, and even ignore, as they create new literary works.

The Victorian poet and critic Matthew Arnold, whom we'll discuss in Chapter 19, argued that literary criticism could (in fact, he insisted that it *should*) help guide a writer's creativity by providing it with "an intellectual situation of which the creative power can profitably avail itself."

And as we'll see in Chapter 14, Toni Morrison explained that her entire approach to reading literature changed when she "stopped reading as a reader and began to read as a writer." What she meant was that her experiences as a writer gave her insight into what other writers were doing in their works, rather like an architect looking at buildings. In a wonderful twist, Morrison then explained that what writers (including herself) are often doing is working out issues that they are not fully conscious of.

IN THEORY

"To ask of what an author is conscious and of what unconscious is as fruitless as to ask which rules of English are consciously employed by speakers and which are followed unconsciously." —Jonathan Culler

In fact, many critics we'll discuss in this book argue that what writers do is the product of unconscious mastery of the styles, techniques, rules, and codes that structure all stories. As we'll see in several chapters, the situation is compared to speaking a language—you can talk all day because you've internalized the rules of grammar, even if you couldn't actually explain those rules. In fact, as we'll see in Chapter 20, Stephen Greenblatt has suggested that great writers have a heightened sense of the grammar of "cultural codes" and are "specialists in cultural exchange."

So you can expect to see some of the critics in this book focusing on the role of the writer or the source of a literary work. Some argue for the author's active, conscious role in creating a literary work, and some look into the unconscious or social forces that prove "one unified person" is never the true source of a literary work.

Stick to the Script

And what about that literary work? What's it doing there, and what are you supposed to do with it? The answers seem obvious—you're supposed to read and interpret it—but they lead to more questions. Are you reading it to discover the author's point? Are you looking for insights into the author's soul? Do you want to uncover influences and draw connections to other works? How about the text's own inner, timeless truth? Do you read to reinforce your personality, change yourself, or explore the effect of literature on society?

Well, whatever you want to do, you're in luck, because there's a theory and a critical approach to support you in any of these endeavors, and more.

Essentially, though, questions of how to approach literature all come down to what you think literature is in the first place. Literary critics don't just disagree with each other regarding interpretations, they disagree over how literature itself should be defined. And this is a very good thing, since writers have never agreed, either.

IN THEORY

"A book is not shut in by its contours, is not walled up as in a fortress. It asks nothing better than to exist outside itself, or to let you exist in it. In short, the extraordinary fact in the case of a book is the falling away of the barriers between you and it. You are inside it; it is inside you; there is no longer either inside or outside." —Georges Poulet

As we'll see throughout this book, but particularly in the chapters of Part 3, theory and criticism help you see literature in different ways. For example, one huge question regarding all art is whether it should be seen as imitation or expression. Should you read a novel, that is, as a reflection of reality or as the expression of the author's feelings or point of view?

If you're interested in the expressive nature of a novel and you push the question a bit further, you have to wonder where those feelings and points of view come from. Do writers express themselves as individuals, or do they express social, cultural, or political points of view? For that matter, are writers really in control of the language they use, or is language itself actually leading the way?

Looking critically at any literary work, therefore, means linking questions of the author, the work, and—as we'll see next—the reader. How you form these links is what theory and criticism is all about. In fact, because of all the linking and interconnections that literature provokes, critics often use the term *text* to describe a literary work, because text, like *textile*, indicates the interweaving that faces you when you try to isolate one or two threads of any aspect of literature. And if you haven't gotten enough of that metaphor, don't worry, because as we'll see in Chapter 17, there's a whole theory behind the distinction between a "work" and a "text." You'll like it; you can make up your own texting jokes.

Real Worlds and Real Words

And then there's the real world. It's part of the interconnected nature of literature, too, of course. Many critics see very little difference, in fact, between reading literature and reading anything else in the world. For some critics, as we'll see, everything we perceive is part of a giant textual interweaving.

Yet no matter how you relate the literary to the nonliterary (if there is such a thing), there's no denying the very real history of literature's effects on human society. The critics discussed in this book (some of whom are also writers of poetry, prose, and drama) embody a wide range of triumph and tragedy in literary history. As we'll see, the dynamic relationship between literature and the world has been a force for both progress and persecution, and many critics have devoted their lives to demonstrating how critical analysis can promote the one over the other. In fact, for some critics, it's the human tendency to confuse progress with persecution that demands new theories of literature and society.

The importance of literary theory and criticism starts with the fact that we make sense of the world and everything in it through images, metaphors, and stories. Critics are readers like you, interested in how this meaning-making occurs. One of the tricks of literature, of course, is that like any art it seems to be happening all at once. That is, literary works often strike us as products rather than processes. Theory and criticism offers a variety of methods for getting at the processes that are part of any literary work's past, present, and future.

Gertrude Stein once wrote about the difficulty she was having in describing a person she knew very well. Stein wanted to write truthfully about that person, but realized how strange it was going to be to transform the knowledge and feelings that she held in her mind "all at once" into a narrative description that would demand time to write and to read. Then she realized that she had in fact acquired all of her familiarity of this person over time as well, so the only unusual part of the whole thing was her feeling that she held knowledge of her friend "all at once" in her mind. So Stein simply accepted both aspects as truths to cherish. She could feel her knowledge and experiences all at once *and* she could create a narrative that would start the whole process over again for her readers. Stein called it "making a whole present of something that it had taken a great deal of time to find out."

In the chapters that follow, you'll have a chance to explore dozens of ideas, theories, and stories. The material in some chapters might seem to blend right in with whatever you're reading (or watching) at the time, while other chapters offer ideas and questions that you may just want to think about for their own sake.

Learning about theory and criticism means finding out how *physical* literature is. All those timeless ideas emanating from novels, poems, plays, and movies take time to develop and then to recall. Theoretical perspectives and critical approaches are just asking for you to perform them. Most critics think that when you do, you'll find your sense of knowing a work or an idea "all at once" doesn't disappear, it just gets some company.

The Least You Need to Know

- People will make meaning out of anything.
- Theory is a way of seeing things; criticism is an approach to analysis and interpretation. Each influences the other.
- Writers have varying levels of awareness of and concern for literary theory.
- Critics describe the very nature of literature in differing ways.
- For some critics, literary theory and criticism is about changing the world.

What's the Word for That, Again?

In This Chapter

- The dance of content and form
- How stories get organized
- What those fictional people do
- How details make it happen

I could say there are hundreds—literally hundreds—of literary terms that you'll need to know before exploring theory and criticism. But I have a very high respect for your time, so instead I'll say there are just eight terms to think about.

Why eight? Because when you read literature, your experience really revolves around a select number of key concepts. And it's these concepts, always interacting and overlapping, that actually account for the variety of drama, humor, suspense, and subtlety of what you read. With each term I'll preview issues that we'll be discussing in later chapters. Revisiting these terms is already a valuable form of practicing literary theory because it raises your awareness of your own reading experience.

Two Sides of the Coin

First up are two terms that always go together: theme and form. We'll talk about them one at a time, but only for the sake of explanation. Otherwise, keep in mind that they always go together. They positively blend into each other. Form and theme can be compared to the common expression "form and content," but with a difference. If you think of *form* as a glass, and *content* as water, then you can see how the two might be separated. In literature, as we'll see, form and theme are combined in such a way that you can't change one without also changing the other. Each side, or dimension, depends on the other in creating a unique literary work.

Theme

Theme describes what you believe a literary work or movie is really about. A theme is not exactly the subject matter of a work, but the work's main concern or even main question. When you talk about theme, you can also use terms like *central idea*, *controlling idea*, or even the work's *statement*.

This gives you rather a lot of room to work with. A theme can be general ("*Frankenstein* is about creation") or more specific ("*Frankenstein* is about how complicated creation is"). Sometimes a theme seems to be stated very clearly, rather like "the moral of the story." In *The Wizard of Oz*, for example, Dorothy says that what she's learned from her experience is that "there's no place like home." She's directly stating the theme of her story, as she sees it. The theme of the movie is simple, then—it's the message that one shouldn't look for happiness anywhere but right at home.

But what if you're not buying it? What if you have a different view? Is there only one correct theme for any given story? Not at all. Most critical perspectives emphasize that identifying a theme is really an exercise in interpretation. Some interpretations seem more natural than others—and any interpretation should be supported intelligently—but any time you talk about the theme of a work, you're really talking about the work's central idea as you see it. This is the case when you state, "It's clear that Mark Twain's *The Adventures of Huckleberry Finn* explores the hypocrisy of so-called 'civilization.'"

APPLY IT

Consider two different literary works that have similar themes. What are their specific thematic issues? Regarding a central issue or question, could you consider one of the works to be a response or a complement to the other?

You should see any theme as an idea or statement that unifies the story. A theme suggests how all of the work's parts fit together, or how they elaborate on a central concern.

Since talking about theme gives you a broad range of possible issues to consider, you'll want to keep the adjective *thematic* handy. This is simply another way of referring to an issue that you think of as central to the work. "Yes, well," you can say, "Dorothy's direct statement is fine for a general moral of the story, but I think there are even more important thematic issues at stake." And when your friend asks "Like what?", you can say, "Why, the commentary on the evils of capitalism that runs through the movie, of course. That's the thematic issue I'm most concerned about." Nicely done. Now get some snacks and explain an example or two that support your opinion.

IN THEORY

"*Frankenstein* is famously reinterpretable. It can be a late version of the Faust myth, or an early version of the modern myth of the mad scientist; the id on the rampage, the proletariat running amok, or what happens when a man tries to have a baby without a woman. Mary Shelley invites speculation." —Marilyn Butler

In this book, we'll see a wide variety of critics identifying and supporting thematic issues. Some critics see certain themes as universal, since similar myths seem to emerge across different cultures (see Chapter 16); some see themes as interpretations of psychological depth (see Chapter 10), or as emerging from readers themselves, rather than from texts (see Chapters 5 and 11); and many see themes as motivated by economic structures (see Chapter 9).

In any case, identifying the theme of a work is not the end of the story. In fact, you may find thematic issues themselves less interesting than the other elements of literature that interrelate with theme, such as plot, point of view, or figurative language. Formalist critics (see Chapters 3 and 4) recognize themes as well, but what really gets their attention are the various operations of form that literature reveals.

Form

So how do you support or illustrate your view of a thematic issue? How do you point to a literary work and show someone that what you see in it is *really* in it? You do that by pointing to what you see on the page. These are elements of form, better known as formal features. In fact, it's through formal features that you develop an understanding of theme in the first place.

The term *form* can refer to many things, from a literary work's structure, shape, or genre to the various techniques used by an author. You experience some formal features clearly and consciously, while others affect you on more subtle levels. One of the best things about literary criticism is how it can raise both your awareness and appreciation of the formal features that contribute to your experience.

Since you develop your opinions and feelings about stories as soon as you start reading, as well as when you revisit the entire story in retrospect, theme and form always exist side by side. You can't experience one without the other.

A related term, *genre*, refers to types or categories of literature, which is particularly important when it comes to expectations. That is, you come to expect certain content to be related to certain forms. With genres, the form predisposes you to prepare for a particular theme. Classical genres include tragedy, comedy, epic, and satire, while later genres include such categories as science fiction, western, romance, mystery, and detective fiction.

The next six terms we'll cover are all examples of formal features.

Order, Please

When it comes to giving shape and structure to a story, novel, or movie, one formal feature—plot—is quite well known. We'll also take a look at motif, a more subtle organizing force in stories.

Plot

Basically, plot is just what you think it is—the arrangement of incidents in a story. Not every story is told in chronological order; in fact, most stories take some kind of liberty with strict chronological order. Take any novel—is the beginning really the beginning? That is, as you read the novel, do you find flashbacks that take you back to a time "before the beginning"? Aristotle, the first expert on analyzing plots (see Chapter 6), famously said that a good story needs a beginning, a middle, and an end. Yes, sometimes the obvious makes perfectly good literary theory.

Still, Aristotle was well aware that beginnings, middles, and ends can be effectively reorganized. Many novels and movies begin *in media res*, which means "in the middle of things." This method puts you right in the midst of the action, gives you questions that must be answered with flashbacks or exposition, and sets you up for future events.

The bottom line is that a plot is rarely a step-by-step recounting of events, but the result of an author making carefully calculated choices regarding the order of those events.

APPLY IT

Some stories, novels, and movies feature rather extreme plot manipulation. You may be interested in checking out any of the following:

"An Occurrence at Owl Creek Bridge," by Ambrose Bierce (1891)

"A Rose for Emily," by William Faulkner (1930)

If on a Winter's Night a Traveler, by Italo Calvino (1979)

Time's Arrow, by Martin Amis (1992)

Pulp Fiction, directed by Quentin Tarantino (1994)

Memento, directed by Christopher Nolan (2000)

Once you've finished a novel or movie, you can reorganize all of the events into chronological order. When you do this, you've created an abstract image of the original story, an image that only exists in your mind, not on the page or screen. The Russian formalists, who thought about this kind of thing a lot (see Chapter 4), called this abstract reorganization "story-stuff," since it's like the raw material that the author organizes into the plot you see. And when you compare the events that you can infer or imagine to have happened with what the author has chosen to include and exclude, you begin to appreciate the craft of fiction.

The more you look into plot, the more you see that it isn't just one thing leading to another, but the arrangement of material into a work of art that makes you think and feel more intensely than a simple list would.

IN THEORY

"If it is in a story, we say 'and then?' If it is in the plot we ask 'why?'" —E. M. Forster

In addition to the Russian formalists, we'll see plot examined in greater depth by Aristotle and other critics in Chapter 6, and by structuralists in Chapter 16.

Motif

Motifs can be obvious and subtle. You can notice them while you read and you can be influenced by them subliminally. You can even ignore them and still feel their effects. The effect of motifs is to help make any literary work or movie more unified, more recognizable, and more distinctive.

When an image or series of similar images appear in a story, like flowers and colors do in Willa Cather's "Paul's Case," you find that you have another formal feature at work, contributing to thematic issues and to the overall effect of the story. While any detail of a story can be significant, the presence of a motif alerts you to something particularly noteworthy, such as the comparison of an image to a character. For example, the images of windows in James Baldwin's "Sonny's Blues" help "reflect" on the characters' pasts.

Characters themselves, as well as character traits, can also function as motifs. In Charles Dickens's *David Copperfield*, the character of Mr. Micawber has a way of speaking that recurs at several points in the novel. In some instances, even before we see him, we know it's Micawber by his quoted or written speech. Another motif associated with Micawber is his repetition of the phrase "something will turn up," which is a rather clear example of form and theme working together: the repeated phrase (an aspect of form) supports the theme of optimism in the face of setbacks.

Motifs can also signal plot turns or character traits, such as the repeated descriptions of the weather in *Frankenstein* and *Wuthering Heights*. A famous example from movies is the motif of the music that signals the arrival of the shark in Steven Spielberg's *Jaws*.

A related meaning of motif, which is important to literary history, is as a topic, issue, or concern that comes to be associated with a specific era or genre of literature. Nature, for example, is a common general motif for the Romantic poets (see Chapter 8), and the motif of mistaken identity can be found in many mystery novels.

Who Are These People?

Narrators and characters involve the people or presences that bring stories into the world. Narrators come in a variety of types, and characters have some surprises of their own.

Narrators

How do you know what you know when you read? I mean literally—who or what gets the words on the page? Every story relies on some kind of narrator in order to exist.

The narrator may be obvious, like a storyteller, or it may be a kind of disembodied voice or eye that reveals the story in what seems like an unremarkable way. No matter what, every story has a *point of view.*

DEFINITION

The term **point of view** loosely describes the way in which the audience comes to understand, or "see," the events of a story.

Literary narratives are generally broken down into the categories of first-person and third-person points of view. A first-person point of view usually reflects the storytelling abilities of a single person and employs the pronoun "I." The author, it's important to remember, is generally not considered the narrator, since authors, even when they sound like they're "just talking," have actually created fictional masks, or personas, for this purpose. Besides, an author is a real person, and the narrator, no matter how closely identified with the author, is made up of words on the page.

Some first-person narrators are characters in the story itself, like Nick Carraway in F. Scott Fitzgerald's *The Great Gatsby,* or Holden Caulfield in J. D. Salinger's *The Catcher in the Rye.* In fact, this type of narrator is sometimes called unreliable, because the author expects you to recognize gaps, biases, or outright misinformation present in the narrator's story. In these cases, you actively read into or through the character in order to get a bigger picture of the story than even the narrator seems to present.

IN THEORY

"If you really want to hear about it, the first thing you'll probably want to know is where I was born, and what my lousy childhood was like, and how my parents were occupied and all before they had me, and all that David Copperfield kind of crap, but I don't feel like going into it, if you want to know the truth." —J. D. Salinger, *The Catcher in the Rye*

While first-person narrators are usually limited to the observational abilities of ordinary people, third-person narrators can do all kinds of things. Some can read minds, be in many places at once, and know all about a character's past, present, and future. Such narrators sometimes exhibit what seems to be omniscience, the ability to see and know everything that's going on in a story, regardless of time and space.

Omniscience, however, is overrated (as a narrative point of view, at least) because being all-knowing can never be translated into all-telling. The artful choice and ordering of events, with its inclusions and exclusions, is always a part of storytelling. Some critics will acknowledge this with the term *limited omniscient narrator*—while the narrator has the potential to see all, it tends to limit what it reveals. I think it's just as effective for us to keep in mind that *all* third-person narrators are limited in what they do. What becomes fascinating is watching *how* the limitations are chosen and used by any particular author.

APPLY IT

A sampling of novels with interesting narrators:

The Moonstone (1868), by Wilkie Collins (multiple narrators unravel a single mystery)

The Sound and the Fury (1929) and *As I Lay Dying* (1930), by William Faulkner (stream of consciousness, multiple narrators)

The French Lieutenant's Woman (1969), by John Fowles (narrator self-consciously interacts with the characters)

My Name Is Red (1998), by Orhan Pamuk (multiple narrators)

Often, an author will limit the third-person narrator to one character's perspective. In Franz Kafka's "The Metamorphosis," the third-person narrator stays closest to the main character, Gregor Samsa. The narrator reveals Gregor's actions and thoughts, and stays with Gregor when he's alone. Most of the information you get about the other characters, therefore, comes from Gregor's point of view, even though he is not the narrator. The term for this is *focalization*. The third-person narrator focalizes through (not necessarily on) or channels a character when telling the story. Focalization leads you to ask "Who sees?" and "Who speaks?" In "The Metamorphosis," Gregor is the character who sees (and hears and feels), but it's the third-person narrator that speaks.

APPLY IT

Notice the focalization in any novel you are reading now. If the narrative is presented in the third person, which character or characters are given the star treatment? Does focalization occur through one or more characters? And—sometimes this is very telling—are there characters whose thoughts are hidden from you throughout most or all of the novel? Joseph Conrad's *The Secret Agent* makes use of focalization with great effect in scenes involving a married couple. In any given scene, the husband's feelings may be revealed, while the wife's thoughts are kept from us—until this subtle formal feature shifts, and … (you'll have to find out for yourself).

When it comes to narrators, it's essential not to think that one type is "better" than another. It isn't the case, for example, that a first-person narrative is always more personal than a third-person narrative. Because of focalization, third-person narratives are rarely objective, but reveal important biases, blind spots, and motivations, just like first-person narrators. Some third-person narratives get extremely close to the characters' thoughts and feelings, closer even than the characters themselves. The Victorian novelist George Eliot, for example, is known for the deep sympathy of her third-person narrators who blend their own "omniscience" with a character's feelings and even vocabulary.

Second-person narratives are rare, unless you're a fan of old-time radio. This narrative style consists of "you" as the narrator. This sounds something like, "Your heart is beating like a drum as you hold out your trembling hand to turn the doorknob. Has it been that long since you last saw her? Your memories spin in your head like leaves in a whirlwind, and you turn the knob …." Really, at the end of the day, this point of view can be rather hard to sustain, and it isn't everyone's favorite. Still, it's been done well—try Jay McInerney's *Bright Lights, Big City* (1984). And for a unique film experience, see *The Lady in the Lake* (directed by Robert Montgomery, 1947), and puzzle over whether the whole thing is told from the first-person point of view or the second.

Characterization

Always keep in mind that most fictional characters have two sides to their motivations. They do what they do in order to reflect human personality, and they also act as part of the overall theme. That is, characters have reality-based as well as symbolic functions. As absorbed as you may get in a character's troubles or triumphs, notice how the character's behavior contributes to the overall scheme of things.

As we'll see in Chapter 6, allegories are an extreme example of the character's symbolic function calling the shots. (When Mr. Greedy and Mr. Irritable go to dinner, you know there's going to be trouble.) But even if you're not reading an allegory like John Bunyan's *Pilgrim's Progress* (1678), with characters named Piety, Talkative, and Giant Despair, you're usually faced with characters who function as part of the work's theme. For example, a character may represent a group of people, an occupation, or a type. A character may serve as the embodiment of an idea or an era. And as we'll see in Chapter 14's discussion of Toni Morrison, a character may actually be reflecting the author's own psychological blind spots or fears.

APPLY IT

In any novel you're reading now, which characters do you see as the most lifelike, and why? Which characters seem to be serving primarily symbolic functions?

Writer and critic E. M. Forster is famous for identifying what he called "flat" and "round" characters. Round characters are fleshed out and change during the course of a literary work. Flat characters do not change, and they tend to support other characters or the plot, like background. Which is which in any given novel? Like most categories in literary criticism, these choices are easily debatable. Forster, for example, cites Mrs. Micawber in Dickens's *David Copperfield* as a classic flat character, and to that I say "Ha!" I happen to think Mrs. Micawber has some very subtle and changing human features, no matter how stable she is in her symbolic functions. Forster also calls Becky Sharp in William Thackeray's *Vanity Fair* a round character. To that I say, "Okay, sure."

No matter how they function, characters must be presented to the reader one way or another. Authors often make use of both direct and indirect characterization in any given work. Direct characterization occurs when the narrator simply tells you what a character is like. Indirect characterization means the text shows you the character doing or saying something, and it's from these external cues that you form your opinion about the character.

Writers Love Details

Hemingway once wrote that "all our words from loose using have lost their edge." Saying that phrase aloud really brings home how much writers like to mess around with language to create an effect. I'll mention more than once in this book that it's almost impossible for you to read too much into a literary work, since the author has gotten there before you and, through inspiration or careful planning—or both—has managed to set out all the details you see. Now this doesn't mean that authors interpret their works better than you do. Hemingway also wrote that "books should be judged by those who read them—not explained by the writer." Authors generally want you to do whatever you can to really notice what's on the page. They want you to love details as much as they do, and make their literature work for you.

IN THEORY

"To get the right word in the right place is a rare achievement. To condense the diffused light of a page of thought into the luminous flash of a single sentence, is worthy to rank as a prize composition just by itself …. Anybody can have ideas— the difficulty is to express them without squandering a quire of paper on an idea that ought to be reduced to one glittering paragraph." —Mark Twain

Imagery

Descriptions on the page can do more than describe things. Descriptions and images can evoke any of the five senses and even extrasensory perceptions, leaving you with strong feelings, impressions, thoughts, and even intense memories. Because of this, imagery—or concrete representation—plays a vital role in literature, contributing to theme and often to your understanding of a character.

The imagery of Bierce's "An Occurrence at Owl Creek Bridge," which appeals primarily to the eye and ear, is very carefully designed to reflect the main character's state of mind and his situation. In this case, imagery contributes to characterization and even point of view.

IN THEORY

"He closed his eyes in order to fix his last thoughts upon his wife and children. The water, touched to gold by the early sun, the brooding mists under the banks at some distance down the stream, the fort, the soldiers, the piece of drift—all had distracted him. And now he became conscious of a new disturbance. Striking through the thought of his dear ones was a sound which he could neither ignore nor understand, a sharp, distinct, metallic percussion like the stroke of a blacksmith's hammer upon the anvil; it had the same ringing quality. He wondered what it was." —Ambrose Bierce, "An Occurrence at Owl Creek Bridge"

The images of nature in Shelley's *Frankenstein* form the "natural forces" motif that contributes to your understanding of the novel's characters as well as its main themes of ambition and dual identity. One of *Frankenstein*'s several narrators even draws on Romantic imagery to consider that no one can look on such images without being affected, since "the starry sky, the sea, and every sight afforded by these wonderful regions, seems still to have the power of elevating his soul from earth. Such a man has a double existence."

Imagery and patterns of imagery have been studied very carefully in poetry, as you'll see in our discussion of the New Critics (see Chapter 3).

Figurative Language

Using language figuratively means asking readers to look beyond literal meanings and dictionary definitions and to recognize the connotations, associations, or coded meanings at work in a text. Figurative language often makes use of "figures of speech," which associate or compare one thing with another. Figures of speech are also called *tropes*, which comes from the Latin word for "turning," which is a good way of seeing figurative language—words are "turned" from their literal meanings in order to create new meanings and effects.

Metaphor is one of the most important and common tropes. Virtually every critical approach discussed in this book addresses metaphor to one degree or another, because the concept of metaphor strikes at the very heart of meaning-making. Metaphor comes from the Greek term for "transferring" or "carrying." A metaphor transfers a word from one context to another. It carries the expressive power of one situation (a word, a person, an action, and so on) over to another.

A metaphor also tends to carry the explanatory power of one situation to another. That is, metaphors are often used to help you understand something unfamiliar by comparing it to something familiar. Writers have long recognized, however, that this is not a neutral process—metaphors don't just do their "carrying" work and then disappear. And that's a good thing. The residual effects of using metaphors are what writers are counting on to help get their points or impressions across.

Recall Kafka's "The Metamorphosis," for example. The story centers around Gregor Samsa's curious situation of waking up one morning and discovering that he has turned into a huge insect. Kafka's story is an example of an extended metaphor (as well as an *allegory*), by which Kafka transfers many of the very specific qualities of this giant insect to Gregor's human situation. Why does he do this? What does the metaphor represent? For years, readers have speculated on this question and come up with all kinds of interpretations: Gregor's repulsive insectlike character is a metaphor for anything from the plight of the handicapped, the social outcast, or the victim of religious persecution to the predicament of a young man going through puberty. Which interpretation is correct? That's a question that may never be answered.

DEFINITION

An **allegory** represents an abstract idea in a storylike, concrete way. Allegories are therefore always understood to have at least two meanings—the literal and the figurative.

But if you ask why so many interpretations are not only possible but *supportable* with specific evidence in the story, the answer is fairly simple, and even humbling. It's because Kafka's story so carefully follows the logic and details of the insect's condition that readers can confidently arrange into new contexts all of the details that the metaphor has carried. Gregor's emotional weight, in particular, is carried by these details. That is, by imagining the details of Gregor's insect life, you arrive at a more powerful sympathy for his condition in real life, whatever that life may be in your particular interpretation.

Now, symbols can be distinguished from metaphors by keeping in mind that symbols tend to mean one thing in any given literary work. That is, a symbol combines two things in order to create more of a correspondence, such as scales symbolizing justice, or "xoxo" symbolizing hugs and kisses. Symbols can also serve as anchors or central images in a literary work, such as the whale in Herman Melville's *Moby Dick* or the scarlet letter in Nathaniel Hawthorne's novel of the same name. In these types of cases, the image's details are not elaborated or investigated like those in a metaphor; instead, the image—as a symbol—stands relatively unchanged, affecting the characters in the books but remaining a kind of force on its own.

The Romantic poet-critics had much more to say about symbols and their effects, as you'll see in Chapter 8.

IN THEORY

"I used at first to wonder what comfort Traddles found in drawing skeletons; and for some time looked upon him as a sort of hermit, who reminded himself by those symbols of mortality that caning couldn't last forever. But I believe he only did it because they were easy, and didn't want any features." —Charles Dickens, *David Copperfield*

The Least You Need to Know

- Theme and form are always interrelated.
- Plot organizes stories, and so does the use of motifs, which indicate patterns and expectations.
- The tale is often about the teller.
- Characters should be seen as acting both like people and like the embodiment of ideas.
- It isn't possible to read too much into imagery and language.

In Theory, How Do You Read?

The chapters in this part look at methods of reading. But isn't reading, well, just reading? It depends on whom you ask. We'll be asking critics ranging from Aristotle to the folks responsible for much of the reading that goes on in college classrooms today. The answers they give offer a fascinating range of perspectives and strategies for approaching literature and even film.

New Criticism Looks Very Closely

In This Chapter

- New Criticism showcases the text itself
- Organic unity brings all the details together
- Returning to the literary experience after analysis
- Criticizing earlier critics
- The business of criticism

When you hear the words *English major*, what comes to mind? Wait, come back. What I mean is, how are you supposed to read if you're an English major? Everyone knows you're supposed to "analyze" literature. It's only natural—an English major examines details, reads deeply into the various meanings of words, and otherwise looks very closely. It's only natural—unless, as it turns out, it isn't natural at all. Instead, it's a specific approach to literary interpretation developed in the first half of the twentieth century.

Conveniently, this approach to reading closely has been branded close reading. And just as conveniently, the style of interpretation I'll be discussing in this chapter distinguished itself from "old" criticism by calling itself New Criticism. Yep, that's how you get it done in the literature business. In fact, New Criticism became the most influential and widespread school of criticism in the twentieth century and remains fundamental to literary studies—no matter how many people try to kick it to the curb (more on that later).

Everything Fits Together

The New Critics started with the idea that any work of literature—let's say a poem—is a specially crafted object made up of all kinds of parts operating in harmony. A poem, they said, is not just an emotional burst of expression, or even a series of emotional bursts strung together. It's the product of a poet's painstaking craft, a unified, constructed object. All of its details fit together, like a well-made machine.

Buy Organic

But wait—the New Critics weren't finished with the analogies. They said an even better comparison is with a growing plant, since all the parts of a plant naturally grow together to form and support the whole. Similarly, any work of literature is actually held together by an organic system of relationships, or, simply, organic unity.

This means all of the details of a good novel, story, or poem—the specific word choices, rhythms of language, elements of plot, character, and setting—can be seen as working together in a natural, unified way to create the effect you feel when you read.

It also means that it's this organic unity that makes close reading different from simply reading closely. True close reading is reading closely with the specific goal of discovering the central idea that makes all the details unified in the first place. The details of the text, in one way or another, are held together with a kind of tension. They all support a central idea, or theme. I'm tempted to say this theme is like the gravitational pull that holds all the details and techniques in the literary work's "orbit," but I wouldn't want to add yet another analogy. Oh, wait—the New Critics used that one, too.

The New Critics wanted you to think of any work of literature as a system that can be studied for its own sake, by looking at how it works. It's not just *what* literature says that's important, it's *how* it says it.

IN THEORY

More analogies! The New Critics also compared organic unity in literature to unity in the other arts, such as the musical key a song is played in, or the selection of a few main colors that an artist uses for a painting.

Can't I Just Read?

The New Critics were almost exclusively actual English professors, unlike some of the other theorists discussed in this book who come from a wide variety of fields. And while you may simply want to read a novel or a poem "because you like it," the New Critics wanted you to be aware of *why* you like it. But before you say, "Well thanks, professor, you've just ruined reading for me," take a look at what they were really up to.

The New Critics sincerely hoped that your experience of literature would *not* be ruined. In fact, they wanted their methods to help heighten your experience of literature and even of life. New Criticism argues that your experience of literature actually depends on several levels of experience happening at once. These levels are the basis of your appreciation of any book, poem, or movie, but because many of these levels are very subtle, you generally ignore them, consciously speaking. New Criticism urges you to study the levels (or layers) separately and very carefully—and even the New Critics themselves admitted this is an artificial thing to do. But the goal is the point. The goal is to have you return to the literary work and re-experience it more fully.

Because of the nature of poetic communication, literature practically demands to be studied more closely. This is because, according to the New Critics, an author isn't just spouting emotions, but constructing the verbal equivalent of emotions and ideas. Then this verbal equivalent has to be interpreted by readers who are faced with a real physical text, not just abstract emotions or ideas.

In Other Words, There Are No Other Words

Since, at the end of the day, it's your actual experience of the literature that matters, New Critics warned against replacing the actual poem or story with a paraphrase of its meaning. The total significance or *true* meaning of a work was much more than a description of the poem, or an abstract statement of the ideas contained in a story or novel. To paraphrase a poem and think that you have figured out and stated its meaning is, the critics argued, "heresy" against what they saw as the practically sacred quality of literature.

New Critics even compared literary works to religious icons. An icon, even if it's a painting, is not just a representation of something else. Instead, it's an object that actually shares the qualities of its subject. The idea is to treat the icon as you would the person depicted in the icon. A poem, in this comparison, is a kind of "verbal icon" that doesn't just represent ideas or emotions, but actually shares those ideas and emotions. The poem *becomes* the thing it represents.

From a more secular perspective, New Critics argued that what makes literature *literature* in the first place is the poet's special use of language. This special use of language marks literature as different from ordinary description and statement. The New Critics called this literary quality of language—wait for it—literariness. I told you they were good with branding.

This reinforces the view that a literary work communicates poetically by giving you an experience that can't be reduced to any simple explanation. Poetic communication is the power behind your experience of literature, and all of the New Critical methods of analysis and interpretation, which I'll turn to in the next section, are intended to help make you fluent in this kind of communication.

RELATIONS

New Criticism is called a formalist approach to literary study, since it emphasizes the importance of formal features, or techniques. Russian formalism also does this—in an extreme way, and with no apologies—as Chapter 4 explains.

Reading Closely for What?

So New Criticism sets out to train you to be both an appreciator and an analyst of literature. Combining these two aspects of your personality will then produce a better experience. The training leads you to perform an explication, or examination, of literary techniques used in any particular work of literature. You're looking for ways that elements of form work together with a theme to unify the work.

Your task, then, is to account for why the work is good and how all of its parts work together in a unified way to create an effect. Such an accounting has several key steps, which I'll explain in the following sections. Also, if anyone asks—and they will—tell them you're "doing a reading" when you're analyzing literature in this way.

There's a Pattern Here

One of the more obvious unifying forces in a work of literature is the presence of repetition and patterns. Songs are unified by their refrains, for example, and novels can be unified through repetition of similar scenes. Poems also often include very clear patterns of meter, rhyme, and imagery as unifying elements.

Let's say you're reading Mary Shelley's *Frankenstein*. Everyone knows the story is about a mad scientist who dreams of discovering the secrets of immortality and creates a living being from dead bodies. But what a New Critical reader would know is that this theme doesn't just show up when we meet Victor Frankenstein (don't call him "Doctor," since he never finished medical school); the novel prepares you for it from the very beginning.

In the novel, the guy who actually tells the story of Frankenstein is the narrator, Robert Walton. In the opening chapters, Shelley has this narrator-character lay the groundwork for a unified novel by telling us about his own dreams of immortality, which parallel Frankenstein's ambitions. Walton also goes on and on about the need for a friend, which also gives us a preview of Frankenstein's own character.

Each time Walton remarks on one of these themes, the novel becomes more unified by drawing another parallel with Victor. The unifying effect is even stronger if you connect Walton's comments with the creature's personality as well, since the creature also obsesses about friends and ambition.

But why stop there? Even the details of Walton's word choices—he uses such loaded words as *revive* and *restore*—help create the patterns that contribute to the novel's organic unity. According to New Criticism, the poetic communication of this novel actually depends on the reader having similar feelings about several characters at once.

APPLY IT

Shelley's *Frankenstein* is incredibly unified. What happens to one character almost always happens to other characters. Try reading the novel with any one of the following themes in mind, and notice how this patterning works: friends, fame, the thirst for knowledge, marriage, childbirth, parenting, orphans, pride, sacrifice, altruism, falling from privilege, giving up on a project, destiny, and fate.

No, You're Not Reading Too Much Into It

Writers love details. It's very, very hard for you to read too much into any work of literature, mainly because writers pay a lot of attention to everything that goes into their works. You might see something in a poem, for example, that seems ambiguous, and you're not sure if it means one thing or another. New Criticism tells you it's okay to see both meanings at once.

Ambiguity, in fact, is one of the most important features for New Criticism. This seems kind of obvious when you think of how ambiguous some stories are: is Gatsby a hero or a victim? Yet the New Critics went way beyond ambiguous plots and characters. For poetry, in particular (and it was poetry they tended to focus on), ambiguous words and phrases are seen as essential to the poem's total meaning.

The New Critic Cleanth Brooks, for example, read the following two lines at the start of John Keats's "Ode on a Grecian Urn": "Thou still unravish'd bride of quietness, / Thou foster-child of Silence and slow Time." Brooks got to the word *still* and had to stop and investigate. He wonders if *still* means "lasting up to this point," or if it means "motionless." Brooks's answer, as you may expect, was that both meanings are valid.

Why? Not because anything goes and you can make up a poem's meaning based on random definitions, but because these two definitions actually support the poem's theme. That is, Brooks feels that the point of the poem involves complex ideas of desire, fleeting time, and the survival of art.

According to the New Critics, these ideas—the theme of the poem—are supported by the experience of seeing one word and having two thoughts in your mind at once. The final effect—the poetic communication of the poem—demands that one word be used and the reader's mind bounce between two meanings. In this way, the poem doesn't just represent the theme of "desire suspended in art," it exemplifies it. It gives you an experience, not a heretical paraphrase or a one-dimensional meaning.

Brooks gave the same treatment to other words, phrases, and images throughout this poem, creating a characteristic New Critical reading—which means lots of discussion about a little poem—and you can imagine this same sort of process at work in your own head when you hear a song you like or even a joke. The effect of the song or joke is so much more than a description of it. It's the experience of multiple meanings at once.

APPLY IT

Bring poetry to your reading group! A single sonnet can even serve as a kind of appetizer for your regularly scheduled novel or short story reading. Have everyone read the poem first, looking up any interesting words or phrases, then bring everyone's comments together in discussion. How do all the comments suggest a New Critical experiential meaning for the poem?

When ambiguity leads to a flat-out contradiction, you get a *paradox*, and New Critics really go crazy about paradox. New Criticism argues that a paradox urges you to see, feel, or experience something that wouldn't be available otherwise. *Noisy* and *silence* simply contradict each other, if you look at the pair analytically. But poetically, the paradox creates something new, something that can't be paraphrased even though you "know what it means."

DEFINITION

A **paradox** is a contradictory statement or phrase, like *noisy silence*.

Ironic, Isn't It?

Like ambiguity and paradox, irony is an aspect of language that helps make language literary. And while irony can mean saying one thing and meaning another, like sarcasm, New Criticism wants you to understand it a bit more broadly. Think of something as ironic when it turns away from an obvious or straightforward meaning and toward contradiction, uncertainty, or surprise.

Let's say you've finished Shelley's original *Frankenstein*, and you're now sitting down to the 1935 movie, *Bride of Frankenstein*. The opening sequence of the film is not about Frankenstein and his creature, but about Mary Shelley, her husband Percy Shelley, and Lord Byron. It's a frame narrative that introduces these historical characters as they bring the audience up to speed by talking, fictitiously, about the events of the first film, *Frankenstein*. Now, what's ironic is that the character of Mary Shelley is played by Elsa Lanchester, who also plays the Bride later in the movie.

This is ironic because it means the introductory part of the movie does not just give you one meaning—watching Elsa Lanchester and thinking "Mary Shelley." Instead, as the movie progresses, you're confronted with Elsa Lanchester as the Bride, which suggests that Shelley and the Bride have something in common—could Shelley be projecting her own personality into the character? Of course this all assumes you're looking at the movie very closely; but being a New Critic, you're doing just that.

What's Wrong with "Old" Criticism?

At this point, you're probably wondering what critics did before New Criticism came along. Basically, and according to one New Critic, they didn't study literature at all, they studied "*about* literature." Earlier scholars would examine an author's biography, for example, looking for clear connections between life and art. Or, they would look at the historical era that produced a work of art, also looking for clear connections between life and art.

> **RELATIONS**
>
> As luck would have it, the kind of "old historicism" that New Criticism denounced would give way, later in the twentieth century, to more sophisticated approaches to historical issues, called—here it comes—new historicism. It's fascinating, and you can see Chapter 20 for more.

Another approach to earlier literary study was simply to swoon over poems in rapt appreciation. Even to the New Critics there was nothing wrong with that—the whole point of reading literature is to enjoy it. But as you've seen, the New Critics wanted readers to be both appreciators *and* analysts. In fact, New Critics themselves knew that all kinds of issues are important to enjoying and understanding literature. History, biography, philosophy, psychology, sociology—everything has its place in literature, since literature is about life. But the primary task of the critic, before everything else, is to examine the literary work for its own sake as a crafted object.

And when you think of it, this emphasis also takes a big weight off of your shoulders as a reader. That is, unlike the earlier approaches to literary study, New Criticism only asks that you sit down with the literary work—and a dictionary—and do a reading. You no longer have to be an expert on the author's life and times. New Critics wanted anyone to be able to claim mastery of a text; they wanted to show that the ordinary reader could claim to be a critic, given the appropriate training.

Feelings, Nothing More Than Feelings

Two famous fallacies, or mistakes in reasoning, deserve a bit of attention before we finish up. The New Critics warned against the affective fallacy, which they called the misguided attempt to analyze literature—or worse, evaluate literature—simply in terms of how it makes the reader feel. They argued that the affect, or your emotional response to a poem, was clearly important, but the point of literary criticism was to explain how the work got you to feel anything in the first place. The remedy for the affective fallacy is to be more objective as a reader and analyst, at least before jumping back in to experience the literature for the full effect.

RELATIONS

See Chapter 5 for a discussion of reader-response criticism, which directly confronts New Criticism by putting the reader's feelings at the center of literary study.

Did the Author Really Mean *That?*

It's pretty common, and reasonable, to hear the complaint, "Oh, the author couldn't have meant *that.*" What's kind of refreshing is that the New Critics response to this question was a very emphatic, "Don't worry about it!"

The intentional fallacy describes the mistake of thinking that the author's intention is the final word in interpreting a work of literature. For New Criticism, it doesn't matter what the author *intended* to say, what matters is what the author has *managed* to say by putting together a literary work. While it might be interesting to know an author's own interpretation of his or her work, the New Critics insisted that the literary work is autonomous and has a life of its own, with any number of meanings.

For New Criticism, the author's true intention is to create a literary work, a self-contained artistic object. The writer and critic T. S. Eliot said that a good author creates an objective correlative, a literary work that succeeds, for astute readers, in provoking an emotional effect in the readers themselves, not just transmitting the poet's own emotional message.

The reader, then, has to experience the work itself to discover its full meaning, not just absorb someone else's meaning, even if that someone else is the author. A poem, story, novel, or movie belongs to the public.

RELATIONS

Speaking of authors not being in control of their own works—take a look at Chapter 10's discussion of psychoanalytic approaches to literature. According to Freudian psychology, authors never really know what they're writing about—until they visit an expert analyst or a good literary critic.

Everyone's a Critic

As I mentioned at the beginning of this chapter, New Criticism is one of the biggest success stories in literary studies. It brought about the discipline of English as we know it, and created a business for criticism, a business that linked professors with institutions, textbook publishers, and writers such as T. S. Eliot and Flannery O'Connor. It was, as one of the founding New Critical books was titled, eminently *Practical Criticism.*

IN THEORY

The writer and critic Ezra Pound (1885–1972) also influenced the development of New Criticism. Among other things, Pound published a neat little book in 1934 called *ABC of Reading,* in which he wrote things like, "A great deal of false teaching is due to the assumption that poems known to the critic are of necessity the best."

New Critics actually started out by emphasizing their amateur status and their role as advocates for the ordinary reader, rather than the literary expert. Their influential books included collections of essays, full treatments of criticism and theory, and some very long-lived textbooks. In fact, unlike many of the approaches or schools covered in this book, some of which were never intended to be named or even to be literary methods at all, several of the New Critic's signature terms and concepts either started or ended up in the titles of their publications. Take a look at the list:

- Cleanth Brooks (1906–1994): *The Well Wrought Urn*

- Cleanth Brooks and Robert Penn Warren (1905–1989): Textbooks including *Understanding Poetry, Understanding Fiction,* and *An Approach to Literature*

- I. A. Richards (1893–1979): *Principles of Literary Criticism* and *Practical Criticism*

- William K. Wimsatt (1907–1975) and Monroe C. Beardsley (1915–1985): *The Verbal Icon*

- John Crowe Ransom (1888–1974): *The New Criticism* and the essay, "Criticism, Inc."

- William Empson (1906–1984): *Seven Types of Ambiguity* (livelier than it sounds—read the epilogue)

IN THEORY

In addition to their readings of Romantic poets like Keats and Wordsworth, the New Critics helped revive and popularize the seventeenth-century metaphysical poets, including John Donne and Andrew Marvell. These poets often developed elaborate metaphors (or conceits) involving science, philosophy, and theology. The complex constructions and multiple shades of meaning made metaphysical poetry perfect for New Critical readings.

Who Begs to Differ?

As you can see by all the cross-references to other chapters in this book, there has been rather a lot of negative reaction to New Criticism over the past century.

One complaint centers around all the "good poem" and "astute reader" comments. That is, the New Critics have come under fire for being evaluative and elitist. As democratic as the New Critics said they were—they did extend literary study to all kinds of people, after all—they still tended to focus on a specific kind of literature. They liked the kind of works that helped support their views of literature as complex yet unified.

Some critics have also claimed that New Criticism prohibits any consideration of nonliterary matters such as history, psychology, or politics. Yet the New Critics themselves had no problem with such aspects of literature. They only insisted that getting to any of these questions was best done by starting with an analysis of what they saw as the text itself.

On a politically theoretical level, the New Critics argued that their methods would help people see the harmony that's always naturally present in ambiguity, paradox, or irony. Other critics, however, say this harmony isn't natural at all, but imposed by New Criticism's utopian worldview, and it's actually just a way of replacing traditional religious claims of unity with literary ones.

Still, as you look at many of the other approaches covered in this book, you'll find them relying on New Critical methods at some point and at some level. After all, many of those approaches developed, literally, out of the New Critical school.

The Least You Need to Know

- Treat literature as a crafted, self-sufficient object.
- Indulge in ambiguities, paradoxes, and irony.
- Don't trust authors to explain their own work.
- After analyzing the text, re-experience it.
- When you see an English major, thank the New Critics.

Russian Formalism Fixates on the Machinery

In This Chapter

- Literature isn't only about ideas
- Turning literary study into a science
- Shaking up old habits of seeing
- Letting readers in on the tricks
- Writers only care about other writers

Russian formalism emerged in the early twentieth century (and as you may expect, out of Russia). It's particularly fun to consider because while it sounds really complicated, its basic principles are actually very straightforward, engaging, and influential. Also, you get to say "Shklovsky," which is neat.

To get at formalism, start with the traditional relationship between form and content. A novel's structure, style, and actual composition—its *form*—is merely the container for the more important content of great ideas or emotions. You're a formalist if you claim this relationship gets things backward, and form should actually be emphasized over content. Paying attention to ideas is not focusing on what makes literature literary. Instead, you need to examine the form of a work, since that's what the writer has real control over. Literature isn't a clear window through which you examine things on the other side; literature is itself the thing to be examined. And for Russian formalists, if you can do this scientifically, all the better.

The actual critics involved only did the Russian formalism thing for a few years—almost exactly from 1915 to 1930—but their influence has been huge. They helped shift literary theory away from the Romantic tendency (see Chapter 8) to emphasize a kind of mystical oohing and aahing at strong emotions, impressive symbolism, or even a writer's biography, and toward an analysis of the text itself. The central question for a formalist reader approaching a novel or poem isn't "What's it about?" but "How does it work?" or "What makes it literature?"

Look *At* the Text, Not *Through* It

When you don't focus on literature as a transparent window, you start to see how it should more accurately be likened to a painting, particularly a painting that doesn't hide the fact that it's a painting. Take van Gogh's "The Starry Night," for example. What really jumps out is van Gogh's emphasis on the paint itself. The appeal is not so much what the visual image represents (a town in France), but that all those colorful blobs, thick smears, and heavy, obvious brushstrokes actually become the aesthetic experience of the work itself.

Not Content with Form and Content

Now, imagine having a discussion about *Frankenstein*. But wait—you haven't read *Frankenstein*, despite our earlier discussions? No problem. Have you seen one of the movies? No? Still no problem. From a traditional form-and-content position, you can just carry on a conversation about the story's so-called content or summary, which you probably have absorbed by osmosis. After that, according to some very nonformalist logic, you can think about the situation and the characters of a novel as if they were real. That is, once you get a running start at the ideas and themes that seem to be in play for any given story, you can have all kinds of opinions about it, whether or not you have actually read the novel. In fact, I know plenty of students (and friends at reading group) who can talk all day about something they haven't read. This kind of literary criticism focuses on the ideas and characters which, once you get a sense of them as real, you can make very sincere judgments based on your own experiences.

You can even describe a fictional event, idea, or character to another person, and *that* person is free to form opinions and views about the story.

To all of this, the Russian formalists say *"Nyet!"*

They argue that simply talking about the ideas behind a work, or talking about the characters as if they were actual people, completely misses the point of literary study. The point is to look right at the text of *Frankenstein* (or directly at the film) and consider how the details *work* and what they *do*. How do these details—chosen instead of any others—make the novel or film a work of art?

In her 1816 novel, Mary Shelley did not just imagine the creation of a monster and a few provocative moral issues, she made specific choices in arranging and presenting the text. She didn't just tell any Frankenstein story, she told this one, with all of its formal features, and they become the focus of formalist theories. For example, Shelley decided to have several different narrators tell different parts of the story. The story does not come from one source or point of view, but from multiple sources, creating remarkably complex layers of letters, testimonies, and narration. For the formalists, a writer's decision to do this is not at all incidental to the "real story" behind the novel, but should be examined as the most important aspect of the art of the novel.

IN THEORY

"The formalists simultaneously freed themselves from the traditional correlation of 'form-content' and from the conception of form as an outer cover or as a vessel into which a liquid (the content) is poured." —Boris Eichenbaum

But wait—doesn't this miss the point of how literature invites us to explore our own world and to build relationships between fictional people, fictional history, and fictional situations and the real ones? Wasn't Shelley *trying* to get us to see the point behind her art? Aren't Russian formalists just privileging style over substance? If you follow this line of questioning, you're reacting the way other critics did when they said, "Sure, sure, but these guys don't really respond to literature, they're just, you know … *formalists*."

A Scientific Basis for Literary Study

The intention—and effect—of the formalists was to redefine what it meant to study literature. The point of investigating literature was not simply to identify which brilliant ideas or themes a writer had divined, as if the poet were valued only as a mystic, seer, or as one critic put it, the "guardian of the mystery." Instead, writers should be valued as physical makers and manipulators of form. A good writer was a successful technician or architect who built works of literary art.

In support of this, formalists argued that literary language is different from other kinds of language. Ordinary language is used transparently—we're supposed to communicate something with language, like delivering a sandwich on a platter. We're not supposed to fixate on the platter and all of its details. To use language in a literary way, however, is to highlight or "roughen" the qualities of language itself. The formalists went so far as to say that the content doesn't even matter—forget about the sandwich; let's obsess over the platter.

Why Did They Do This?

Russian formalism may seem like a pretty dry approach to literature. It's explicitly scientific, refuses to focus on ideas and emotions for their own sake, and, depending on your mood, it sounds like a tone-deaf response to the vital way literature echoes and accompanies our lives. The formalists, however, felt perfectly justified in their perspectives, and offered several provocative explanations.

It's What Art Really Is

First, they basically said, "Tough luck, that's what literary theory is all about."

They argued that if you want to just speculate on themes and ideas and images, then go ahead, but what you're doing is not specifically literary in nature. If you discuss a fictional event as if it's real, or simply consider its themes, you miss out on what makes it literary, which is the mastery of technique and form.

At the same time, there is still an important connection between literary form and the outside world. The Russian formalists explained that technique and form have the power to revive your perceptions, especially your perceptions of everyday objects and events. Basically, the argument is that your senses become dulled to what is going on around you in everyday life, and it takes the right kind of literature to bring new life to the things we would otherwise overlook. And the right kind of literature is the kind that defamiliarizes something that has become habitual.

Habit Dulls Our Perception

"Perception becomes habitual, it becomes automatic," wrote Viktor Shklovsky, describing the primary predicament that art can help remedy. His point is understandable. As we go about our daily lives, we tend to turn down our sensitivity to things. This can be a good thing, since we can't always be aware of everything and function normally. But this dulling down is definitely bad when we become so habituated to important features of life that we simply skip over them, often thinking that we are noticing them, but not really doing so.

Formalists pointed out that there's a difference between recognizing something and really seeing it. They argued that as important as it may be for people to recognize and know things, those terms actually describe people *not* perceiving. You look at a tree and make a match: yes, that's a tree. Your job is finished—you've recognized the tree and can move on. Shklovsky wants us to perceive the tree—really look at it as if we haven't seen it before, and as if we do not recognize or know it. That way, you look at a tree and really see it, fresh, without the automatic process that comes from habit.

IN THEORY

"All of our habits retreat into the area of the unconsciously automatic; if one remembers the sensations of holding a pen or of speaking a foreign language for the first time and compares that with his feeling at performing the action for the ten thousandth time, he will agree with us. Such habituation explains the principles by which, in ordinary speech, we leave phrases unfinished and words half expressed." —Viktor Shklovsky

Habit forces us into operating on the principle of "it's already understood," and it makes us unconscious of what is actually going on. In conversation, as Shklovsky noted, you can talk comfortably with friends without finishing words and sentences, but you can also get annoyed when you're trying to say something to someone (maybe not a friend), and that person keeps nodding his head before you're finished, as if he knows exactly what you're going to say before you say it.

It's that kind of automatic, rushed, and presuming response—which robs the actual object of its well-deserved attention—that the formalists wanted to put a stop to. Shklovsky took this matter very seriously, arguing that automatic responses lead you to miss out on everything important, "so life is reckoned as nothing. Habituation devours work, clothes, furniture, one's wife, and the fear of war."

Of course, each generation brings new challenges. Long before texting, Shklovsky considered that one example of extreme habituation would be if someone stopped using full words altogether and only used—get this—the first letter of each word in a sentence. His example is a schoolboy writing "TSmab" instead of "The Swiss Mountains are beautiful." Can you imagine? LOL! Okay, let's move on.

The solution to dulled perception, like the solution to the annoying person nodding his head in anticipated agreement, is to shake things up, formally speaking. It's to manipulate language so that your reader cannot simply skate along the surface of your words, or, to change the metaphor, your reader can't just look *through* your words and ignore them on the way to an already understood point.

Make the Ordinary Strange

Shklovsky is most closely associated with defamiliarization. The point here is very simple and not exclusive to Russian formalists—depict ordinary things and events in artistic, unusual ways, preventing readers from having automatic, habitual responses.

IN THEORY

Consider this example from Robert Browning in 1855:

We're made so that we love
First when we see them painted, things we have passed
Perhaps a hundred times nor cared to see;
And so they are better, painted—better to us,
Which is the same thing. Art was given for that. —"Fra Lippo Lippi"

This is from a wonderful story-poem which suggests that the whole point of art is to revive our appreciation of something by providing a new way of looking at it. We may see something every day and pass it by without much thought; it isn't until we see it painted, narrated, or otherwise made more artistic and less familiar that we start to appreciate it.

Shklovsky's own examples of defamiliarization often featured Tolstoy, who, in one famous instance, has a horse narrate part of a story—but Tolstoy doesn't explicitly tell us it's a horse narrating part of the story.

Being a horse, the narrator would have a defamiliarized perspective on human matters, and he would lack most of the familiar vocabulary for describing what he sees. So Tolstoy has the narrating horse describe human matters involving property laws, physical punishment, and marriage. Each subject is presented in a way that frustrates an automatic response; nothing is taken for granted by the narrator, so nothing can be presumed by the reader. Tolstoy produces a successful critique of these institutions by bringing their absurd but often overlooked premises into the foreground.

APPLY IT

"I was delighted when I first discovered that a pleasant sound, which often saluted my ears, proceeded from the throats of the little winged animals who had often intercepted the light from my eyes." —Mary Shelley, *Frankenstein*

Here, Frankenstein's creature, like Tolstoy's horse, has no access to the expected vocabulary for describing "tweeting" and "birds." You know what he's talking about, particularly as the sentence proceeds, but the way he says it helps defamiliarize the familiar scene. The fact that the sentence sounds *overdone* proves that we already have a sense of how the description is *supposed to be done,* which is exactly the kind of habitual understanding that the formalists wanted good literature to unsettle.

There are several other ways to achieve defamiliarization in literature. A writer can draw out a description with extreme detail, or otherwise interrupt an ordinary depiction. Defamiliarization in movies is often produced through slow-motion shots and extreme close-ups. In some shots, you don't even know what you're looking at until it dawns on you: "Hey, that's a beach ball!" or "I never realized how graceful the snow cone vendor was until I saw him slowed down like that." Again, it's this effect of not knowing what you're looking at that the formalists are after, because the time you spend not knowing is the time you are most fully *perceiving* whatever is in front of you, on the page or on the screen. As soon as you know what you're looking at, recognition kicks in, and your brain tries to go back to auto-pilot. Check out the film *Koyaanisqatsi* (*ko-YAW-nis-COT-see*), a modern classic of defamiliarization directed by Godfrey Reggio (1982).

Unfortunately for Tolstoy, formalist principles led to some trouble. Shklovsky noted that when Tolstoy defamiliarized certain traditional religious rituals, he was accused of blasphemy, since he wasn't depicting them according to tradition, but trying to get people to question their own understanding. Indeed, Tolstoy came to feel that his own faith had originally been based on recognition, knowledge, and habit, rather than genuine perception.

"Art exists," wrote Shklovsky, "that one may recover the sensation of life; it exists to make one feel things, to make the stone stony." That stony stone sums up one of the first principles of formalist theory—literature should lead to a revitalization of perception and feeling. The second principle of formalist theory turns you, as a reader, into a scientific researcher. The point is to show how literary language is different from ordinary language, and to identify the features of a literary work that prove this difference.

> **RELATIONS**
>
> Be sure to distinguish between the Russian formalist approach, with its emphasis on defamiliarization and its scientific aspirations, and the American New Critics (see Chapter 3), with their concern for organic unity and the "anyone can do it" method of criticism. Each group, in its own way, is focused more on formal features of the actual literary text rather than any external factors, such as psychology or biography, and so they are both considered formalist.

Make the Artistry Obvious

So while it's okay for ordinary language to be transparent, even for the Russian formalists, literature is different. Literature uses language in ways that call attention to itself; it actually reminds you that you are reading, and it wants you to be aware of language's unique characteristics. Think of this as reinforcement of the first formalist principle: if the purpose of literature is to get us to perceive things more clearly, then one of the things we get to see more clearly is literature itself. One of the ways a writer can help us see a literary work more clearly is to let us in on the secrets of a work's workings.

Revealing the Tricks

Russian formalists really want to know the secret to the magic act. Not only that, they want exposing the secret to be the central part of the act. From this theoretical approach, the most interesting literature doesn't try to hide its tricks, techniques, structure, and form. This is literature that "lays bare its construction," or "bares its *devices.*"

DEFINITION

For Russian formalists, a **device** is any technique or feature that writers employ in their art in order to make literary language different from ordinary language. Examples include personification, point of view, metaphor, parallelism, and so on.

Movies that bare their devices point to their own construction as movies. One of the most famous Daffy Duck cartoons, *Duck Amuck*, openly shows the main character being manipulated by his animator. On the screen, you not only see Daffy Duck but the brushes that paint him and the eraser that causes trouble. Daffy also walks out of frames with scenery into blank frames, asking, "Who's in charge here?!" Sounds are manipulated to emphasize that noises in cartoons are not just representations of real sounds, but sound effects selected from libraries and arranged for specific artistic purposes. The cartoon is not simply telling a story, but commenting on its own medium—on the formal features of its medium. Shklovsky must have loved it. The *Scream* movies are also very self-conscious, relying on the fact that audiences know the rules of horror films and can play along. Simply put, these rules, when discussed openly in the movie, become bared devices.

RELATIONS

The Russian formalist emphasis on baring the construction can be related to other, more extreme theories of self-conscious art, such as Brechtian theater (see Chapter 9) in which actors break the fourth wall by directly addressing the audience and never letting the audience forget that it's watching a form of art.

Shklovsky's own central example of literary construction is an eighteenth-century English novel by Laurence Sterne, *Tristram Shandy*. This comic novel, from start to finish, emphasizes that it *is* a novel by including direct address to the reader, blank pages (even blank chapters), diagrams, and so on. The novel makes a point of puzzling over what it means to be a novel. It explicitly focuses on the formalists' main concerns as it explores the relationship between the real world and the characteristics of literary art. In one instance, the narrator lets us know that he's not just telling a story but constantly relying on the conventions of literary art:

Imagine to yourself;——but this had better begin a new chapter.

Chapter IX.

Imagine to yourself a little, squat, uncourtly figure of a Doctor

In this way, the novel calls attention to plotting, images, characters, and even sentence and paragraph structure. Pages offer typographical jokes by being blank, or covered in scribbles or designs, and all of this emphasizes that the novel's form is also its content. That is, pondering over the manner of telling a story is precisely the point of the story. Since the novel is a kind of fictional autobiography, this kind of self-consciousness also makes thematic sense. The novelist is exploring *how* a person can tell his life story in a medium—literature—that is not the same as his life.

At one point, the narrator provides four wavy and convoluted lines that he says represent the way the story had progressed in the first four (yes, four) volumes. Then he offers one more line to illustrate the fifth volume:

——In the fifth volume

I have been very good,——the precise line I have described in it being this:

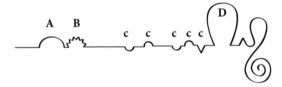

By which it appears, that except at the curve, marked A. where I took a trip to *Navarre*,——and the indented curve B. which is the short airing when I was there with the Lady *Baussiere* and her page,——I have not taken the least frisk of a digression, till *John de la Casse's* devils led me the round you see marked D.——for as for c c c c c they are nothing but parentheses

By showing this, the narrator is letting the reader in on the overall design of the novel, with its segments of smooth plot, its digressions, asides, and other features. Like a magician explaining a trick, or an architect showing you the plans for a building, the novelist is not letting you get lost in the story, but asking you to see the story as a crafted, artificial thing. For Shklovsky, this is a prime example of how a novel can highlight the literariness of literature.

Plot vs. Story-Stuff

Sterne's use of wavy lines to diagram the form of his story is one instance of the scientific approach suggested by Russian formalism. Another is the attempt to segment, analyze, catalog, and outline the literature you read. For this, the formalists argued that fiction should be thought of as having two dimensions: a dimension of plot and a dimension of "story-stuff."

For Russian formalists, plot remains the arrangement of events in a novel or film. Story-stuff, on the other hand, can be thought of as the raw material for a novel. It's like the entirety of the fictional world, from which the novel selects and arranges events for you, the reader. You can also think of it as the events in the fictional world arranged into chronological order, and complete—no gaps. The plot is the result of selecting and arranging *some* of the fictional events and including them in the novel. Sometimes the concept of story-stuff is referred to simply as *story*, which is fine ("Hey, look how the arrangement of the plot in this novel reverses the story"), but I think using *story-stuff* gets the point across better and frees up the word *story* for the usual, less technical purposes.

So why is the distinction between these two dimensions important? Because separating out plot from story-stuff helps you recognize the literariness of what you're looking at. It emphasizes the author's role as a technician, as someone who has to craft a finished product, not merely as someone who just imagines a good story. In fact, it's common to see an author take a story that everyone already knows and then, cleverly using the formal features of literature (or film), turn that story-stuff into a new work of art.

Of course, you recognize the need for selection and arrangement in fiction all the time, and it's the plot versus story-stuff distinction that allows you to think about this more systematically. For example, you can always imagine events that would have had to take place in the story but don't make the cut into the actual plot. How often does the plot skip over events that must have happened and time that must have passed? A character may be shown eating dinner, then the next thing you get is breakfast.

When Russian formalists examined literature, they analyzed how a writer made use of the story-stuff as raw material and offered arguments for how any given text was more literary than another. They also considered how writers would get readers to imagine events that never actually appeared on the page. *Tristram Shandy*, as you've seen, emphasizes the selections and arrangements that turn story-stuff into plot. Movies like *Pulp Fiction* and *Memento* make it a point to force you to reconstruct the story-stuff world behind the arranged plot.

APPLY IT

Consider how plot and story-stuff are related in any novel or movie. How else could the story-stuff of the fiction have been presented? If you were to retell the story, which omitted events would you include or even play up?

When you separate out plot and story-stuff for the sake of analysis (since in practice they are always interacting), you can also investigate how a writer makes use of motivation. Motivation refers to those aspects of the story-stuff that must be included in the plot of any given version of a story. For example, every Cinderella story has to include certain features—such as the put-upon Cinderella losing something so the prince can track her down—in order for the story to still be a Cinderella story. Features like this are called motivated, and the formalists thought they weren't as important as the *un*-motivated things a writer did, since unmotivated touches were the true signs of art. Nobody's going to gush, "Gee, that's so clever that you gave Cinderella a fairy godmother," since Cinderella *always* gets a fairy godmother. (It's demanded, or motivated, by the story-stuff.) What the formalists wanted to see were details and modifications that don't have to be in every version, like adding dress-making mice (Disney's film—and of course the mice sing, unmotivatedly), or making Cinderella a guy (seen Jerry Lewis in *Cinderfella* lately?). In more elaborate examples, an author can even craft a challenging backstory for a classic novel, as Jean Rhys did with her *Wide Sargasso Sea*, based on the story-stuff of Charlotte Brontë's *Jane Eyre* (see Chapter 21 for more on this adaptation).

RELATIONS

The Russian formalist distinction between plot and story-stuff is a precursor to the structuralists' project of cataloging different versions of the same fairy tale, as discussed in Chapter 16.

Literary History Is the Interplay of Form

Russian formalists also had a pretty technical view of literary history. That is, when they asked how new literary forms and styles arose, and then you suggested they arose because "times change and literature reflects the times," the formalists rolled their eyes, sighed, and prepared to set you straight. For them, form doesn't follow function, but function follows form. As Shklovsky put it, "A new form appears not in order to express a new content, but in order to replace an old form, which has already lost its artistic value."

Writers see something being done, and they copy it. And more importantly, writers see something being done too much and decide to try something new. Russian formalists saw literary history as a series of changes in form and style. A particular form emerges as new and refreshing, and for a while it helps defamiliarize what you had started to ignore. But then, of course, the new becomes the norm, and you begin to take the writing for granted again.

IN THEORY

"Try and write straight English; never use slang except in dialogue and then only when unavoidable. Because all slang goes sour in a short time. I only use swear words, for example, that have lasted for at least a thousand years for fear of getting stuff that will be simply timely and then go sour." —Ernest Hemingway

So what does this cycle of formal change look like? Is it as simple as the progression through types of stories, like, "Oh, we're so tired of westerns, let's make musicals now"? No. Is it like Ernest Hemingway's style, which barged in on the 1920s literary scene and said, "Enough with the omniscient narrator thing; here's a stripped-down, just-the-facts form of writing"? Sort of. What the Russian formalists wanted to analyze were the complex interactions of forms, tracing their contributions—fresh or stale—to any given situation. Remember that the difference between literary language and ordinary language is a matter of context. For example, if you want to call attention to language itself when ordering dinner at a restaurant, you might say, "Prithee, dost thou have any victuals drawn from the tempestuous sea?" Yes, you might say that, and in addition to it being really annoying, it would be an instance of challenging the context by saying something in an unexpected way.

If, on the other hand, you're writing a story in which everyone is *supposed* to use "prithees" and "dost thous," then the best way to call attention to literariness is to bring in a contrasting form. The Russian formalists called this foregrounding, or highlighting a device against a more typical background. Look for an extended example of this in Mark Twain's *A Connecticut Yankee in King Arthur's Court*, which emphasizes how strange (and even powerful) ordinary language can be when heard in another context. As you might expect, one effect of this shifting of contexts is to raise your consciousness regarding language itself. You don't just absorb meaning, you notice how and why something is said the way it is said.

In this way, the formalists could develop quite elaborate schemes of formal change, interaction, influence, and evolution. They wanted to show that writers were aware of what was normal, fashionable, effective, and ineffective in literary form, and that writers based their creative decisions on the literary environment, rather than on social or even personal circumstances.

In fact, since Russian formalists went so far as to consider form to be *prior* to content, they saw literature as capable of changing the way we actually see the real world. Formal features are not just aspects of literature that we can take or leave. They are the organs through which we perceive, think, and even feel. It's the influence of artistic forms, so goes the argument, that leads to organizing and understanding everything around you.

The Least You Need to Know

- Form is the proper object of literary study, not ideas.
- Form determines content, not the other way around.
- Defamiliarizing what has become habitual is the central purpose of good literature.
- Plot is a way of organizing and presenting story-stuff.
- Literary history doesn't simply reflect the times, but is a series of changes in form and style.

Reader-Response Criticism Watches Itself

In This Chapter

- Subjectivity and literary meaning
- The effect of a reader's transactions
- How texts create their readers
- Reading habits and their causes
- Meaning and historical reception

What's really going on when you read? Are you hoping to immerse yourself in a good story? Trying to figure out what the author is saying? Exploring new places, people, or concepts? The critics I'll discuss in this chapter have another idea. They want you to think about how much your interaction with the text actually creates the literature that you think you are simply reading. You, in other words, are as much the author of *Pride and Prejudice* as Jane Austen is.

You're welcome.

In the Eye of the Beholder

It may seem extreme to say the reader is the author, but this approach starts with a concept that's easy to recognize: subjectivity. People see things in different ways, and when people look at literature, they often come away with very different reactions.

Why is this? Do some people have the correct response, while others get it wrong or don't get it at all? If this is the case, then you have to assume the novel you're reading holds all of its meaning like a puzzle waiting to be solved. This is generally what the critics in the last two chapters emphasized—the objective nature of any literary work.

New Critics and Russian formalists generally argued that literary study should be grounded in literary works alone. A poem or novel, they said, is self-sufficient; it sits there like a beacon and broadcasts the same meaning to everyone. Your job, as a reader, is to look closely at it to see what it's saying.

The critics in this chapter are not a unified group like the New Critics, but they do agree, in one way or another, that the novel you're reading is not simply and objectively there.

Reader-response criticism, as it's usually called, wants you to see a more active and interactive process at work. And it's the process itself that deserves to be the focus of your attention.

IN THEORY

"Good, Sweet, Honey, Sugar-Candied Reader …" —Aphra Behn, from the preface to her play *The Dutch Lover* (1673)

As you'll see, it really comes down to where you think the meaning comes from when you read. Consider your options. Meaning comes from (A) the text: there it is, sending its objective message to you and anyone who looks at it; (B) your response: only you can transform marks on a page into a meaningful story; or (C) somewhere in between.

Exploring "C"—the exact nature of this middle space—is what this chapter is all about.

Making It Up as You Go Along

The middle space is between two ends of a spectrum. One end is the text and one is you, and the transaction between these is the process that creates meaning. In fact, according to some of the reader-response critics, that novel you're reading doesn't even exist until this transaction takes place. All you have is a text without meaning until reading comes along. The marks on the pages may be there (call them "the text"), but they don't become "the novel" until you make it happen.

IN THEORY

"The convergence of text and reader brings the literary work into existence …. This virtual dimension is not the text itself, nor is it the imagination of the reader: it is the coming together of text and imagination." —Wolfgang Iser

According to reader-response criticism, then, the text is a potential structure that you actualize—or "concretize," as they liked to say—in the transaction of your reading.

This means that as you work your way through a novel, you should acknowledge the steps of this interactive process. You should notice the active transactions taking place, rather than assume you're only a passive recipient of the novel's information.

Show Your Work

One way to do this, according to the American critic Stanley Fish, is to be honest about your actual reading experience. Fish suggested a mode of criticism that carefully follows a reader's thoughts while reading the words of any literary work.

Here's one of Fish's own brief examples. It's from John Milton's poem *Lycidas* (pronounced *LIH-sid-duss*), and Fish says it shows how a reader's reaction is part of the literary work's meaning.

> He must not float upon his wat'ry bier
> Unwept ...

Okay, stop snickering at "wat'ry bier." *Bier* here means a platform for a casket, so the image of a watery bier indicates a funeral on water. Now, that first line says, "He must not float upon his wat'ry bier" ... and then the line stops. Fish says that when the line stops, your mind pauses, too. And when you pause, you think, "He must not die!" because that's the meaning of the single line.

But then you keep reading, and you see "Unwept." Aha! So it's not that the guy shouldn't die, it's that he shouldn't die *without being mourned*. Fish's point is that while you read you think one thing at one point ("The guy shouldn't die!") then you think another thing at another point ("The guy shouldn't die without being mourned!").

The payoff? Other critics want you to wait until you've got the complete picture before making a judgment about meaning. They want you to wait until "the end" to comment, rather than pay ongoing close attention to all the different adjustments you make while reading. Sometimes these thoughts seem rather minor, and you may not even bother to notice them all, but for reader-response criticism, they're fascinating.

Fish argued that the meaning of a literary work is not confined to your final pronouncement. The meaning of the text is what it *does*, not just what it *says*. And part of what this poem does is provide you with one phrase that actually moves you through two different ways of thinking about poor Lycidas. It leaves you with a layered understanding of him, rather than a static one.

Draw a Blank

Next up: your response to things that aren't there.

If literature is all about the spectrum of transactions between the text and you, then according to reader-response critics, you really get to shine when there are blank spaces or gaps in the text.

Wolfgang Iser (pronounced *EE-zuh*) paid very close attention to the way a text activates your creativity. For Iser, reading is really a process of combining what is physically in print with what you make up in your mind—and very often you don't even think about the difference between the two. It's okay, though—everyone does it.

The idea, of course, is that texts never tell you absolutely everything, and when the author doesn't give you a particular detail, you may supply it yourself. It can be as simple as when a character "hears a rapid knock on the door," and you naturally assume that someone wants in. You might also be told by the narrator that the woman who comes through the door "is wearing a perfectly lovely hat," but you are left to imagine the details of that hat. In fact, when you remember the scene later, you might even "remember" the details of the hat, as if they were part of the text, when they are actually your creation.

Moreover, reading the same novel twice actually creates two different novels, because you fill in the blanks so differently during your first and second trips through the text.

Iser called the whole process of reading an example of "meaning projection," because you don't just draw meaning out of the text, but you project the novel's meaning outward, in collaboration with the printed text.

And this brings us back to you and Jane Austen.

Iser pointed out that the writer and critic Virginia Woolf (1882–1941) was a big fan of Austen precisely because of the way Austen would leave gaps for readers to fill in. Woolf said that Austen often "stimulates us to supply what is not there" in her texts, and this brings us even closer to the novel's characters and events.

In the famous opening scene of *Pride and Prejudice*, for example, two characters are involved. The first few paragraphs include at least three significant gaps for you to add information, assumptions, or other information.

> It is a truth universally acknowledged, that a single man in possession of a good fortune, must be in want of a wife.

However little known the feelings or views of such a man may be on his first entering a neighborhood, this truth is so well fixed in the minds of the surrounding families, that he is considered the rightful property of someone or other of their daughters.

"My dear Mr. Bennet," said his lady to him one day, "have you heard that Netherfield Park is let at last?"

Mr. Bennet replied that he had not.

Now it's your turn. Since the sentence "Mr. Bennet replied that he had not" isn't a direct quotation, we don't know exactly what Mr. Bennet says, and even more, we don't know exactly *how* he says it ("No, dear, I haven't"? "No, darling"? "By golly, I sure haven't, Mrs. B"?). Of course, most readers have already started making inferences here.

The general idea is that Mr. Bennet is the patient listener, while Mrs. Bennet talks on. The fact that the text does not say this in actual words supports the idea that it's you, the reader, who really has to fill out the picture, taking your cues from what you're given—such as the subtle shift away from direct quotation—and then "writing" what turn out to be crucial aspects of the novel.

The passage continues:

"But it is," returned she; "for Mrs. Long has just been here, and she told me all about it."

Mr. Bennet made no answer.

Your turn again. If Mr. Bennet made no answer, why does Austen include this comment? Can't she just move on, since Mr. Bennet didn't say anything? It must be important that he doesn't say anything. Mr. Bennet's "no answer" is a classic gap to fill in, and again, most readers have filled it in with the assumption that he doesn't care about (or doesn't want to seem interested in) what Mrs. Bennet is saying.

And finally:

"Do you not want to know who has taken it?" cried his wife impatiently.

"*You* want to tell me, and I have no objection to hearing it."

This was invitation enough.

You've probably already caught on that "filling the gap" can also be roughly translated as "reading between the lines." In this case, you know, as a reader, that Austen is developing these characters' relationship as you had expected. You can then safely translate the line about an "invitation" to mean that Mrs. Bennet is about to proceed with her story.

Now, with all this imaginative co-authoring going on, Iser still cautions that you can't just read anything at all between the lines. You can't go completely crazy and start filling in the blanks of *Pride and Prejudice* with zombies, for example.

Oh wait. That's been done, hasn't it? Well, Iser would say that *Pride and Prejudice and Zombies,* by Jane Austen and Seth Grahame-Smith (2009), is more of a creative revision rather than reader-response, since the book adds physical words to the page (hence the two author names on the book's cover).

Strictly speaking, reader-response criticism relies on the idea that the printed text serves as the "potential structure" of any novel. The novel—as a novel—is the virtual dimension that exists only in your mind as you read.

Still, what if you can't help but read *Pride and Prejudice* and think about zombies? Or, put another way, what if you read a text and you don't fill in the blanks correctly? And who's to say what "correct" is, anyway?

Glad you asked.

Crack the Code

The success in filling in the blanks, or in imaginatively interacting with a text in order to create a novel, presumes a lot. It presumes you're reading in a certain way. It presumes, for example, that you understand what Jane Austen is implying in her text. If you don't get it, much of the meaning is lost on you, like a joke that goes over your head. Luckily for us, there's a theory behind this.

The theory of communication as a process of encoding and decoding argues that information doesn't just go from one person's head to another, but goes through at least a couple of steps. First, the senders of any message can't really say anything without dealing with their own various worldviews, vocabularies, and contexts (such as motivation) for communicating.

This means any message is encoded when it gets spoken, written, or whatever—and any recipient has to make sense of it as a code. And since recipients, in their turn, have their own ways of looking at the world, their own vocabularies and personal contexts, they may or may not decode the message the way it was intended.

Put another way, it isn't so much this:

$$Sender \rightarrow Message \rightarrow Recipient$$

It's more like this:

Sender's worldview, way of saying things, and immediate context
↓
Coded message
↓
Recipient's worldview, way of saying things, and immediate context

But wait—doesn't a lot of what we say seem perfectly natural and not coded? Aren't we just communicating? Reader-response criticism says no. It says you might feel like you're just communicating, but you have only succeeded in naturalizing the codes. That is, the codes have become so much a part of you that you don't even recognize them as codes anymore.

IN THEORY

"There is no intelligible discourse without the operation of a code …. There is no degree zero in language." —Stuart Hall

And think of where this logic leads. If reading a novel always requires a process of encoding and decoding, it means interacting with the text by imaginatively filling in the text's gaps has rules. Yes, rules. Like the subtle rules that make a joke funny or not to any particular person. You know the feeling when someone tells a joke and you "get it," but you still don't think it's funny? In fact, you might even find the joke teller offensive because he expects you to play along and see the humor the way he does, and you'd rather not. Same thing with literature. Just whom does Jane Austen think she's writing to?

Like a joke teller, an author presupposes a certain kind of audience. And interesting things happen when you ask whether *you* are the text's intended recipient or not.

RELATIONS

The chapters of Part 4 consider several important ways that readers have reacted to the "preferred codes" of literature, such as the code of having to read from a male reader's perspective, no matter who you are.

Making You Up as It Goes Along

Reader-response criticism would seem to be doing you a favor by emphasizing your role in the creation of literature. But there's a flip side to the idea that the reader creates the literature, which is that the literature, in various ways, creates the reader.

"You" Are There

Wolfgang Iser alerted people to the general idea that reading makes your mind into a kind of hybrid, mixing up the text's material and the "you" who reads. It isn't hard to see how this works. In the joke comparison, for example, you hear the joke, and while one side of your mind plays the part of the intended audience by getting the joke, another side of your mind monitors things, and might even resist and move on.

Iser calls the two sides the "implied reader" and the "actual reader," and they always operate together when you read. The implied reader is the side responsible for filling in the gaps according to the text's inner, fictional logic. It's also the "Dear Reader" that the narrator sometimes talks to.

The actual reader more actively—and sometimes critically—compares what's going on with all kinds of other, external aspects.

You know the term *suspension of disbelief,* which means you can read about made-up things without worrying about real-world logic? That's your implied reader at work. And when you decide that one novel is better than another? That's your actual reader at work.

APPLY IT

About that novel you're reading now: Do you think the author is talking to *you?* What kind of reader does the text seem to expect, and how can you tell?

And what about that author? If "you" aren't you, is the "author" the author? Of course not. It's only fair.

The implied author, according to the American critic Wayne C. Booth (1921–2005), isn't the actual human author responsible for a literary work. Instead, it's what you imagine the author to be, based on the literary work in front of you. It's a kind of image of what you think organizes and holds the novel together.

Of course, sometimes this is very similar to the narrator. As we saw in Chapter 2, the narrator might be anything from a named character to a presence that tells the story, but it isn't the same as the actual author. Booth's implied author goes a bit further to suggest that even behind the narrator lies the author figure that you create from the text. And each reader's implied author is different from any other reader's implied author, because it's a reflection of your own reading experience.

So it's come to this. You're not only as much the author of *Pride and Prejudice* as Jane Austen is, you're also the creator of "Jane Austen."

You're welcome again, dear reader.

Group Dynamics

But before you go getting overly excited about your individual creative abilities, Stanley Fish would like to have a word with you about interpretive communities. An interpretive community describes the set of strategies or codes that any group uses to approach literature. And yes, you have to belong to one.

According to Fish, all that ability you have to imaginatively interact with the text is not natural, but learned. You become a part of an interpretive community through education, religion, popular culture, and any other shared experience of making sense of texts. The reading strategies of an interpretive community tell you what to look for in a literary work, what to find important, and what to ignore.

The most important thing about the strategies of an interpretive community is that they influence the way you read everything because they exist even before you read, predisposing you to have certain responses to what you read. Like a scientific paradigm that determines what gets taken seriously as a fact or not, interpretive communities call the shots when you read.

In fact, Fish said you can see and read only what your interpretive principles let you see and read. You'll literally screen out anything that doesn't fit the model you're used to. And you'll always find what you're looking for in a novel, because you'll cause it to be there in the first place.

APPLY IT

Is it possible to become more self-aware of your own interpretive communities? Consider what you find valuable or interesting in the novel you're reading now. Do you often look for the same features in other novels?

Getting Real

Now, while some reader-response critics locate a literary work's true meaning in an individual reader's experience, or in the interpretive community responsible for the reader's experience, others want you to consider how meaning emerges from many layers of reading experiences over time.

For example, Hans Robert Jauss (1921–1997, pronounced *Yowce*) sees everyone's reading experience as an active, interactive engagement, just like the other reader-response critics, but he went a bit further to consider how all of these responses should be considered together in their historical perspective.

So according to reception theory, that novel you're reading means what it means because of a kind of historical inheritance of responses. As a reader, you inherit much of the historical weight of the novel, and your expectations and judgments come from that inheritance. Jauss called this your horizon of expectations, and it's made up of what you imagine should happen in whatever you're reading.

Once again, you're predisposed to expect and value certain things in certain types of literature. If you're reading a Jane Austen novel, for example, you might expect to find characters that speak indirectly, plots that hinge on marriages, and lots of irony. On the other hand, if you're reading modern poetry, you'll have a different horizon of expectations. Horizons of expectations can be especially important for parody, when, for example, an author wants to mess with the traditional approach to a book by, say, adding zombies.

IN THEORY

"Any new literary work evokes for the reader the horizon of expectations and rules familiar from earlier texts, which are then varied, corrected, altered, or even just reproduced." —Hans Robert Jauss

In this way, then, history is made because you, as part of the reading public, contribute to a literary work's future horizon of expectations. Your responses become part of the work's inheritance of reception (particularly if you're a critic).

Regaining Consciousness

And finally, as you've been expecting, it's time to consider what happens when your experience as a reader turns into the spiritual union between your mind and the author's consciousness as it exists in the artistic universe of the literary work. I'm sure you saw that coming.

IN THEORY

"Criticism is primordially consciousness of the consciousness of another, the transposition of the mental universe of an author into the interior space of the critic's mind." —J. Hillis Miller

According to critics of the Geneva School, literature is literally a form of consciousness. In fact, it's the only form of the author's consciousness that's available to you. It's out there, open to inspection and careful reading, while any other form of consciousness would be, well, locked inside the author's head.

Geneva School critics took very seriously the idea that true literary meaning is found between the reader and the text. They set out to actually enter the consciousness of writers, like Dickens and Flaubert, through "creative participation" with the author's texts, letters, notebooks, and anything else they could get their hands on. By carefully reading these works, the critic (and regular readers can do it, too, in their way) would inhabit the author's mind.

Pride and Prejudice, in other words, doesn't just offer you insights into Jane Austen's mind, but it invites you to become Austen's mind itself, because the novel is an emanation of her consciousness.

Don't mention it, dear reader.

The Least You Need to Know

- The text doesn't just give you meaning—reading creates meaning.
- Literary works are filled with gaps for you to fill.
- You are preloaded with rules and conventions for filling in the gaps.
- A literary work's true meaning is reflected in its reception over time.
- Literature lets you merge with an author's consciousness.

Aristotle and Friends Plot the Course

In This Chapter

- Aristotle approves of fiction
- Literature's emotional release
- How plots work their magic
- Journey to the center of a novel

Why do you read sad novels? Why do you watch violent movies? What's wrong with you?

It's a very old question: why does anyone bother with made-up stories, particularly if they're sad, violent, or otherwise filled with unfortunate behavior? We all like to lose ourselves in made-up stories from time to time; there doesn't seem to be anything wrong with that. Of course, some influential people—and I'm looking at you, Plato (see Chapter 7)—have suggested that made-up stories are in fact bad for you, since the pretend world gets in the way of understanding genuine reality. Then there are the folks who say that fictional violence and misery are models for—and maybe even causes of—the wrong behavior in real life.

To these charges, Aristotle and some of his friends in literary history have said (and I'm paraphrasing), "Now calm down and let's look at these issues more closely. You can and should enjoy literature and other made-up stories. They can be entertaining and even good for you. Of course, a lot depends on exactly how you read, so we'll advise you on that. Also, terms and conditions apply."

Reading for Fun and (Intellectual) Profit

Aristotle (384–322 B.C.E.) started it off for the Western tradition by arguing that as a human being, you are naturally attracted to imitation. You not only enjoy seeing things imitated, but you also learn from seeing things imitated. You did this as a baby, and you'll continue to do it your whole life.

Philosophically, this is a very important move, since it directly answers Plato's challenge to prove literature can be as good for you as, well, philosophy. The trick is in getting this inherent human connection with fiction to work for us, not against us. According to Aristotle, it works for us when we actively understand some of the central features of literary and dramatic imitations. On the other hand, our attraction to imitation works against us when we don't really know what we're looking at, and when we look at the wrong kinds of imitations—such as too much violence or too many "bad examples." Sorry, kids.

But even with violence and bad examples, there are some ways around the danger. In fact, Aristotle made a point of saying that you can productively look at things in fiction that you wouldn't want to see in real life, and that you can even learn from bad examples. The key to getting anything good out of imaginative literature is to read things that both entertain and teach you, and to keep in mind the overall shape of the story you're reading. Think of that novel or movie as its own crafted object, rather than simply an imitation of something else. Plato had said that if fiction is defined as just watching some guy holding a mirror up to reality, you're better off turning to look at all the real life instead of mere reflections.

Aristotle and his friends want us to look more closely at that guy holding the mirror. They thought that if we really are hardwired to enjoy and learn from representations of things, then we should try to find out where the value comes from.

IN THEORY

"Since the mind of man does naturally tend to, and seek after the truth; and therefore the nearer anything comes to the imitation of it, the more it pleases."
—John Dryden

And since you asked, by "Aristotle's friends" I mean two groups of critics in particular, and I'll discuss their views in this chapter along with Aristotle's own views. One group, the *neoclassicists* of the seventeenth and eighteenth centuries, popularized those ideas of literary taste, decorum, and moral education that sound so stuffy to us now.

And they are stuffy, but they're also very clever and useful. The other group, emerging in the middle of the twentieth century, is typically called the Chicago School or the neo-Aristotelians.

> **DEFINITION**
>
> **Neoclassicism** refers to the idea that literature, art, and criticism should follow models set by ancient Greek and Roman (or classical) writers. The "neo" or new guys that we are concerned with in this chapter are critics who put a high value on order, appropriateness, and the rationality of general concepts in literature. Neoclassical criticism is often contrasted to Romantic criticism, as we'll see in Chapter 8, which puts a higher value on individual experience.

Delightful Instruction

When it comes to imaginative literature, our time is best spent with works that both "delight and instruct," a phrase primarily associated with the Roman writer Horace (65–8 B.C.E.), but used in one version or another by many other critics. Aristotle explained that literature doesn't get in the way of understanding real life, it actually helps us understand real life. Appreciating imitation—and any form of representation—is an intellectual virtue. Reading and studying literature, therefore, does not detract from understanding reality, but actively contributes to your knowledge of truth. You learn something about reality by looking at imitations of it.

Neoclassical critics—like John Dryden (1631–1700), Alexander Pope (1688–1744), and Samuel Johnson (1709–1784)—sought to bring classical values, including the "delight and teach" view of literature, to their own society as a way of keeping things civilized. Literature was beginning to spread very quickly and widely among all kinds of people, and the neoclassical critics wanted to uphold standards of taste. While an older, more exclusive and aristocratic group of readers may have claims to defining culture, the emerging middle class—"common readers"—could and should also be influenced by literature's moral and social values. The good ones, that is.

In the twentieth century, the *neo-Aristolelians* of the Chicago School created new college courses and an entirely new curriculum to take advantage of the "instinctive pleasure in learning" that all people get from storytelling and plots. Like the New Critics, the Chicago School created a business in academia and changed the way English majors get their degrees. But more on that toward the end of this chapter.

DEFINITION

Neo-Aristotelian was a label given, unsolicited, to a group of critics at the University of Chicago in the 1950s who didn't actually argue for a return to all of Aristotle's principles, but did revolve around Aristotle's fundamental view that criticism should develop organically out of actual literary examples.

What these two schools of criticism share with Aristotle is a concern for the intellectual virtues of reading literature. And central to this concern is seeing each literary work as its own crafted object, leading to its own kind of appreciation and critical analysis. Learning from literature doesn't come through simply thinking about the subject matter or what literature reflects or imitates, although that's important. Instead, real literary appreciation and judgment comes from viewing each work as an artistic totality—seeing what it's trying to do as a work of art.

What does this mean for you? Three things. First, it means you can read fiction with a clear conscience, which is nice in case you ever run into anyone who wants to give you a hard time. This approach to literature and criticism supports the idea that literature can be seen as a leisure activity and still be good for you, even raising the reading of literature to a level equal with any of the sciences.

Next, it means you can even read for fun! Sort of. According to these critics, you can go right on enjoying literature, as long as you learn something from it. The "delightful" part of the equation can and should lead you to learn something from that novel or movie, whether you know it or not at the time.

Third, evaluation is back! That is, it's okay to make judgments about what you're reading, based on literary as well as moral arguments. Analysis is one thing, and we'll get to that in this chapter, but good old-fashioned opinion by an ordinary reader carries a lot of weight with these critics, so feel free to extol the virtues of a stunning novel like Alice Walker's *The Color Purple*, even though parts of it make you cry like a baby.

Get It Out of Your System, or Not

And this brings us back to those sad and violent stories. What is it that makes unpleasant real-life situations not just bearable, but positively attractive in literature?

IN THEORY

"For there are some things that distress us when we see them in reality, but the most accurate representations of these same things we view with pleasure."
—Aristotle

One answer is suggested by the line, "It's only funny when it happens to someone else." In other words, you find something in literature appealing because it isn't happening to you. The problem with this explanation, what makes it only a partial solution, is that it doesn't account for empathy. At least part of the attraction of reading about someone else's misfortune is the compassion we feel for the character.

One of the most famous terms associated with Aristotle offers a way of understanding the complex relationship between characters, our own feelings, and empathy. The term is *catharsis*, and there are three interpretations these days of what Aristotle meant by the term.

The oldest definition explains that "having a catharsis" means getting something out of your system. It's like having second-hand emotions through literature instead of through real-life experiences. When a play or any other work of literature is successful at bringing about a catharsis in the audience, it helps purge or relieve that audience of these uncomfortable feelings. The idea here is that any work of fiction is a controlled environment, so crying at sad parts and being afraid at scary parts actually leaves you feeling better when you're finished.

IN THEORY

"The chief advantage which these fictions have over real life is, that their authors are at liberty, though not to invent, yet to select objects, and to cull from the mass of mankind, those individuals upon which the attention ought most to be employed; as a diamond, though it cannot be made, may be polished by art, and placed in such a situation, as to display that lustre which before was buried among common stones." —Samuel Johnson

Another definition of catharsis is purification. According to this view, Aristotle sees fiction as having the power to purify your emotions by showing you the right things to worry about. Turns out not every instance of sadness and fear is worth your time, morally speaking. The best emotions for writers to represent, according to Aristotle, were pity and fear. Pity is good, because it's your experience of seeing bad things happen to (generally) good people. Fear is good because, well, everyone feels fear and needs to do something about it. Because of the controlled environment of fiction, according to the neoclassical critics, a writer can guide you to feel pity for the right characters and fear for the right reasons.

The third interpretation sees catharsis as a form of clarification. What's being clarified? Well, let's take a classic Greek example of big-time pity and fear—the Oedipus story. In this play, a fairly well-meaning guy kills his father and marries his own mother without knowing who they are, then ends up discovering the considerably pitiful and fearful truth at last. Seriously, who wants to see that?

Apparently a lot of you want to see that, and Aristotle would say it's because you're not just watching the pitiful and scary events; you're watching the pitiful and scary events in an arrangement and in an artistic whole that helps you understand how such horrible things can happen. The fictional context and especially the fictional boundaries (you can see everything from beginning to end) allows you to think about all the stages of Oedipus's story, and this helps clarify your understanding of things like tragic flaws, human choices, and plain old bad luck. In this way, catharsis-as-clarification brings you the very Aristotelian pleasure of learning about human nature and fate.

Mime in a Box

So if pity and fear are good, extreme pity and fear should be even better, right? Nope, not for these critics, and not in this chapter. There are limits to this, because there are rules for what fiction should imitate. Creating and enjoying made-up stories should revolve around noble, dignified people and events, rather than "inferior" ones. Except comedy. There's room in comedy to imitate disreputable folks and their antics. Still, according to Aristotle and his friends, you should learn something even from comedy. Like not to stick your tongue to a frozen flag pole.

IN THEORY

"It is justly considered as the greatest excellency of art, to imitate nature; but it is necessary to distinguish those parts of nature, which are most proper for imitation: greater care is still required in representing life, which is so often discolored by passion, or deformed by wickedness." —Samuel Johnson

It really all boils down to how you define literature itself, something we'll be investigating in more detail in the chapters of Part 3. For now, think about some basic options: just like a painting, a literary work can be seen as a creation, an expression, or an imitation (or any combination of these three, with one in the lead). As a writer, is your main goal to create something new, to express yourself, or to represent some aspect of life around you? And as a reader, which of these three expectations do you bring to a novel?

Aristotle's legacy is to highlight imitation or *mimesis* as the artist's goal, yet it's a particular type of imitation. For one, it's an imitation of actions, not just of people and things. Unlike paintings, fiction allows for the representation of actions occurring through an ordered series of steps. And Aristotle insists that it's by imitating actions that fiction can accurately represent truths about people and things. That mime trapped in a box? He's not announcing his predicament in a simple statement, he's imitating actions that make you feel his frustration. Wait until he has to fight the wind with a broken umbrella.

DEFINITION

Mimesis (pronounced *my-MEE-sis*) can mean imitation or, broadly, any kind of representation. It can refer to wordless plays (miming) as well as the kind of representation you see in realistic painting.

This all leads to Aristotle's emphasis on the writer's role in *organizing* the elements of that imitation. It's the organization of imitated actions that makes all the difference; it's what gives literature its power. People, things, and events of real life are not just reflected but transformed by the "mirror" of art into something that can have a very different effect on you than reality does.

Plot Changes Everything

Plot, described most simply, is the playing out of events in a story. The plot begins, there's a conflict or two, one thing leads to another, a surprise turn here or there, then there's a resolution and a conclusion. And while Aristotle may start with his famous definition, "I mean by plot the arrangement of incidents," he and the other critics quickly turn to the more subtle and remarkable aspects of plot.

For starters, according to these critics, a good story should be constructed so that you don't even have to read the actual novel to feel a reaction. For example, your emotions of pity and fear should be aroused simply by hearing the plot of a good story paraphrased (don't tell the formalists). Aristotle said that's definitely what would happen to anyone hearing the plot of *Oedipus* described. Even a bad storyteller could get mileage out of a good plot, since it's the deceptively simple-sounding arrangement of incidents that powers the entire fiction.

The Rules of the Game

Plot's effect is so strong, in part, because there are rules to it that keep reappearing in all kinds of stories. Even Plato recognized that good stories ought to be shaped organically, like the human form, with a head, body, and feet. Not to be outdone, Aristotle decreed that a good narrative should include a beginning, a middle, and an end, in that order. Really, once you make plain speaking your shtick, you can get away with anything.

Still, even this basic setup for plot gets nicely complicated and very interesting. Think of all the novels you've read or movies you've seen in which the beginning is really an event taken from the middle of the overall story. Or stories in which the importance of the ending lies in the sense of a new beginning. (For more on critics' approaches to these kind of neat plot twists, see Chapters 2 and 4.)

Writers have relied on classical models of plots ever since they were described. For example, writers recognize that events are better when they're linked by cause and effect, rather than just lined up as random episodes. Classical writers also liked plots that featured characters who are respectable and likable, yet have tragic flaws. A character's tragic flaw leads to trouble, and the character's fortunes suffer a reversal. Aristotle really liked it when a character's own recognition of something previously unknown rounds out the tragedy—like Oedipus figuring out what he'd done.

Then there are the three unities. A French dramatist, Pierre Corneille (1606–1684, pronounced *kor-NAY*), is well known for encouraging aspiring playwrights to stick to the "unities of time, place, and action." This meant that any good play should be unified in action, so that the entire plot takes place only in one room (or in as much space as the stage allowed); unified in time, so that the time depicted on the stage was the same as the time of the performance (Corneille would have loved the real time of the TV show *24*); and unified in action, so that all the incidents of the plot are unified around a single, central idea.

Naturally, some writers thought this was gold. Finally, a cookie-cutter approach to success in the theater! Just as naturally, others thought that adhering to the three unities was much too limiting. Samuel Johnson, in particular, while writing about Shakespeare's rather free-flowing plot style, was especially hilarious in condemning the three unities. Johnson explained, in so many words, that audiences weren't stupid, they knew they were watching plays and not real life, and they had paid to see a good show, so give them what they want. (Although, he added, do be sure to instruct as well as please; I mean, we have to keep up civilized standards of taste and decorum no matter what.)

One Ring to Rule Them All

Now, while Aristotle himself did not prescribe all three unities, he was clear about the unity of action. For Aristotle, when a story's action is unified, it means that all the pieces of the plot fit together. So not only can you follow a unified plot more easily than one that isn't unified, but you can analyze its various parts to see what each of them contributes to the overall story.

For all you fans of Charles Dickens, this means those multiple subplots can and should be brought into your appreciation of his painstakingly plotted novels, like *Great Expectations*. Unity of action is highlighted in complicated or multilayered plots, because the effect of the overall story relies on tying up loose ends and showing how details, no matter how minor, can be related to a novel's main story line.

IN THEORY

"You will find it infinitely pleasing to be led in a labyrinth of design, where you see some of your way before you, yet discern not the end till you arrive at it." —John Dryden

For the critics of the Chicago School, unity of action was huge. They saw plot as a sign of something absolutely essential to understanding a work of fiction. They called this something *form*, but if I use that term in this discussion we'll get into a dreadful tangle with other uses of the word. Luckily, they also used the Aristotelian term *first principle* to describe the same thing, so let's use that.

A literary work's first principle is the logic and power behind the plot. It's the reason everything is arranged the way it is. And I mean everything. All aspects of that novel you're reading are coordinated by this first principle, or principle of construction.

Not only are the incidents of the plot arranged because of this principle, but all the characters do and say things because of this principle, and the setting and imagery appear in order to manifest this principle.

When you think of the plot, therefore, you're really thinking about the most visible sign of the principle, logic, or power that unifies the work you're reading. The critics of the Chicago School didn't want you to think of plot as just one literary element among others. You shouldn't break down a novel into separate pieces like plot, character, and point of view, and think of plot as a mere framework of action for all the other literary elements. Instead, you should consider how the plot leads you to understand the true center of the literary work.

This gets pretty interesting in practice. The Chicago School critics would approach any given literary work with the goal of discovering its first principle, then of exploring how the various aspects of the work contribute to this principle. These critics reacted against relying on formal features that were said to operate pretty much the same way in any work they appeared in, as the New Critics had argued (see Chapter 3). The Chicago School critics emphasized that each work is distinct, and the reader has to find out how each work makes use of formal features, rather than the other way around.

IN THEORY

"We tended to see most stories as more like people in action than like well-wrought urns or efforts at communication." —Wayne C. Booth

Here, the contrast is between the New Critics viewing a literary work as a "well-made container" for formal features, and the Chicago School emphasis on the action that defines a work's real meaning.

Characters, for example, don't even have to function the same way in all novels. That is, in one novel a character seems to do and say things based on human personality, while in another novel, a character operates like an allegory. Take Edith Wharton's *The House of Mirth*. In this novel, the main character, Lily Bart, starts off like a "normal" human character, and that's what really keeps the reader interested. But then, according to many readers, Lily makes some choices that suggest her actions are actually guided by the logic of an allegory. Lily *represents* something, and that's why she does what she does. Her actions have to imitate the concept or message she's representing, not just a human personality.

Or, consider reading a simple allegory in which characters named Mr. Greedy and Mr. Irritable go to a restaurant together. Among other things, Mr. Greedy keeps asking for more bread, while Mr. Irritable complains about everything. Why, oh why do they act like this? They have to. Can't they ever change? No. The first principle of an allegory is not to explore fully human characters, but to illustrate a lesson.

The Chicago School critics stressed the importance of finding out what any given work is trying to do before you go trying to prove that it's doing it well or badly. Appreciating a novel means finding out if the novel is guided, for example, by the principle of following a psychological character, or by an idea or philosophy, or even by the demands of representing a historical era.

APPLY IT

What do you think is the first principle of a novel you have read recently? Think of the steps and stages of the plot, and consider what they seem to be driving at. Do most of the incidents suggest character development? Allegorical interpretation? A lesson in morality?

They're Just Guidelines, Really

With all this talk about discovering the first principle of a literary work, you might be tempted to ask, "Sure, but what if my view of the first principle is different from my friend's? Who's right?" Good news—you're both right. Of course, there are conditions: you have to support your view of the text's main power or logic with details from the actual text. And you have to know the text and its contexts (including cultural contexts) well enough to get inside the author's head. But as long as both of your interpretations are involved and informed enough, there's no reason why they can't both be valid—and interesting.

Wayne C. Booth wrote a terrific essay, "Pluralism and Its Rivals," in which he shows how a single short story can be usefully interpreted in very different ways. For each of the interpretations, he drew on exactly the same source material—James Joyce's story, "Araby"—but develops distinct readings by identifying different first principles. Booth illustrated that when you begin with different starting points or perspectives, you inevitably emphasize certain features of a text, and you'll make connections between those features that legitimately form convincing interpretations.

Such an approach to literary criticism—known as pluralism—asserts that there is not simply one interpretation to be discovered in any given work. Instead, the activity of critics, or readers in general, is to explore what they have made of the text. "Each of us constitutes our own 'Araby,'" Booth wrote, not because we can make any story mean anything we want, but because it's the very nature of literature to draw different interpretations from a thinking individual who is offered concrete details arranged into a pattern.

The pattern, however, as Booth points out, is like any particular person's view of a cone. Yes, a cone. If you're directly above the cone, what you see looks like a round circle, and if you're to the side you'll see a triangle. If you look at the cone from anywhere else you see things with complicated math names. The point is, reading and criticism is all about doing the best we can to explore and explain what we do see.

The Least You Need to Know

- Literature is based on imitations of actions.
- Fiction's rules and boundaries help you understand reality.
- Good literature should please and instruct.
- Literary works are powered by a central principle of construction.
- Critical pluralism recognizes the validity of any well-developed interpretation.

What Is Literature, Anyway?

Simply defining what literature is has turned out to be one of the most vital and fascinating aspects of theory and criticism. In the chapters of this part, we'll discuss some definitions that you may find familiar, along with others that might strike you as unusual but stimulating.

The story begins with Plato, who disapproved of literature in general and dared poets to explain the value of their art. This set off a storm of responses that continues to this day. The poet-critics get their say, so you'll hear from Shelley, Keats, Wordsworth, and others. You'll also explore the essential political and psychological definitions of literature, and see how defining literature with respect to language itself leads to some fascinating current investigations into the science of the mind.

Plato's Fundamental Gripe Against Literature

In This Chapter

- Plato's idealism
- The false world of appearances
- Why literature is dangerous
- Inspired by the muses
- Plato's endless legacy

Someone once said, "All of Western philosophy is but a footnote to Plato." You could also say that all of literary criticism is just a series of love letters to Plato. Sometimes it's a letter that says, "Oh yes, Plato, you're the only one for me!" Or it's a letter that says, "Oh Plato, why don't you love me back?" And sometimes it's a letter that says, "I am so over you; give me back my key."

Why is this? What did Plato say to get everyone so excited? And I mean everyone. Well, the guy who made the "footnote" remark claimed it was because Plato said pretty much everything there was to say about life, death, and knowledge, so the only thing left for everyone else to do was humbly cover some of the same ground in their own inferior ways. I would say you can just think of Plato as that very early crush you'll never, ever forget, whether you want to or not.

Of course, you should also think of Plato as the ancient Greek philosopher who argued that literature was bad for society and ended up as the fundamental friend or foe of practically all literary theory and criticism ever devised.

He was that good.

What's the Big Idea Here?

For Plato, art is all about usefulness, not artistry. Plato would look at a painting of a horse and say—well, he wouldn't say anything for a while. First he would look really closely at that painting of the horse, staring suspiciously at the details, then he would raise an eyebrow and say, "I'm no expert, but this horse's reins don't look right." And he'd read a description of someone driving a chariot and say, "So is this accurate?" Plato had a serious case of preferring content over form.

If this were the whole story, we'd just be left with Plato as a cranky old guy who didn't understand what artists are trying to do. But there is a lot more to the story, mostly involving Plato's fundamental view of the relationship between truth and imitation, a view that's still very much in circulation.

The problem with all imaginative art, Plato said, is that it's fake. And you say, "Okay, that's fine, I can see that this painting of a bowl of fruit is an imitation of a bowl of fruit, not the real thing. Why is that a problem?" Plato said it's a problem because the number-one goal for all of us is to understand true reality.

By true reality, Plato meant something that we'll be looking at more closely in this chapter, but for now, think of it as the model or ideal version of that horse's reins, or the chariot, or the bowl of fruit. And it's not only the model, ideal, and perfect version of those things, it's the actual source of those things showing up in the first place.

Because of this unequal relationship between things and ideals, spending any time away from pondering actual reality and instead reading mere imitations or fictional stories will tend to be, according to Plato, a giant waste of time. And for thousands of years, as we'll see, critics have found it ironic, hypocritical, maddening, hilarious, and profoundly inspiring that Plato made most of his points by writing stories.

Me and My Shadows

Plato's most famous story is the allegory of the cave. In this dialogue, Socrates explains the state of human knowledge by comparing it to a group of people sitting in a cave watching shadows on the wall.

There they are, having a great time, watching these shadows move around, like a puppet show. And this group of shadow watchers really gets into the show. Some of them just look and laugh, or cry, while others study all the details very carefully, comparing their opinions and arguing about what the shadows mean and how to link together all the older episodes. They even give each other awards for coming up with the best theories about the shadows and making the smartest observations about them. Heavens, these people must spend a lot of time looking at these shadows.

IN THEORY

Who's who? To keep the order straight, from oldest to youngest, head to the SPA:

Socrates (ca. 470–399 B.C.E.)

Plato (ca. 428–347 B.C.E.)

Aristotle (384–322 B.C.E.)

Socrates was Plato's teacher, and he's featured in many of Plato's writings conducting conversation with people he met in Athens. Plato recreates these conversations, or dialogues, combining actual details from Socrates' philosophy with Plato's own views. Socrates himself never wrote any of his philosophy down, so we owe it to Plato and a few other writers for his place in history. Socrates was executed at the age of 70 by the Athenian government for "corrupting youth" with his unorthodox views. Aristotle (see Chapter 6) was then one of Plato's best students, and like students often do, Aristotle set out to correct and revise his teacher.

It turns out they have to spend a lot of time looking at the shadows because they're all chained to their chairs and can't even move their heads to turn around. They're completely stuck in this cave looking at shadows all the time. And I mean all the time. Behind the watchers are some people holding up objects, such as little cut-out houses or bunnies, so that the light from a fire casts each object's shadow on the wall in front of the watchers. And since they can't move, the watchers have no idea what's going on. They think what they're looking at is real.

Plato said this cave is a metaphor for the whole visible world. Everything you see around you right now is just a shadow image of some object held up in front of a flickering light source, and you're mistaking it for true reality. Feel free, as many have, to think of this like a movie theater instead of a cave. The details of Plato's comparison are so carefully arranged that they seem to predict film technology (yes, even digital projections if you want to go there). He was that good.

Anyway, there you are, chained into your seat watching movie after movie after movie, in the dark, with no other thought than that you're watching the real world. Then, according to Plato, someone grabs you out of your chair, spins you around and says, "Ha! Look! It's a projector that's been creating your so-called reality!"

Naturally, you get really annoyed and you can't see a thing, because the direct light from the projector hurts your eyes like crazy. The guy who dragged you out of your seat is trying to tell you that the reality you thought was real is only a show of images, not the real thing. He even shows you the little cut-out houses and bunnies—I mean the celluloid film—and he says this is the source of your "reality."

You look at the film frames carefully and say, "No way, what I saw was much more real; I'm going back to my seat." But the guy won't stop. He drags you out of the theater completely, right into the sunlight (it's a daytime showing), and says, "Now look—this is really real."

Naturally, you cover your eyes and shriek. Much too bright. Then a bit of time passes. You get some coffee. As your eyes grow accustomed to the new situation, you look around and realize the annoying guy was right. This is real reality. It's bright! You can touch it! It's incredibly beautiful! Oh, how could you have ever spent so much time in that miserable theater, even though *Grand Illusion* was excellent?

So you resolve to go back into the theater to help out your friends by bringing them out of the dark and into reality as well. Good luck with that. As soon as you go back inside, you can't see anything, you stumble around, make a lot of noise, and everyone tells you to be quiet. You say, "But wait, come outside, it's real out there and fake in here. Trust me, I know; I've been there!"

They say, "Okay, smarty, if you're so enlightened, prove you know more than us by saying something intelligent about this movie, just like you used to." And of course you can't, since it's still too dark and you don't care about these stupid movies anymore, and of course your self-satisfied friends are now sure you've lost it. It's probably best just to leave the theater and never go back, although Plato said we all have a moral obligation to keep trying to help our deluded friends.

Plato also said that if you annoy your friends too much by trying to drag them into the light of truth, and if they get sufficiently angry, they'll actually kill you just to keep their lives comfortable. Sounds rather extreme, but then look at what happened to Socrates.

In any case, here's what you're left with. Everything you see in the visible world is really an illusion. Not only that, but the sun isn't even the sun in this allegory. The sun you see—the real sun in the sky—is, according to Plato, only the projector's light. When we see things, we're looking at false images or imitations of true concepts, and we can thank the physical sun for lighting them up for us.

In the allegory, the "sun outside" actually represents the power behind pure thought or ideas. It's what starts everything else in motion. It enables our reason and our knowledge of true reality. Leaving the theater and moving into the world illuminated by this sun means living in the "intelligible realm," or the realm of pure ideas. So instead of living in the physical world you're used to and that everyone else seems to be living in, you live in a state of true awareness. Oh, and one other thing, it's not exactly all of you that gets to live in this realm, just your soul.

The best part? Just as Plato is getting to the real heart of explaining the allegory, he says this: "Whether it's true or not, only the god knows; but this is how I see it."

Now that's a philosophy that will get people talking.

A True Original

Plato's system, in which truth is at the top and only knowable by the soul, logically places literature much lower in the scale of things. In the system, God or nature is the first author, or maker, of things. These things are often called forms. Each form is the perfect model or idea behind the object it resembles in the visible realm. One of Plato's favorite examples is a bed. Maybe he was tired. In any case, the form of "bed" exists in a realm of pure thought, and it provokes people to make beds. These people are called bed makers. The beds they make may be nice, but they're only copies of the true original form of the bed. Philosophers also like to call Plato's forms unchanging nonsensibles, which is really charming. This would be in contrast to things called sensibles, which means anything you can sense with your, um, senses. A nonsensible can only be thought about, and they're unchanging because they are absolutely eternal.

Remember seeing cartoons of Greek philosophers drawing geometric diagrams in the dirt with sticks? There's a reason for that. You can think of Plato's forms like geometry truths: you've heard of a 90-degree angle or a circle? Of course! But have you ever really seen one? I mean, really seen one and experienced its absolutely flawless 90 degrees or its perfect circularity?

Look at any nearby angle right now. Looks pretty good, doesn't it? Yet if you measured it microscopically, you would discover the flaws and variations that are part of its actual physical nature. The only time you can come close to experiencing the absolute nonsensible truth that stands behind any worldly version of this angle is when you think the concept "90 degrees."

Okay, back to bed. While the timeless ideal form of the bed sits in the intelligible realm, the one you can only think about, a bed maker makes a copy of that form and it becomes your bed. Then, according to Plato, an artist draws a picture of your bed, and that becomes a copy of a copy. Artists, including writers, don't really make things, they make copies of things. Artists can't copy the ideal forms, they copy the physical versions they see on earth. So literature ends up being two big steps lower than truth. Plato's opinion is pretty straightforward: a poet or novelist "is the imitator of images and is very far removed from the truth."

RELATIONS

Note that while Plato saw artists as imitators, Aristotle (see Chapter 6) argued that artists are legitimate makers. In fact, Aristotle's use of the word *poet* emphasizes that word's derivation from the Greek word for "maker."

Making copies of copies is not only unsatisfying to Plato because you end up being "removed from reality," as he says. Beyond that, Plato warned of another danger. Remember that artists can't copy the forms themselves. The copiers of forms are those specialists who make the horse's reins or arrange a bowl of fruit and actually make something.

Artists or writers just imitate what they see other people making, and they'll inevitably ignore or even misrepresent some of the minute details of the actual products. If you're a doctor and you've seen a TV medical show lately, you know what I'm talking about. Plato was very worried that anyone who didn't have specialist knowledge of what is represented in art could be led into a dangerously false state of knowing what the truth is like.

Plato, of course, would take one look at contemporary culture, see how much we absorb our ideas about "reality" from the imitations in the media, and shake his head in dismay. Part of the problem is certainly our very human vulnerability to the lure of imitations, but part of the blame has to go to those unscrupulous imitators who know exactly what they're doing as they mislead us with their copies of copies.

Cheat Sheets

Then there's writing. Not just the writing that writers actually do, but writing itself. Plato had a complicated relationship with writing. You'll recall that Socrates is often the main character in Plato's dialogues, and that this Socrates character is based on the actual Socrates. The actual Socrates didn't write his philosophy down in anything like a textbook. Instead, he would walk around talking to people, questioning them in what has become known as the Socratic method so that whoever he was talking with had to understand right then and there whatever it was Socrates was getting at. It's also called dialectical argument or dialectical reasoning, and according to Socrates it's the only way to truly learn things—by sharing and testing your thoughts with other people. It's these kinds of conversations that Plato puts into the dialogues, like little plays of what might happen on any given day of Socrates' real life.

Socrates himself, however, was very suspicious of anything that took you away from immediate contact with knowledge. Anything you truly know should be in your head, not on a piece of paper. Anybody can walk around with a notebook full of brilliant things to say, but Socrates wanted you to draw only from what was in your head, since that was the only knowledge you could really call your own. Anything else is cheating.

IN THEORY

"For this invention [writing] will produce forgetfulness in the minds of those who learn to use it, because they will not practice their memory. Their trust in writing, produced by external characters which are no part of themselves, will discourage the use of their own memory within them." —Plato

In fact, memory becomes very precious when you look at knowledge this way. For Socrates, memory meant a direct connection to the true knowledge that you had in your head, which was itself aspiring to the even truer knowledge of the timeless forms. Writing ruins this immediacy and is condemned by Socrates as a kind of alien—and alienating—system. Want to have some fun? Walk up to Socrates at a party and show him your smartphone.

The point is, Socrates is setting a pretty high standard for knowledge, but you can see the logic in what he's saying. Writing and reading fool you (and sometimes others) into thinking you know more than you really know. Of course, the irony here is pretty clear, too. That is, if writing and reading are so bad, why did Plato write all that stuff down, and why did people take it seriously when they read it?

There are three ways to follow up on this irony (well, four, if you count the option to stop reading this book). One, take a look at Chapter 17's discussion of deconstruction, which is an approach to literature and philosophy that looks very, very, *very* carefully into the "can't live with it and can't live without it" relationship that Western philosophy has with writing. In essence, Plato is deconstruction's starting point. Two, keep in mind that Plato himself argued that you shouldn't take writing too seriously, and instead strive to gain true knowledge through actual human interaction.

And three, notice how Plato uses the dialogue style of his writing to recreate in writing something of the spirit of conversation. Many critics have pointed out that this style prompts you, even as a mere reader, to become a little more like a performer, or a participant in the dialogues. Instead of responding passively to a lecture, you're likely to actively question what Socrates and the other characters say, and this activity, argues Plato, might even contribute to true knowledge.

Writers Blocked

So Plato could see the value of some kinds of writing, but definitely not all. He was on a mission, after all, and it was to educate and improve mankind. He did this in part by founding a school in Athens called the Academy, where society's future leaders would be trained. And they would be trained in math, philosophy, and political science, not literature. In fact, the best guardians (men or women) for society would be philosopher-rulers who worked to reach true knowledge through study and dialectical argument.

Given this goal of social improvement as Plato saw it, the adjective *Platonic* refers to any theory or criticism with a primary (or even significant) interest in moral and social issues. This kind of criticism looks at any work of literature and asks first and foremost, "What good does it do for society?" And since the answer to this question has often been "not much," Plato recommended that all the poets—and makers of fictions in general—should be banned in a perfect society.

Bad Influence

This brings us back to the central question of why Plato saw literature as dangerous. If the point of society is to constantly improve itself, then many professions will be needed, such as medicine or agriculture. Plato called these activities arts, and he considered anyone who practiced them to be producing genuinely useful things. As we've seen, however, poets and other artists only imitate the things they see around them, they don't actually make anything.

In fact, because people will often be drawn to colorful and exciting imitations more readily than to reason, truth, or socially useful actions, the imitations of poets, painters, and other artists can actually have a terrible influence. Plato suggested that such imitators are "associates of an inferior part of the soul," and that by strengthening this part of your soul they weaken the good, reasonable part. And he hadn't even seen any *Three Stooges* movies.

> **IN THEORY**
>
> "And the same may be said of lust and anger and all the other affections, of desire and pain and pleasure, which are held to be inseparable from every action—in all of them poetry feeds and waters the passions instead of drying them up; she lets them rule, although they ought to be controlled, if mankind are ever to increase in happiness and virtue." —Plato

Plato did acknowledge that some imitation might be useful. Specifically, if you are able to look at mere "earthy copies" of such good qualities as justice or temperance and see through them to the absolute and true "nature of that which they imitate"; in other words, if you can read correctly and see what the text is really supposed to mean, then you might be well served by fiction. However, Plato said very few people are able to pull this off. As you'll see later in this chapter, medieval neo-Platonists actually made it their job to help people do this.

Madness and Magnets

Then, just when you're ready to give up on Plato because of his cranky, anti-artistic moralizing, he comes out with another theory of literature that's positively inspiring. Inspiring because Plato argued that poets are literally inspired—or breathed into—by divine forces. And it's this divine breath going through the poet and onto the page that creates literature.

In one of his dialogues, Plato shows Socrates talking with a young rhapsode, or performer of poetry. This rhapsode, named Ion, explains how proud he is that he can perform and comment on practically anything the great poet Homer ever wrote. Socrates says, "Oh, how wonderful for you, tell me more," which, if you know Socrates, means trouble, because he's about to lead you through that dialectical Socratic method and you'll end up admitting you're completely wrong about whatever it was you wanted to claim.

Which is exactly what happens. Socrates tells Ion that he can't possibly be an expert on anything Homer wrote because he, Ion, isn't an expert on any of the subjects Homer wrote about. For example, Homer writes about warfare, politics, and horses, and Socrates says that Ion is only imagining what these things must be like, since he can't possibly examine them with the eye of a true expert of warfare, politics, or horses. Ion's just a performer and critic, after all. Ion says, "Yes, that must be true, Socrates," which, if you know Socrates, is always the right thing to say.

Then, Plato goes further. He has Socrates argue that Homer himself, as the poet and so-called creator of his work, can't really be considered the true creator, because even Homer wasn't an expert in the subjects he wrote about. He was just a poet, after all. So how do you account for all the plot, characters, and details, not to mention the entertainment and educational value of Homer's work? How do they get there, if Homer hasn't made them?

"I'm not sure, Socrates."

So Socrates explains, and gets Ion to agree, that Homer was actually out of his mind when he wrote, and that Ion himself is out of his mind when he performs. Homer was out of his mind when he wrote because his mind was taken over, or inspired, breathed into, by the muses. It's divine inspiration that really brings the literature into existence.

As we know from the discussion about imitations, Socrates could have argued that Homer was just mimicking what he saw around him, creating copies of copies. But now the argument is somewhat different. Here, the point is that writers create literature because of divine influence, and that divine influence is also felt by the performers and commentators of that literature—including readers, who "perform" and comment during their silent reading. Socrates is therefore arguing that both writers and readers are out of their minds or under the influence when they deal with literature. What else, Socrates asks Ion, could account for all those feelings of fear, joy, or sadness when nothing in real life is causing these emotions? The only explanation is divine inspiration, acting like a magnet.

"A magnet, Socrates?"

Yes, a magnet. One magnet can pull on a little piece of metal, and then that little piece of metal can attract another piece of metal, and so on, with the original force traced back to the first magnet. The little pieces of metal might think they're the ones with the attractive force, but they aren't the real source. This is like the power of the muse, causing the writer to write and then the reader to react. The mere mortals may feel like they're the ones making it all happen, but the true power comes from outside.

"Yes, that must be true, Socrates."

In this way, Plato reinforces the primary status of truth and the secondary nature of art and literature. Maybe. After all, historically speaking there's a huge Platonic "but" on the way, which will take up most of the next chapter. Basically, it's the question, "But Plato, if poets are like the channels or conduits for divine knowledge, shouldn't we see them as our best hope for actually drawing closer to divine truth, not as threats to the truth?"

Yet even before the Romantic poets got their hands on this argument, various groups of philosophers, writers, and theologians roughly categorized as neo-Platonists weighed in on the positive value they saw in the idea that a divine source flows through literature.

Famous Platonic Relationships

Some of the earliest neo-Platonists were instrumental in shaping early religious principles anywhere between the second and fifth centuries. Just imagine the stakes. Plato had said that writers were inspired or possessed by gods when they wrote, and he said that any reader's goal in understanding writing was to draw closer to the divine. When you apply this to the need to interpret sacred texts, and when you draw a comparison between Plato's ideal forms and your own view of God, you end up with particularly powerful systems of literary criticism.

One of the most significant influences in this regard was the third-century philosopher Plotinus (pronounced *plo-TYNE-us*), who elaborated on several of Plato's ideas concerning *metaphysics*, or theories of the connections between what we see and what we can't see. His work expanding on the "ladder rungs" or levels that lead from physical human experience to the realm of the pure soul was particularly influential for Christian and other religious doctrines.

DEFINITION

Metaphysics describes the kind of philosophy that investigates "first principles" or the truths that must underlie existence.

Medieval Christian theologians took Platonism even further, developing sophisticated systems for interpreting sacred texts. Plato had said that ideals of beauty and truth, along with the ideal of the good, must be interrelated, since they all draw human nature to the highest goal. Regarding the attraction of literary works, St. Augustine (354–430) said that human language, which we can perceive directly, is given to us by

God to reflect God's own word, which we can understand only indirectly. Literature, for Augustine, can lead you to true spiritual knowledge as long as you read correctly. And "correctly" often meant reading in an allegorical manner. What you read has to be understood as operating on several levels, including literal, figurative, moral, and mystical levels.

From the medieval period through the Renaissance, Plato's argument that physical beauty should be seen as an emanation or reflection of ideal beauty really took off. Writers such as Dante, Edmund Spenser, and Baldassare Castiglione, among others, wrote poems of "courtly love," in which a lover sees his or her attraction to a beloved as a reflection of love for the soul. By contemplating earthly beauty and love, the lover would draw closer to the divine beauty and truth of God.

Then there are the Romantics, who, even as they defend themselves against Plato's charge that they don't belong in a perfect society, are unashamedly neo-Platonic as well. When Plato charges that poets are merely the irrational, inspired, magnetized delivery systems for timeless beauty and truth, the Romantics say, "Bring it on, man." And regarding Plato's own abundant use of stories, dialogues, and metaphors, more than one Romantic poet simply said, "Plato was essentially a poet."

He was that good.

The Least You Need to Know

- Anything you perceive with your senses is just a reflection of an ideal form.
- Writing alienates you from true thoughts and keeps you from developing your memory.
- Art, including literature, needs to prove why it belongs in a perfect society.
- Writers write because they are possessed by divine spirits.
- Plato knew exactly what he was doing, and he wanted you to wrestle with his theories.

The Romantics Get Defensive

In This Chapter

- Romanticism's response to Plato's challenge
- Nature's central role
- Theories of emotion, imagination, and beauty
- Poetry as knowledge
- Romanticism and society

Birds chirping. Nice breeze. Magnificent mountains in the distance. When you think of that dreamy poetic genius, sitting under a tree composing verses that spring from his (usually his) soul, you're thinking of the Romantics. Sometimes it seems like this is the only picture you can imagine for what literature must be all about. Of course, if that's the case, you haven't been paying close enough attention to the previous chapters. But why do I nag? Don't worry about any of that now, because in this chapter it's all about the imagination, man.

The *Romantic* view of literary creation sounds so familiar, natural, and, well, artistic because we still live in a Romantic world in many ways. People generally put a high value on creativity and consider it worthwhile when artists "express themselves." It seems to be simply the way things are, artistically speaking. Yet consider what we've seen so far in the history of literary theory and criticism. In much of his theory, for example, Plato didn't bother with poets who expressed themselves; he criticized them for simply imitating things they saw around them.

What we're faced with, theoretically speaking, are two different ways of looking at the arts. That is, you can look at literature as an imitation or you can consider it an expression. Imitation is holding a mirror up to nature, while expression is literally ex-pressing something out of you. Imitation emphasizes the external world. Expression emphasizes internal faculties.

DEFINITION

The word **Romantic** comes from "in the Romantic tongue," or those languages derived from Latin but not Latin itself. Latin was the language of learning and law, while romance languages (the vernacular languages) tended to reflect more popular subjects. In fact, medieval fables in verse are called romances. As a term, Romantic grew increasingly broad (too broad, for many scholars), referring to any kind of literature deemed sad, bizarre, pleasant, or sentimental. Eventually, German and British writers in the early 1800s came to use the term in the way we'll see it in this chapter, as an adjective describing an emphasis on the imaginative and expressive aspects of art.

Quick test of two examples: The *Mona Lisa* versus a child singing. Which one is imitative and which one is expressive? The painting is obviously imitative, since it's an attempt to capture something external—the model for da Vinci's portrait. The song, on the other hand, is obviously expressive—it's just the kid's inner feelings coming out in music.

On the other hand, maybe da Vinci was not just imitating the model but trying to express himself, trying to paint what he saw in the model or how he felt about her. And maybe the singing child could be trying to imitate a bird or even some other music she's heard.

Seems that while it's definitely useful to distinguish between art that imitates and art that expresses, we're also finding throughout this book that the categories are not set in stone. Some critics emphasize one over the other, some blur the lines between the two, and some redefine what the terms even mean.

What brings the critics in this chapter together as Romanticist is an emphasis on the expressive function of art, no matter how differently each critic defines this. And expression for these critics is intimately related to the powers of the imagination. More than just pretending, the imagination serves art by being the fundamental basis of creation, perception, and appreciation. And while they're at it, Romantics will tell you that the imagination also represents your highest form of consciousness.

Plato II: Revenge of the Poets

So the choice is between imitation and expression. Or, as an influential book by the critic M. H. Abrams put it, the categories suggest "the mirror and the lamp." Do you see writers as trying to reflect the world around them, or do you see writers as lamps, lit from within, casting their creative light outward? And if they are lamps, do you prefer to see the light itself as the main attraction, or are you interested in how an artist's creative light helps you see things in the world?

As for the mere imitative function of art, Abrams quotes the twentieth-century writer Rebecca West, who concluded, "A copy of the universe is not what is required of art; one of the damned thing is ample." No need, say the critics we'll consider in this chapter, to pursue simple or naive imitation. Yet this doesn't mean that expression completely excludes imitation. Even with the wildest imagination, there is some aspect of mirroring going on. Personally, I can't keep the image of a disco ball out of my head, but there are more sophisticated metaphors for the Romantic artist's activity. Shelley wrote that poets are "the mirrors of the gigantic shadows which futurity casts upon the present," which brings to mind Plato's allegory of the cave (see Chapter 7). It's as if Shelley is saying, "Okay, if shadow-puppet plays are all we humans really get in this world, then let's give some credit to the puppeteers."

You'll recall that Plato said two main things about poets (and, by extension, other fiction writers). He said that poets either imitated what they saw in this physical world, or they were possessed by gods and spouted divine truths without even knowing it. In either case, the idea that writers could produce something valuable by expressing their own thoughts or feelings was left for others to defend. And defend it they did.

One of the first to reply to Plato was his student Aristotle. As we saw in Chapter 6, Aristotle not only countered Plato's charge against poetry by pointing out its benefits, but established ways of analyzing plot and other literary features that still influence how we read.

Along with Aristotle, Plato's other respondents throughout history have shifted the literary critic's emphasis toward the relationship between the writer and the work. Instead of ignoring or downplaying this relationship, critics have pointed to a writer's imaginative and creative processes as central to appreciating literature. And for you aspiring writers out there, note that many of these critics were also poets, and their criticism inevitably helped justify and promote their own poetry with theoretical principles.

A Sincere Apology

Sir Philip Sidney (1554–1586) wrote what is generally considered the first full work of literary criticism in English, called "An Apology for Poetry." It wasn't an apology in the sense of being sorry for what poetry has done, but rather an explanation for how poetry works and what it means. Sidney wasn't sorry at all about poetry. He loved, loved, loved it. "An Apology for Poetry" is filled with the kind of grand, exuberant declarations that can be mistaken for mere gushing about poetry, but Sidney's zealous yet methodical explanations clearly struck a nerve with poets and readers alike, and has continued to influence criticism to the present day.

Sidney's signature point is that while they may reflect and represent the things of this world, poets do so in ways that actually improve on nature.

IN THEORY

"Nature never set forth the earth in so rich tapestry as diverse poets have done; neither with pleasant rivers, fruitful trees, sweet-smelling flowers, nor whatsoever else may make the too much loved earth more lovely. Her world is brazen, the poets only deliver a golden." —Sir Philip Sidney

In a direct response to Plato's charge that anything less than exact imitation will distract you from reality, Sidney explained that poetic imitation—with its expressive supplements—is actually good for you. Poetry is your first teacher, argued Sidney (along with Aristotle), and its simple rhymes and beautiful images help you get to the point where you can take on "tougher knowledge" later.

According to Sidney's argument, even philosophy needed to learn its truths from poetry first. Plato and the other philosophers all benefitted from poetry's "delightful instruction" and then tried to condense the so-called intellectual content into classroom lessons taught by philosophers who turned around and condemned "their masters" by banishing poets from a perfect society. Sidney pointed not only to Plato's constant use of poetry to support his theories, but also to Plato's use of the dialogue—a poetic form—as the delivery system for knowledge.

Also in response to Plato (you can get out your scorecard and check off the following items), Sidney argued that

- Poetry is actually good, not bad, for your memory, since rhymed verses can be recalled much easier than regular prose.

- Poets don't just reflect but actually make things, since, as Aristotle explained as well, the Greek word for poet means "to make."

- Not only does poetry *not* get in the way of virtue, but its plots and characters actually urge you toward virtuous actions, rather than just insist on virtuous ideas, which is what philosophy does. In other words, if the point of knowledge is to get you to right action, then poetry gets you there better than philosophy.

- Poets don't lie or deceive. They can't, because to lie means to affirm that something which is actually false is true. Poets don't claim what they say is true, so it can't be lying. Or, as Sidney wrote in his most famous line, "The poet, he nothing affirms, and therefore never lieth."

- Poetry in general wasn't actually banished by Plato from his perfect society, it was poetry that depicted bad things. Plato "banned the abuse, not the thing."

- "And while we're talking about banishing immorality from our perfect society, Plato," said Sidney (and I'm paraphrasing), "you'd better look to your own house, since there are some terribly racy details depicted in your dialogues that I find disgusting."

And this is from someone who actually liked Plato.

Sidney also remarked on the poet's imagination, likening poets to God, since poets can write about "the divine consideration of what may be," not just imitate what is. If God is the first maker/poet, we should see poetry as a reflection of the divine impulse. In addition, Sidney claimed, Jesus himself was a poet, what with his parables and all.

It's Just My Nature

By the time we get to the eighteenth century, the hunt for the best philosophical explanation of human creativity and imagination was in full gallop. At the head of the party was Immanuel Kant (1724–1804), whose theory of the mind set the main direction for Romantic theory.

Kant argued that the relationship between your mind and nature was not as simple as "your mind" and "nature." It may seem like it, but you don't open the door and just perceive and absorb the world out there. Instead, your mind itself gives meaning to everything you perceive—starting with time and space. Seriously. For Kant, time and space are not just out there waiting to be experienced, but they are products of your mind. Time and space are the first "forms" that are stamped on whatever is out there in order to make them meaningful to humans. And you're not even aware of it, since this process is part of awareness itself.

After the first two stamps have done their work so that you find yourself just "naturally" looking around thinking, "Gosh, look at all the stuff out there in time and space," then, according to Kant, the doors are open for all kinds of other operations that your mind conducts on this so-called reality. The upshot of the whole theory is that it makes the human mind very, very important. If Plato wanted you to find real truth out there in the unchanging ideal forms, Kant says you'll only find them in your own mind. It's very groovy.

What's particularly groovy is the way Kant and others used this view of the mind to support theories of the imagination. Kant himself argued, for example, that you have two kinds of understanding—rational and intuitive. Rational thought is good, but its actions are passive and follow along lines that classify and divide your thoughts. Intuition is part of the creative faculty of imagination, which is able to break through the barriers set up by rational thought. The imagination, for Kant, is not completely wild and free, since it follows its own laws, but those laws allow the imagination to perceive another nature distinct from the one your rational side wants you to see. This can also lead to the *sublime*, which the Romantics considered a particularly powerful aspect of human experience.

DEFINITION

Attributed to the ancient Greek philosopher Longinus, the concept of the **sublime** was important to both the neoclassical poets and to the Romantics. The word *sublime* itself means "up to the threshold," and came to describe a particularly strong emotion caused by something more than beautiful and involving a vastness or grandeur beyond ordinary comprehension. Kant suggested that feelings of the sublime were hints of the reality that existed beyond our built-in sense of time and space.

Other philosophers who contributed to the main currents of Romanticism around the world included Friedrich von Schiller (1759–1805), who argued, in a Kantian way, that the imagination is particularly important for helping you tolerate concepts and situations that seem out of your rational control, particularly in society, which was changing very quickly as modernization increased.

Germaine de Staël (1766–1817) emphasized the key Romantic principle that the subject of art isn't just nature, it's nature as its appears to you—well, at least as it appears to poets who have a heightened awareness and can portray this awareness in their writings. De Staël was an early advocate of this kind of sensitive poet and was instrumental in popularizing the term *Romanticism* in France.

IN THEORY

Jean-Jacques Rousseau (1712–1778) not only had an important impact on Romantic literature, but his writing, which included fiction, influenced writers in dozens of fields, including philosophy, religion, education, and politics.

Johann Wolfgang von Goethe (1749–1832), one of the greatest of all German poets, explored the relationship between allegory and symbol, explaining that allegories perpetuate logical thinking while symbols can prompt you to actually experience complicated concepts in concrete images.

Ralph Waldo Emerson (1803–1882) was an American poet and critic who met many of the European Romanticists during a tour of that continent in 1832. Among other pronouncements, Emerson claimed that nature was like a poem to be read by sensitive types: "The world is a temple whose walls are covered with emblems, pictures, and commandments of the deity" (see Chapter 22 for more on Emerson and ecocriticism).

Clearly, then, what these and other Romantic critics share is the view that nature, what you may mistake as simply the external world, is always nature as you specifically experience it. That means knowing anything about nature takes more than science or reason, it takes intuition, imagination, and feeling, man.

Put an even stronger way, if there is a mirror at work in art, then it's the mirror of your soul—an internal mirror—that truly reflects reality. Since reality isn't simply a set of objects outside of you, but a combination of human nature and "nature nature," the best works of art are creations that both reflect and expresses your awareness.

And now, on to the Fab Four of Romantic criticism. These are the poet-critics who significantly set the scene for viewing literary works primarily as products of the imagination, and influenced generations of readers, writers, and artists of all types.

Wordsworth's Emotional Rescue

"Good poetry is the spontaneous overflow of powerful feelings," wrote William Wordsworth (1770–1850). It's common to hear this as your take-home quote for Romantic literary theory, but as you might expect, there's more to it. First, there are conditions regarding those feelings, and second, you know you want *overflow* defined a bit more specifically.

Feelings tend to start with nature. Wordsworth agreed with Sidney that poetry is our first and best teacher, but he went further to emphasize that what poetry teaches us best is nature. And not just any nature, but the poet's experience of nature. That is, a poem doesn't teach you about nature in general, but nature *for* someone. That's a good thing, because this someone is a poet, and when nature is understood by the poet, you end up understanding what nature really means.

As for overflow, or the actual characteristics of the poet's expression, Wordsworth explains that what actually ends up on the page should be "emotion recollected in tranquility." What this means is that the poet doesn't just have a peak emotional moment staring at a sunrise and suddenly explode into expression right then and there. Instead, it means the poet calmly sits down after seeing the sunrise and brings it back to mind. From this initial tranquility of memory, the poet gradually becomes emotional again through the operations of memory, then spontaneously puts the emotion into words.

Why, then, is a poet the best teacher of this recollected experience of nature? Because a poet has a "more lively sensibility, more enthusiasm and tenderness" than ordinary folks. Not only that, but the poet "has a greater knowledge of human nature, and a more comprehensive soul, than are supposed to be more common among mankind." In fact, the poet's superior qualities are so numerous that Wordsworth, in his description of them, goes on as above for at least a dozen more lines, finally concluding that the poet "has acquired a greater readiness and power in expressing what he thinks and feels," especially when those thoughts and feelings are not just the spillover of an immediate reaction to nature, but a recollected poetic experience.

Did I mention that Wordsworth was writing this as part of his preface to a volume of poetry he had written with Coleridge?

Yes, Wordsworth held a rather high opinion of poets, like all of the Romantics, but he also emphasized that no matter how great the poet with his admittedly "divine spirit" may be, poetry itself is just a dim reflection of actual emotional states and actions. What poetry loses in this reflection, however, it gains back by being more helpful to other people. Poetry, simply put, communicates what might otherwise be isolated emotional experiences.

So while Wordsworth's goal in his poetry is to "illustrate the manner in which our feelings and ideas are associated in a state of excitement," you would expect to find him writing about such highly emotional situations as the mother-child relationship, strong reactions to extreme beauty in nature, or the approach of one's own death. In this, he doesn't disappoint. But Wordsworth made a point of writing about less dramatic, positively humdrum experiences as well. "The human mind," he argued, "is capable of being excited without the application of gross and violent stimulants." Common life, for Wordsworth, held all the ingredients needed for a full appreciation of human emotions and natural beauty. And Wordsworth matched common life to common language. Despite traditional opinions to the contrary (consider the neoclassicists discussed in Chapter 6), and charges of writing in an uncouth and scandalous manner, Wordsworth preferred ordinary language rather than flowery diction. Poetry, Wordsworth maintained, could even sound like prose, if that would help get the emotional effects across. Oh yes he did just say that.

APPLY IT

Recommended Wordsworth readings: some poems that most clearly illustrate his critical views include "Tintern Abbey," which examines how the poet's view of himself and nature have been intimately mixed at different stages of his life. The "Lucy poems" are powerful and brief meditations on mortality, natural cycles, and love, as are the brilliant sonnets "Mutability" and "Surprised by Joy." If you like some of these shorter poems, you'll definitely want to settle into *The Prelude*, a book-length poem published in 1850 in which Wordsworth traces "the growth of a poet's mind." You could also read the earlier, shorter version, the "Two-Part Prelude" of 1799.

Emotional effects were very important to Wordsworth, because they can make you do things; they can lead you to right action.

Wordsworth cited Aristotle as arguing that poetry is "the most philosophic of all writing," and while Aristotle didn't actually say that, Wordsworth's point is still a good one. Since poetry imitates emotions as well as actions, it becomes a very effective teacher. According to Wordsworth and the other Romantics, feelings will get you closer to truth than reason. The best service a poet can do, therefore, is help people understand how to feel, not just how to know.

But if Wordsworth thought that ordinary language was so important, why did he write in verse? Rhyme and meter are rarely features of ordinary conversation. Wordsworth said it was because verse actually teaches better—it's easier to follow and remember—and it's charming. Literally. That is, poems charm you with regular meter and unifying rhymes into a calm and receptive state, rather like the poet's own tranquility, from which your emotions can naturally develop. With this idea, Wordsworth anticipates T. S. Eliot's related notion of the objective correlative (see Chapter 3).

Also, because poetic verses can echo other poetic verses, you may find your response to one poem affected by unconscious memories of another poem. Wordsworth saw this as yet another benefit of an artistic form whose goal was to link individual emotions with the shared qualities of human nature.

IN THEORY

Poetry's "object is truth, not individual and local, but general, and operative; not standing upon external testimony, but carried alive into the heart by passion."
—William Wordsworth

Coleridge's Fevered Imagination

Samuel Taylor Coleridge (1772–1834) spent a lot of time thinking about the imagination—where it comes from, where it goes, what it does. While Wordsworth tended to emphasize the reader of poetry in his criticism, Coleridge focused on the effects of the imagination on poets themselves. Unfortunately, he also focused on the effects of opium on himself, spending more than 13 years struggling with addiction.

For Coleridge, the imagination was a "synthetic and magical power" central to art's status as a way of knowing. As we've seen, an aesthetic theory is any approach that holds art to be a way of knowing, in contrast to arguing that knowledge can only come from rational analysis. Coleridge was influential in elaborating some of the details of Romanticist aesthetic theory through his own criticism as well as through the ideas of German philosophers—ideas which, every now and then, Coleridge would present as his own.

IN THEORY

"All knowledge rests on the coincidence of an object with a subject …. During the act of knowledge itself, the objective and subjective are so instantly united, that we cannot determine to which of the two the priority belongs." —Samuel Taylor Coleridge, with an assist from Friedrich Wilhelm Joseph von Schelling (1775–1854)

Art, argued Coleridge, is so powerful because it shares an important characteristic of the human mind in general. That is, when the mind knows something, it cannot really distinguish between object and subject. When you look at a cow, your subjective reaction to that cow is so fundamentally blended with the cow that even thinking about "the cow itself" is meaningless. (If you're thinking of Immanuel Kant at this point, that's fine; so is everybody else, including Coleridge.)

This leads Coleridge to suggest that you possess two kinds of imagination. Primary imagination takes the unformed stuff out in the world (what Kant called *noumena*, and what we can call the "cow who cannot be known without being processed by your mind") and turns it into impulses that you recognize as being something (what Kant called *phenomena*, and what we can also call phenomena—or, if you want to be specific, the cow). Primary imagination for Coleridge, therefore, is not just fun and games, it's the faculty that allows us to orient ourselves mentally in the world. It's literally a divine power that makes the world for us.

Secondary imagination is then the operation of the artist, doing what the mind has already done, but on a different level. Secondary imagination transforms what the poet sees into something else, or contributes subjective details, or combines phenomena in creative ways. Look, a thoughtful cow wearing a hat!

In Coleridge's own words (maybe), primary imagination is "the living power and prime agent of all human perception," and a reflection of the infinite act of creation. Secondary imagination is "an echo of the former … differing only in degree," which "dissolves, diffuses, dissipates, in order to recreate."

Coleridge also drew a helpful distinction between two terms sometimes considered synonyms: imagination and fancy. Imagination is what we've just discussed, an active, creative faculty. Fancy, however, is just "a mode of memory emancipated from the order of time and space." In other words, fancy is just making or mixing things up without arriving at a truly creative new image or emotion.

This same distinction separated allegory from symbol for Coleridge, Goethe, and many of the other Romantics. An allegory may be useful and clever, but it's really just trading in abstractions. The whole point of an allegory is usually to get you to understand something better analytically and intellectually. A symbol, on the other hand, unites an image with a concept in order to make you experience and feel something. In fact, it's better to think of the symbol uniting an image with a concept that doesn't even exist yet, because it's the symbol itself, when it appears, that brings the concept into existence. Coleridge says of the symbol, "It always partakes of the reality which it renders intelligible." Like an icon, a symbol doesn't just represent something else, it is part of that something else.

APPLY IT

The Coleridge readings you may have heard about include "The Rime of the Ancient Mariner," with that albatross hanging around a guy's neck, as well as "Kubla Khan," which would later be referenced in such classic films as *Citizen Kane* and *Xanadu*. But for a really good time, try "Christabel," a long fantastical poem filled with sexuality, mysticism, and a wild gothic setting. Coleridge left the poem unfinished, however, on account of being too strung out on opium to keep writing, and then running naked through the streets. At least that's what they told me in college.

When it comes to the poet's craft, Coleridge sees the imagination leading to the genuinely organic development of poetic form. Organization must come from within the nature of the work itself, not imposed through external rules, as many of the Romantics charged the neoclassicists with doing (see Chapter 6). Any sort of imposed form is simply "mechanical regularity," like molding clay into a certain shape, whether the clay likes it or not. Organic form "shapes, as it develops, from within," so poems grow, like nature and its forms. Of course, this emphasis on the organic unity of a literary work leads straight to the American New Critics, as we saw in Chapter 3.

So the point is not to abandon all rules, but to make sure all the rules originate in the work itself. Not only that, but once you begin creating a literary work according to its own inner laws, you'll find that all of its parts contribute to the whole. You'll find (again like the New Critics would) that each part is meaningful on its own as well as in concert with all the other parts, like any leaf of a tree. In fact, as Coleridge said, genius is "the power of acting creatively under laws of its own origination."

IN THEORY

"The reader should be carried forward, not merely or chiefly by the mechanical impulse of curiosity, or by a restless desire to arrive at the final solution; but by the pleasurable activity of mind excited by the attractions of the journey itself."
—Samuel Taylor Coleridge

Keats and Beautiful Truthiness

So when you find yourself endowed with Wordsworth's advanced emotional sensibilities and Coleridge's transformative imagination, deciding on the best object to turn your attentions to is easy to figure out, said John Keats (1795–1821). It's beauty.

Keats declared, "What the imagination seizes as beauty must be truth." As we know, seeing beauty as truth and truth as beauty goes back at least to Plato (see Chapter 7), but Keats made this principle quintessentially Romantic during the few years he had to live and write. Trained in the medical profession but preferring to pursue a life in poetry, Keats learned at the age of 23 that he was suffering from tuberculosis. He died three years later.

Since Keats never wrote any formal criticism, his literary theory was really comprised of comments he would make in letters to friends.

IN THEORY

"With a great poet the sense of beauty overcomes every other consideration, or rather obliterates all consideration." —John Keats

In his remarks on poetic theory, and in his poetry itself, Keats reinforced the aesthetic idea that beauty is a form of knowledge, and a unique one at that. For Keats, it wasn't just any set of emotions or any type of imagination, but beauty that would teach you things that reason cannot.

Keats called rational thought *consecutive reasoning*, because it always tries to get to a determined destination, or resolution. Keats argued that such a striving only creates boundaries that seem like truth and satisfy us with mere "understanding." The creative process of the poet can break down or bypass these boundaries and get at real truth. Keats's famous term for this quality is *negative capability*, which is the ability to remain undisturbed when a so-called resolution of conflicting emotions is not available. It means, that is, "capable of being in uncertainties, Mysteries, doubts, without any irritable reaching after facts and reason."

According to Keats, Shakespeare definitely had negative capability. As an example, Keats said to look at all the unpleasant things that happen in *King Lear*. Most of them are presented in the play without any clear indication, on Shakespeare's part, regarding their resolution. Instead, Shakespeare offers you the chance in *King Lear* to "bury its repulsiveness" in "momentous depths of speculation" and an "intensity, capable of making all disagreeables evaporate." This kind of creative suspension, for Keats, is an approach to tragedy far superior to having the poet give you all the answers or resolutions.

Keats also weighed in on memory, noting that poetry "should strike the reader as a wording of his own highest thoughts, and appear almost as a remembrance." Without fear of contradiction (appropriately enough, given the right amount of negative capability), Keats argued that poetry's power to reflect truth in beauty comes from the fact that a recalled object or event often seems more beautiful and more "elevated" than it seemed at the time it was first experienced. In such case, the truth of the event is in its recollection just as much as in its past actuality.

In an interesting turn related to Coleridge's distinction between imagination and fancy, Keats also took pains to distinguish poetic memory and imagination from mere "belief." For Keats, belief actually relies, logically, on discursive, consecutive reasoning, not on a true, creative response to beauty.

And finally, when having to choose sides between poetry and criticism, Keats went with the creative poets, who did what he saw as the real work, rather than the critics, who could get away with less effort, since "it is easier to think what poetry should be than to write it."

… But then there's Shelley, who did it all.

Shelley Gets Played Like a Harp

Percy Bysshe Shelley (1792–1822) saw poets as instruments that both responded to beauty and created beauty. He popularized the image of the Aeolian lyre, or wind harp, as a metaphor for the poet's mind. The harp was receptive, feeling the delicate force of the breeze passing through its strings. And it was creative, since the vibration of the strings produced music. In a nice touch, Shelley notes that the breezes that strike the poet's creative strings can be generated by both "external and internal impressions," which means if you're writing poetry you can produce music just as well from your own thoughts as from the world outside.

So to Plato, who first laid down the bet that the gods breathed their inspiration into unthinking poets, Shelley said, "Okay, I'll see your divine inspiration, and raise you a creative human imagination that creates ultimate truth in beauty."

IN THEORY

"A poem is the very image of life expressed in its eternal truth. … It acts in a divine and apprehended manner, beyond and above consciousness: and it is reserved for future generations to contemplate and measure." —Percy Bysshe Shelley

Shelley is perhaps best known for doing everything. He wrote poetry, literary criticism, political and religious (atheistic) tracts, moved in with Mary Wollstonecraft of *Frankenstein* fame when he was still married to someone else, travelled extensively in Europe, slept around most of his life, and died just before his thirtieth birthday in a boating accident. By all means find time to read about his life (you could even see Ken Russell's film, *Gothic*), but for now we'll focus on his central role in Romanticism.

Shelley's *Defense of Poetry* (written in 1821 but not published until 1840) directly replied to Plato and others who demanded that poets justify their value to society.

IN THEORY

George Gordon, Lord Byron (1788–1824), in life and in death, was the very image of the Romantic poet-hero. He spurred generations of writers, artists, composers, and even fictional characters (*Wuthering Heights*'s Heathcliff) to adopt "Byronic attitudes" of gloomy creativity and swagger. He hosted Percy and Mary Shelley in Switzerland when Mary came up with the *Frankenstein* story. He wrote enormously popular works including the play *Manfred* and the long poems *Childe Harold's Pilgrimage* and *Don Juan*. He wrote the line, "She walks in beauty, like the night." He fought for Greek independence and died at the age of 36. And while Byron certainly wrote poetry "with a full but soft emotion/Like the swell of summer's ocean," he didn't write much literary theory.

Shelley started his defense, as we have seen other Romantic poets do, by maintaining that the poetic faculty is equal and complementary to reason, if not even more important for human society. Consider the following high praises, which represent only a small portion of Shelley's quotables:

- Poetry is "the interpenetration of a diviner nature through our own."
- Poetry "redeems from decay the visitations of the divinity of man."

- Poetry "makes immortal all that is best and most beautiful in the world."

- Poetry "is the record of the best and happiest moments of the happiest and best minds."

- Poetry "defeats the curse which binds us to be subjected to the accident of surrounding impressions."

In fact, regarding Plato's banishment of poets from the Republic, Shelley argued that poets have been essential to society since the beginning. Not only was Plato himself a poet, Shelley noted along with Sidney, but "the great instrument of moral good is the imagination" and poets are actually the "unacknowledged legislators" of society.

Shelley's vigorous social argument for poetry is based on the idea (which would be familiar to the Russian formalists we discussed in Chapter 4) that poetry revives and enhances our perceptions. Dead thoughts and language tend to hold us down, but poetry recreates the universe after it has been "annihilated in our minds" through old repetitive habits, expressions, and ways of seeing and feeling. Because we actually see reality through the forms poets create, Shelley argued along with Coleridge, then when language decays, culture will decay.

IN THEORY

Poetry "awakens and enlarges the mind itself by rendering it the receptacle of a thousand unapprehended combinations of thought. Poetry lifts the veil from the hidden beauty of the world, and makes familiar objects be as if they were not familiar." —Percy Bysshe Shelley

This emphasis on the social importance of poetry, in fact, made Shelley's *Defense of Poetry* a significant work of both literary theory and history, a narrative making sense of man's role in the world. It reminds us that Romanticism was not simply a self-contained artistic movement, but was fundamentally related to the social and political changes taking place in the late 1700s and early 1800s. Factors contributing to the need for new explanations of social interactions included the increasing complexity of modernization and industrialism, and the deepening contact with past cultures through archaeology (the big new academic discipline) and present cultures through colonialism, trade, and travel. Shelley's arguments offered responses to some of the biggest questions of the day, while, helpfully, keeping poets in the front lines of the solutions.

The spirit of poetry, according to Shelley, should even be recognized as the force behind all religions, the abolition of slavery, and the emancipation of women, so far as Shelley understood it. To Shelley, almost anything creative was poetry: "Language, color, form, and religious and civil habits of action, are all the instruments and materials of poetry."

With a logic that also illustrates the Romantic aesthetic, Shelley argued that since "we have more moral, political and historical wisdom, than we know how to reduce into practice," and since we definitely have more scientific and economic knowledge than we know what to do with, society is in need of another way of understanding the world. Of course, that other way is poetry, which, Shelley explained, has always been an aspect of political, scientific, and economic systems, but hidden from obvious view. You could even see all of human history as one "great poem" that all poets have been working on "like the cooperating thoughts of one great mind." Focusing on poetry itself, therefore, will help reveal the true meaning of the world's various facts. Poetry illuminates the arrangements and rhythms that make us human in a world filled with seeming chaos.

Still, and without backing off from his commitment to the social scope of poetry, Shelley recognized that poetry in "its more restricted sense" meant verse and meter. Romantic through and through, Shelley treated the actual crafting of poetry with a formalist's zeal. He held that poetry was "that imperial faculty, whose throne is curtained within the invisible nature of man. And this springs from the nature itself of language." For Shelley, rhythm, rhyme, and sound were as important to poetry as the meanings of the words themselves. In drafting his poems, Shelley would often compose pages and pages of nonsense syllables just to get the "music" correct first, then fill in the words to match the melody he imagined. For example, before he wrote this: "O World, O Life, O Time, / On whose last steps I climb," he wrote this: "Ah time, oh night, oh day / Ni nal ni na, na ni." It was rather like Paul McCartney's "Yesterday" starting out as "scrambled eggs," and I'm sure neither poet would mind the comparison.

APPLY IT

Recommended Shelley readings: "Mutability" establishes Shelley's guiding paradox of the fleeting ephemeral nature of endurance, or the enduring nature of fleeting ephemera. "Alastor; or, The Spirit of Solitude" is a longer poem that allegorically follows the protagonist through a sexual wakening and the complications of associating earthly love and beauty with what seem to be their divine counterparts (think Plato). Shelley's retrospective poem, "The Triumph of Life" masterfully surveys humanity's attempts to make its way through love, passion, nature, spirituality, and any number of big issues. The biggest question of the poem is, of course, "Then, what is Life?," which Shelley asks in the final lines … just before dying, with the poem unfinished.

The Least You Need to Know

- Sidney argued that poets create a better nature.
- Romanticism emphasized that human consciousness actually creates our reality.
- Wordsworth saw poetry as recollected emotion.
- Coleridge theorized the imagination as a creative force.
- Keats equated beauty with truth, and vice versa.
- Shelley defended poets as essential to society.

Marx Sees Through the Material World

In This Chapter

- Capitalism's secrets
- Idealism versus materialism
- Ideological strategies
- Realism's pros and cons
- Speaking of subtexts

Let's go back to Plato's allegory of the cave. For Plato, the point of the story is that we're all prisoners of the cave, watching false shadow-puppet shows on the wall, and our ultimate goal is to escape into the truth of light outside. The Romantic poet-critics responded by saying something like, "Well, those shadows mean something, too, so let's hear it for the inspired, creative, poet-puppeteers who bring the truth to you!"

Marxist critics have a different interpretation. They want to show you who's really behind those shadow-puppets, and it sure isn't a group of sensitive artists connected to divine inspiration. The real puppet-master is the capitalist system, keeping its captive audience entertained and imprisoned at the same time.

The system wants you to stay in your place and accept its imaginary stories as truth. Marxist critics want you to see that the shadows are not natural or neutral, but they have an agenda; they even have histories. Not only that, but even the most escapist stories you're enjoying are integrally connected to your humdrum material life, and vice versa.

Why are these critics being so mean?

Immersed in the System

Marxist critics aren't really being mean, they're being helpful. They argue that, because you're a social being, everything you read, watch, build, buy, and use is related to everything else in the social system on some level. And these levels can go very deep. You can immediately recognize some of the levels, such as knowing that any product you buy is probably the result of a long, complicated process. Cars and shoes don't just grow on trees, you know. Other levels are more subtle, and Marxist critics have shown that literary analysis can actually help illuminate the deep connections as much as the more visible ones.

Why do you need to work so hard to see these connections? Because, according to Marxist critics, it's a built-in feature of any existing economic system—and especially capitalist systems—to hide, or mystify, their real operations behind a false worldview. According to Marxists, capitalist systems exploit your labor and manipulate your human potential for the benefit of the rich and powerful. The last thing the system wants (even if some of the rich and powerful themselves don't mind, although they usually do) is for you to really understand how this exploitation works, since that would help you fight the system. Central to Marxist criticism, then, is the project of revealing how your real, basic social relations are hidden behind the false images perpetuated in society.

IN THEORY

Karl Marx (1818–1883) was a German philosopher who, like a lot of German philosophers, studied Greek philosophy and wrote Romantic poetry in his youth. Cowritten with Friedrich Engels (1820–1895), Marx's key works include *The German Ideology* (1846), *The Manifesto of the Communist Party* (1848), and *Capital* (1867). Marx and Engels lived and worked mostly in Victorian England. Their writings paved the way for further developments in virtually every academic field, from philosophy, economics, and social theory, to history, psychology, and aesthetics.

But still, you might ask, isn't literature different? Doesn't art provide a space of imagination and creativity that offers a break from real-world issues? Marxist critics say yes and no. What you see as escape, they see as actually becoming more imprisoned in the system. The more you simply absorb stories without thinking of their connections to real-world operations, the more actively you become part of the dominant class's exploitative agenda.

IN THEORY

"The philosophers have only *interpreted* the world in various ways; the point is to *change* it." —Karl Marx

For Marxist critics, every literary work is a product of its time. It doesn't matter whether Jane Austen or Stephen King actively thought about sociopolitical issues when they were writing—although they probably did. Intention like that isn't necessary, because evidence of the author's involvement in the world can always be found in their work. In other words, Marxist critics begin with the understanding that the elements of human social interaction always flow through any human production. Developing new ways of acting on this knowledge means improving the human condition as well.

Alma Mater-ialism

Marxist critics also begin by seeing the material world as the basis of all consciousness. This might seem obvious—it sounds pretty organic, after all—but we often think of the relationship exactly backward.

When you ask Plato or the Romantics to tell you how you get ideas into your head, they'll say it has to do with inspiration of one kind or another. For Plato, ideas exist in pure form outside of the physical world, but divine forces—and philosophers—can help you get closer to them. The Romantics will tell you it has to do with imagination and the natural creativity of the human mind—and poets can help you with that. In both cases, ideas come first. Getting to the truth for them means getting closer to an ideal. Ideas and ideals, in fact, team up very nicely in the term *idealism*.

Marxists argue against idealism and for materialism. They explain that ideas and everything else in your head—your whole way of seeing things—develop out of your involvement in human society. This orientation toward consciousness is called materialism, because it begins with the material world as the driving force behind any abstractions or ideas you end up calling your own. And for Marxists, the material world is specifically defined as a world of economic and political organization and social interaction. Being human means being a social animal, one that learns—consciously and unconsciously—from its own manufactured environment.

IN THEORY

"It is not the consciousness of men that determines their being, but, on the contrary, their social being that determines their consciousness." —Karl Marx

But wait, there's more. Every social environment has two interrelated aspects. A society's economic base is the foundation of economic realities in any given society—who owns property and controls wealth, how things get made, how labor is organized, and where profits go. A society's superstructure is made up of all those features and institutions we generally think of as that society's defining characteristics—its philosophy, art, and cultural traditions, but also its religions, laws, and even political parties. Marxists emphasize that the superstructure is made up of all the social beliefs and institutions that the economic base needs to ensure its own survival.

Really? To ensure its own survival? Yes. Sociopolitical systems are incredibly self-serving. Marxist critics emphasize that capitalist superstructures work very subtly and successfully to mystify their operations and keep you from understanding your contribution to the economic base and how material circumstances, rather than so-called freely formed ideas, shape your consciousness.

Let's Simplify Things

One aspect of this mystification is getting you to see processes as products. Reification (pronounced *REE-iff-ih-KAY-shun*) is what happens when you think of anything created through human labor as simply an object, and you ignore its economic and political dimensions. When you reify things—and you can reify people, too—you see them in isolation, as products, rather than as integral parts in a system. In fact, you tend to see reified things and people like precut puzzle pieces that fit into whatever worldview or story line is dominant at the time.

Think of manufactured goods and technological processes, for example. Many things can seem so complicated that we just disregard any sense of detail and go along with the reification of processes into commodities. We just use the phone or the coffee-maker, wear shoes, or click through the internet, without having to face the historical forces and human associations of a product's development, the material demands put on workers, or, in the case of the internet, the exhaustive collection of data by commercial interests.

Clearly, it's a lot easier, for most of us, to think of buying, selling, using, and craving commodities rather than processes. Forget about all the detailed history, labor, and seemingly endless complications—just give me the *stuff*. This, by the way, is also what Marx called a commodity fetish. We're drawn to the end product to satisfy our desires, and we're alienated from the processes involved. Marxist critics argue that this alienation is bad for you in two ways. As a consumer, alienation from processes helps you mindlessly contribute to the system's exploitation of human labor. As a producer, you eventually find it difficult to recognize even your own participation in a "finished product," a relationship, or in society.

APPLY IT

Marxist criticism, by definition, applies to any and all literary works, since all art is created in social contexts. According to Marxist critics, therefore, you should look at *every* work of literature with an eye to material history and ideology. Meanwhile, of course, some literary works have been written with Marxist principles clearly in mind:

George Gissing, a contemporary of Charles Dickens, wrote novels with social-ist themes, including *New Grub Street* (1891), *The Nether World* (1889), and *The Emancipated* (1890).

George Orwell's *Animal Farm* (1945) offers a harsh critique of the Russian Revolution specifically in order to highlight the need for genuine socialism.

As you might imagine, when Marxist literary critics consider the New Critics' argument that literary works should be studied as "well-wrought urns," "verbal icons," or other unified organic wholes (see Chapter 3), they see reification. And while Marxist approaches to literature come in a variety of styles and always adapt to new social circumstances, they all see literature as a material process. What you're looking at when you read is not an autonomous, self-contained work, but part of a socioeconomic system.

Living the Dream

Reifying literature, therefore, strips away a text's history, relations, and encodings as part of the superstructure. As a remedy, Marxist criticism urges you not to take texts at face value merely as products, but to investigate their involvement in social processes and even mystification. And when you do this, when you try to uncover or decode the ways that the superstructure hides the harsh motivations of the economic base, you get the kinds of rereadings that make Marxists Marxist and tend to aggravate non-Marxists.

For example, did legal marriage first develop out of love? No, the superstructure merely offers you this fantasy to hide the system's real motivation, which involves property rights for men. Celibacy for the clergy? That's all about property laws, too, ensuring that nothing can be inherited by children, just the church. Religion in general? Marx covers that with his famous line that religion "is the opium of the people." Legal systems? They're designed to keep all the power and money where it is, in the hands of the few. Educational institutions? They serve to mass produce new generations of capitalist workers. Leisure time? Not designed for escape, but conditioned by the economic system to reinforce your willing participation in labor and consumerism.

APPLY IT

If you're looking for an over-the-top science-fiction, alien-invasion action movie that's also an effective allegory of exploitative capitalist mystification (you know who you are), check out John Carpenter's movie *They Live.*

An important term for the stories that societies live by is *ideology*. It's a common term and not used exclusively by Marxist critics. For example, if you say that someone has a liberal or a conservative ideology, you're referring to that person's consciously held beliefs or point of view. For our discussion, however, ideology is used a bit differently. Here, it refers to the whole system of mystification that turns the unfair and exploitative aspects of an economic system into an agreeable narrative, or worse, a narrative presented as simply inevitable—"that's just the way things have always been." Either way, ideologies serve to *legitimize* society's dominant economic class interests.

RELATIONS

See Chapter 19 for a discussion of important twentieth-century critics who examined the social and political implications of popular culture, from Mickey Mouse and television to punk style.

Wake Up and Smell the Ideology

What's particularly interesting about Marxist literary criticism is that ideology can be seen in two different but related modes. In one mode, ideology is emphasized as a kind of brainwashing, or a set of ideas that keep you from seeing reality. This has also been called false consciousness.

But in another mode, ideology is emphasized as the actions you perform on an everyday basis. That is, you don't just think ideology, you live it. Ideology goes from being an illusion that keeps you from seeing the truth, to being a lived reality, a set of practices and enacted beliefs that physically produces the system's fictional worldview.

IN THEORY

"An ideology always exists in an apparatus and its practice, or practices. This existence is material. ... The 'ideas' of a human subject exist in his actions." —Louis Althusser

The history of ideological critique and Marxist literary theory is vast, various, and deeply related to world history.

Get Real

In the years following the Russian Revolution (1917), one of the most significant literary movements to emerge from the Soviet Union was socialist realism. This was a movement expressly designed by Communist Party leaders to bring revolutionary messages to the masses. Writers, according to Stalin, were to be the "engineers of the human soul," building up the consciousness of the working class through depictions of the strength, optimism, and progress of communist society. In this regard, literary works were regulated in order to have the most beneficial impact.

Needless to say, many writers reacted against the strict imposition of style and subject, leading to subversive variations of the official theories, exile, and even imprisonment. Advocates of socialist realism maintained that such stringent artistic rules were necessary for the good of society and that "making labor the principle hero of our books" was perfectly good propaganda. In fact, while it has a generally negative connotation, the term *propaganda* actually comes from the Latin term for propagating religious faith and is used approvingly for any form of art that sends a specifically desired message.

APPLY IT

Take a look at Sergei Eisenstein's 1925 film *Battleship Potemkin,* both for its Soviet propaganda and for its extremely influential early film techniques. A very different film, Warren Beatty's *Reds* (1981), tells the story of an American writer leaving his circle of novelists, playwrights, and actors, to travel to Russia to support and report on the revolution.

While the realism in socialist realism was reduced to only those aspects of life that glorified the working class, one of the most important Marxist literary theories of the early twentieth century took another look at the kind of realism we're more familiar with, the realism of the nineteenth-century European novel.

The Hungarian critic György Lukács (1885–1971, pronounced *LOO-cawsh*) has become associated with the term *reflectionist* to describe a Marxist approach to literature that values the depiction of life without the idealization demanded by socialist realism. Yet why would reflecting life as it appears be specifically advocated by a Marxist critic? Because, according to Lukács, good realist novels do not just reflect details mindlessly, like a mirror. Instead, they reflect, in all their details and multiple plot lines, the social contradictions important to the Marxist worldview. In this way, reflectionism suggests both "mirroring" and "reflecting on" a society's actual arrangements and inequalities.

Lukács pointed to the work of authors such as Charles Dickens, George Eliot, Leo Tolstoy, Walter Scott, Honoré de Balzac, and Thomas Mann as showing realistic characters struggling against real problems. Advocating what he called critical realism, Lukács argued that readers of these works were offered an "intensive" or artistic totality that reflects the "extensive totality" of society itself. The novels, in other words, can reveal what is really true about a society, not just what it looks like even to its participants. Realism, in this way, reflects on the whole system, all due to the artistic transformations achieved by the writers. As Lukács put it, the fictional worlds created by realist novels gave readers "reflections of life in the greatest concreteness and clarity and with all its motivating contradictions."

 IN THEORY

"Art could be seen as reflecting not separated objects and superficial events but the essential forces and movements underlying them." —Raymond Williams

Does this mean Lukács thought all these writers were socialists themselves? Not at all. He explained that it didn't matter whether or not the authors themselves were *trying* to be revolutionary in their depictions. Like Engels himself, Lukács greatly admired Balzac because despite being a reactionary (the political opposite of a revolutionary), Balzac produced works with the same kind of richness and contradiction as society itself, and these works would then be open to being understood in a socially progressive way.

The concept of contradiction is important to Lukács and other Marxist critics because of a process called dialectical materialism. This comes down to the idea that any existing society may look coherent and whole, but within it exist contradictions and tensions, such as the inequalities and exploitation within the capitalist system. According to dialectical logic, these internal contradictions increase in severity until they overturn the existing society (as in a revolution), and the result is a new system in which the earlier contradictions are resolved. And, you guessed it, the process starts over again, since any new system will contain contradictions. The three repeating steps are also referred to as thesis, antithesis, and synthesis. Marx argued that when a truly Communist society was achieved, classes would no longer contain the internal contradictions that lead to dialectical development.

According to Lukács, when you read *David Copperfield*, *Middlemarch*, or *Anna Karenina*, you are given the chance to see events, objects, cities, and above all, people, not as isolated entities but as parts of a working system. Lukács was vitally opposed to the fragmentation and alienation that he saw society inflicting on people, and because of this, he not only championed realism, but condemned much of modernism.

Shocking Audiences Worldwide

Marxists certainly appreciate modern progress, but Lukács was specifically opposed to modernist literary works that depicted fragmented, static, and introverted views of life. What he meant was that much modernist literature, the kind of works published by James Joyce or Virginia Woolf, for example, featured characters and situations that seemed static, without time or history. Rather than depicting society as a whole, modernist works overemphasized, in Lukács's view, the alienation from society that characters felt. The technique of stream-of-consciousness narration, for example, in which you seem to read narrators' thoughts from within their own minds, was particularly troubling. Here was a character's isolated, alienated self on display for all to see, with none of the realist benefits of context and dialectic. Simply put, Lukács said that while alienation was an actual social truth, simply depicting it in literature was not going to help anybody.

Seen from this critical approach, all modernism was doing was reflecting the alienated state of modern life itself, uncritically and without giving the reader a way out. It's a "surrender to the subjectivity" that you should be trying to improve or escape. Lukács, thinking of writers like Joyce, Kafka, Beckett, Faulkner, and Musil, wrote "Man, for these writers, is by nature solitary, asocial, unable to enter into relationships with other human beings." Not only that, but there's another problem—modernism doesn't historicize. By isolating characters and their thoughts, the very inner world of a human being is turned into a cynical, frightening, directionless spirit.

While Lukács condemned modernist techniques that depicted individuals in fragmentary, frightened isolation, another Marxist critic—a German playwright, in fact—celebrated modernism for those very same reasons.

Bertolt Brecht (1898–1956) argued that art was needed to wake people up to the capitalist exploitation they experienced but usually ignored or couldn't understand. Mystification and ideology are powerful weapons, Brecht knew, and he worked to counter them with modernist art forms that he hoped would be just as powerful.

Fighting fire with fire was the basis of Brecht's alienation effect, by which audiences of his plays would be confronted with nontraditional features, such as posters and placards describing the actions onstage, actors talking directly to the audience (sometimes in groups like a Greek chorus), plot lines left unresolved, and any number of surprising or shocking methods of keeping the audience from merely "watching" a play. Calling himself "anti-Aristotelian," Brecht did not simply disregard traditional artistic rules, but highlighted them in exaggerated ways so that they could never be taken as natural. Brecht wanted to provoke and maintain the audience's awareness of the constructed nature of the play, and, by extension, of society.

Like the Russian formalists (see Chapter 4), Brecht believed that defamiliarization helps people really observe what they only think they see every day. The active role the audience had to play when at Brecht's theater was the active role citizens should take as they faced their alienation and exploitation at home and at work.

To this end, Brecht's alienation effect was achieved through presenting social contradictions and inequalities as brutal or shocking, showing them to be unnatural, not just unfortunate. Brecht's message was (and is), don't let "the price of bread, the lack of work, or the declaration of war" seem inevitable, like acts of nature. Show their historical dependence on human exploitation. This is a message that responds directly to the dominant ideology by calling its bluff on the spin it gives to actual power relations.

Return of the Repressed

Marxist critics in the latter half of the twentieth century began developing a wide range of ideological critique. The British critic Terry Eagleton, for example, urged an emphasis on the mode of production for any given work. What matters in a literary work, that is, is not just its content, but its own material existence. Oral literature differs from print, and print differs from online texts, in ways that should be factored into an investigation of how the work functions in ideology. Eagleton also called attention to the multiple ideological spheres that a work might be examined in. We've been talking primarily, for example, about ideology in its general circumstances, concerning all of society. But a work can also be analyzed with regard to the specific ideology of its author, or to the ideology of the artistic principles that dominate any given era.

Speaking of analysis—another area of Marxist theory that developed in the 1960s combines ideological critique with psychological analysis. These theories suggest that ideology, as the socially acceptable version of real economic relations, acts to repress things that are unacceptable, namely, all those contradictions and tensions in capitalism. Repression pushes these unapproved features away, keeping you from getting a good look at them.

Literary analysis, however, can uncover or reveal what's being repressed, or at least indicate that something has been repressed in the first place. The French critic, Pierre Macherey, and the American critic, Fredric Jameson, for example, have argued that you can investigate this repression by first recognizing that all literary works actively try to reconcile the inconsistencies between the ideology of what a society imagines itself to be and the material arrangements of what it really is.

That is, literary works *try* to do this, but they always fail. Solutions to the problem of covering up contradictions are "tried out" in texts that seem to create coherent, unified systems (such as realist novels, as we've seen), but ultimately the solutions fail to fully uphold the ideology. Critics of this sort, therefore, read rather like psychoanalysts, looking for what David Richter has called "blind spots left by what the ideology of [an] age is unable to talk about." And this is even true of nonfiction writing as well. Marx himself, according to a later Marxist critic, read books on economics with an eye for gaps and slips, evidence of what the authors were unable to face and incapable of expressing (see Chapter 17 for how the deconstructionists approach gaps and slips in the text).

So what Jameson called the "political unconscious" becomes the basis for analyzing literature. In fact, for Jameson, it's not only literature that can be studied this way, but all the arts, including architecture and pretty much anything else made or even interpreted by human sensibilities (see Chapter 19's discussion of postmodernism for more).

The bottom line? You live in and rely on a social system loaded with unfairness and exploitation, and while you try to ignore the contradictions and live according to a more reasonable story line (ideology), your political unconscious is always at work trying to expose the illusion. At some level, you feel guilty. In fact, the whole system feels guilty.

The real solution? Work toward understanding and improving the social and historical forces around you. If that doesn't do the trick, well—Dr. Freud will see you in the next chapter.

The Least You Need to Know

- Economic systems hide their true nature.
- Examine things as parts of a process, not as isolated objects.
- Ideology creates and employs literary features.
- A literary work's content can be seen to reflect society's contradictions.
- A literary work's form can be seen to reveal society's inability to keep its story straight.

Freud Sees a Symptom

In This Chapter

- Freud's map of the mind
- Getting past the censors
- Tell me your dreams
- Discovering the true, instinctual meaning

The thing about Freud is that he fundamentally and systematically influenced the way we think about egg salad. I mean human creativity. Why did I say egg salad? That's so embarrassing. I'll start again.

Classical Freudian theory is based on the idea that all of our actions are really symptoms of our necessarily divided selves. That is, we're never in complete control of our lives, including our utterances, but always locked in a struggle to coordinate the various levels of our minds with the instinctual demands of our bodies.

Your mind, according to Freud, is dynamic and busy with parts and processes always at work. Your "thinking" is not a single-stage event, but a messy negotiation with your past (some of it remembered, most of it unknown even to you), your present circumstances, and your expectations for lunch. I mean the future.

Thinking Big

So what does this have to do with literature?

It has a lot to do with literature and any of the arts because it changes what many people think of as the basis of art in the first place. We've seen that art can be seen as an imitation or mirroring of the world, and we've seen that art can be seen as an expression. Freud's approach to the human mind sees art as a symptom; it's something you exhibit without complete conscious control, like a sneeze. It's a symptom of a problem, and when you repress it, your head might explode.

> **IN THEORY**
>
> Sigmund Freud (1856–1939, pronounced *Froyd*) grew up and spent most of his life in Vienna. He earned his medical degree in 1881 and in the 1890s began to develop his theories of psychoanalysis. His own psychoanalytic practice was enormously successful and he became quite famous in his own time. When the Nazis invaded Austria he fled to London "to die in freedom." One of his children, Anna Freud, became an influential psychoanalyst as well, and Freud's grandson, Lucian Freud, was a more-than-prominent British artist whose career spanned the second half of the twentieth century.

Literature's true causes, according to Freud, are difficult to see without expert training, so what gets all the attention is the symptom. Freud began a systematic theoretical approach that analyzes psychological factors—psychoanalysis—as a method for not only uncovering the root causes of the symptom called art, but as a means of helping people recover from their ailments.

In this way, psychoanalytic approaches to literature are not just "literary" theories. They're inherently related to a specific view of human nature. Freud argued that psychological processes are at work in all art, in all eras, whether or not an author is concerned about them.

Psychoanalysis is one of the theories discussed in this book, like Marxism, that makes a claim about the human condition, not just about art. So Freud's theories, just like Marxism, won't let you say things like, "But the author didn't mean that," or "You're reading too much into that," because the whole point of the approach is to uncover the forces that produce the text, and these forces are, according to the theory, always hidden from direct view.

> **RELATIONS**
>
> As you saw in Chapter 9, critics primarily associated with Marxism have developed theories that also incorporate psychoanalytical principles. Throughout this book you'll read about many other instances of Freud's influence, particularly in Chapter 18.

It's because these forces are hidden that they need to be tracked down and exposed by expert analysis. For Freud, it's all about the ongoing improvement of the patient's psychological health. Each of us suffers in some way from neurosis, the emotional conflicts between the various parts of our minds, or, more clinically, our psyches (pronounced *SIGH-keez*).

You know the stereotypical image of Freud's method, sometimes called the "talking cure": A patient lies on a couch and talks to an analyst, who deciphers what's really going on in the patient's head. The patient feels better, then makes an appointment for the next week.

Time to go beyond the stereotype.

But before we do that, two reasons why discussing Freud is so helpful for anyone interested in literary theory. First, it clearly reminds you of the relationship between theory and criticism. Freud's theory is his proposed overall explanation for how the human psyche operates and how literature fits into the picture. Freudian criticism, then, is the method of analysis resulting from this explanation. Critics like to say that theory *informs* practice, and so you can say that Freud's theory currently informs a wide variety of psychoanalytic approaches.

Second, it reminds you how neat it would be to have your name become an adjective. Theoretically, it could happen to anyone, but when you hear the term *Marxist* or *Freudian*, you know it means an entire field in which people may agree and disagree, but they're at least sharing the same way of talking about things. This shared way of talking is sometimes called a discourse. In this sense, discourse means more than just talking—it sets out the rules for talking, as we'll see in many of the chapters to come.

What Do You Have in Mind?

Classical psychoanalysis and Freud's general map of the mind were in place by 1920, and that's what we'll be discussing in this chapter. Throughout his life, Freud made many changes to his theory, but he himself did not fundamentally alter the views that have become so influential in literary theory and criticism.

IN THEORY

"Ladies and Gentlemen,—Today we will proceed along a narrow path, but one which may lead us to a wide prospect." —Sigmund Freud

Freud's view of the divided, conflicted mind contrasts with an image of the mind as the stable basis for self-knowledge. And where would you even get the idea that your mind is a stable basis for self-knowledge? Probably from René Descartes (1596–1650, pronounced *day-KART*).

Descartes is the philosopher famous for saying "I think, therefore I am," which has led to all kinds of arguments about whether or not this really proves your existence (run that around with a philosopher next time you're at a party), but what it definitely presupposes is that you can be aware of your own thinking. If someone sees you as having this kind of disembodied, spectator-like mind, you're being seen as a Cartesian subject. (*Cartesian* is how Descartes's name was turned into an adjective. Kind of good news/bad news for him in the discourse department, you know?) Anyway, the Cartesian subject is defined by the mind's ability to know itself and by the promise of a rational, intentional basis for behavior. That is, there is a "you" that you can know, and you can willfully control yourself with your rational mind and intentions.

Freud's theory says there are forces at work in "you" that make it impossible to fully know your thoughts or yourself, and that your actions are significantly motivated by forces you'll never see or control directly.

Consider what this means for literary works. The Cartesian model of the mind is generally responsible for seeing literary works as carefully constructed, unified objects, as the New Critics liked to emphasize (see Chapter 3). Neoclassical critics, as well, relied on the rational side of creativity with their emphasis on rules, order, and decorum (see Chapter 6). In both cases, critics saw literature as something that could be analyzed with a pretty high level of confidence in the rational mind, no matter how imaginative the literature might be. For the Freudian critic, the task of the critic is to investigate precisely what is hidden from the rational mind.

The famous split, therefore, is between the conscious and the unconscious aspects of the human psyche. The unconscious is a part of your mind that is completely and forever blocked off from direct view by your consciousness. You can never gain immediate access to the unconscious, according to Freud, so you'll have to look for signs of it indirectly, in the things you do and say. Sort of like looking at the wake from an invisible boat.

You've probably heard of Freudian slips, in which people say things they didn't expect to say (egg salad). Freud argues that such simple, everyday occurrences are evidence of the deep and never-ceasing movement of the unconscious, which always seeks to give your conscious mind a hard time.

For Freud, such slips are not accidental, but linked to the activity of your psyche in ways that can be studied and explained. Literature and art, in all their variety, can be seen the same way.

What's responsible for all this hidden psychological activity? Freud explained that the specific regions or structures of the psyche include the id, the superego, and the ego. The id (Latin for "it") resides entirely in your unconscious. It's made up of disorganized energy just waiting for release. This energy is generally oriented toward control, dominance, sexual gratification, and possession of anything pleasurable. Simply put by Freud, the id "is the dark, inaccessible part of our personality."

And not only is the id the Tasmanian Devil of your psyche, but it never goes away. It doesn't know time, and whatever wishful impulses it had when you were a baby, they're still there. According to Freud, since you can't calm it down or wait it out, the only way to deprive the id of its energy is through analysis. You have to link your current thoughts, utterances, and actions to the immortal wishful energy of the id in order to obtain any temporary relief.

But wait. If you've got this id churning away inside your mind, why don't you just act on its impulses all the time? Come on, id, what's keeping you down?

Two things keep your id in check. Or rather, two other structures of your mind are always negotiating with your id. There's the superego, for one. The superego, most prominently, is made up of your conscience. It's your internalized acknowledgement of society's rules and conventions—anything that would keep you from always acting like a baby. I mean *really* like a baby. The superego is also made up of self-observation and the desire to maintain your ideal self. And while it helps you look civilized, the superego is also a big pain in the neck.

Freud points out that much of the superego is in your unconscious as well. Your "internal acknowledgement" of social conventions and laws, or your conscience, is actually developed at a psychological level that you don't have direct access to, just like the id. This means, among other things, that your conscience can go way overboard and make you feel deeply guilty over something very trivial. The superego shows no mercy in its punishment.

To the rescue comes what Freud once called "His Majesty the Ego, the hero alike of every daydream and of every story." The ego (Latin for "I") tries to balance the demands of the id and the superego and create a real, livable self. However, don't jump to conclusions thinking that the ego is your rational conscious side while your id and/or superego is your irrational unconscious side. Freud emphasized that much of the activity of the ego itself is unconscious. I know! This means hardly anything goes on in your head that's fully conscious. Even memories, which you can call to mind willingly, are only *pre*conscious, since as soon as they aren't front and center in your conscious mind, they recede again.

In any case, the most important mechanism at work in this kind of mind, for literary study, is the action of repression. Repression is any of the many forms of denying your unconscious urges their release. Most obviously, repression is what happens to the id when it can't just show up and do anything it wants. Freud argued that repression will always lead to the compulsion for expression. You can't keep a lid clamped on a pot of boiling water without steam eventually escaping.

Now if you change the metaphor from steam escaping to something else, like Freud did, you get to the motivation for the entire history of literature. What is that other metaphor? Censorship.

Dream Weaving

Freud argued that repression is a kind of censorship that leads your unconscious to operate in all kinds of sneaky ways in order to get its message out. Many of these strategies are closely related to literary techniques, and Freud first studied them in dreams. It was during sleep, Freud explained, that elements of the unconscious try to make their way past the various levels of resistance put in place by the superego and ego. The unconscious elements, or dream-thoughts, can only get into the dream you remember, or dream-content, by disguising themselves. Freud called the process of disguise and transformation the dream-work.

Freud also called the dream-work the "factory of thoughts," and what it does is turn stuff that is *latent*, or potential, into something that is *manifest*, or that actually exists. A psychoanalyst listening to patients tell about dreams, therefore, is presented with manifest content—a story. The analyst's task, as mentioned before, is to figure out the true meaning behind the story created through the dream-work's strategies.

APPLY IT

Legendary though it may be, Freud's work can actually be very approachable and even enjoyable. His most important early works include *The Interpretation of Dreams* (1900), *Beyond the Pleasure Principle* (1920), and *The Ego and the Id* (1923). The best recommendation I have, however, is to read one of the books Freud wrote for the benefit of nonspecialists as well as psychoanalysts, including *New Introductory Lectures on Psychoanalysis* (1933), which begins every chapter with the cheery greeting, "Ladies and Gentlemen." In addition, Freud's book *Wit and Its Relation to the Unconscious* (1905) is not only informative but hilarious.

One strategy is called condensation. Freud compared this to an image produced by "several photographs on the same plate." Condensation takes several images from the unconscious and turns them into a single superimposed image in the dream you remember. Why? Because any of the unconscious images (really just urges or impulses at that stage) on their own would be too much for you to handle. So they combine several of your day's "residue" of images and come up with a hybrid image that gets several uncomfortable impulses past the censorship of your ego at one time.

Freud pointed out that artists sometimes reflect what the dream-work does, like when they imagine "centaurs or fabulous beasts" which combine elements of several animals into one creature.

Another strategy of both the dream-work and of literature, according to psychoanalytic approaches, is displacement. Displacement occurs when the ego simply latches on to an image as a substitution for an unconscious impulse. The image isn't emotionally related to the impulse—in fact, it can't be; the point is to distract the mind by getting something unacceptable past the censor in the guise of something acceptable. Defined this way, displacement is the sort of "master strategy" of all art.

Displacement also takes the form of sending something into the dream that seems completely insignificant, but the analyst can see that its insignificance is just a strategy to distract the ego's censor. You tell a dream of an elaborate dinner party, but your analyst discovers that the key to your anxiety is the bird you heard singing on the way in, which barely seemed important to you at the time.

IN THEORY

"Once again the dream, like the one we first analyzed … turns out to have been in the nature of a self-justification, a plea on behalf of my own rights." —Sigmund Freud

You might be wondering when we'll get to phallic symbols and all that Freudian stuff. Freud files these matters in the category of symbolization. In symbolization, any image that makes it to your dream-content *is* related in some way to the unconscious impulse. At least it's related in your own mind or experience. It's still a form of displacement, broadly speaking, but the symbols that appear in your dreams (or literature) all resemble or have some association with your own past experience. And because the id's energy primarily involves sexuality, many of the symbols it provokes will evoke safe images, like euphemisms, that represent their more racy origins. Analysts, critics, and ordinary readers have always been able to spot some of the more familiar examples: loaves of bread, rosebuds, train tunnels, mountain ranges, Oscar Hammerstein.

The point is, for Freud no detail is insignificant. And while you may be tempted to repeat the saying, "sometimes a cigar is just a cigar," Freud would insist that isn't the case. Every detail of a dream for an analyst—and every detail of a text for a psycho-analytic literary critic—is fair game for interpretation.

In fact, when you define literature as a written symptom in which every detail may stand for something else and true meaning is never immediately evident, you also need to radically modify your reading approach. Freud suggested approaching the dream-content like a rebus. Here's one:

You've probably seen rebuses before, so what is this one supposed to mean? Yes, of course, Freud would probably say it's about sex. But what we want to consider now is what this rebus can tell us about reading.

After looking at the images in this rebus, you end up with the phrase, "I left my heart in San Francisco." But think about it—your reading strategy for this little puzzle is actually a very complicated process. You have to shift from one mode of interpretation to another. The equation is something like: "eye which rhymes with I" "LEFT-handed mitt" "MY" "symbol of HEART" "IN" "image of bridge that many people recognize as the Golden Gate in SAN FRANCISCO."

If you try to interpret this rebus with one strategy or too narrowly, you run into dead ends: "I mitt my heart in bridge." Instead, you have to recognize the *manner* in which each image is being used, and this manner changes throughout the sentence. "Eye/I" is a rhyme, but "mitt" (or "glove") isn't. You change gears and see what the image of the mitt is getting at is the word "left." The image of the heart is pretty straightfor- ward. The image of the bridge is not being used for either a rhyme or for its specific detail (like the mitt), but for its *association* with the city of San Francisco. So what happens if you don't recognize the Golden Gate Bridge? You're out of luck. If you do recognize it, maybe the mitt was difficult to decode. In that case, you may have left it for the end, and after interpreting "my heart in San Francisco," you look back and say, "Oh, I get it, it's a *left* glove." So, "I left my heart in San Francisco."

Freud explained that this complex kind of reading is what the analyst does. For the analyst, the dream-story is made up of multiple codes and types of representation. A single system of decoding won't work, because you need to discover what kind of work each image is doing in order to make the whole equation work. Rhymes, specific detail, and associations are examples of the strategies used to get painful impulses into the dream you remember. Once they're in the dream, the analyst can't just take them at face value, but must consider the various ways that the human mind sends messages.

You might think of it this way: this rebus, which once appeared on the inside of a bottle cap (there are lots of examples on the web), is the psychologically coded way of saying what must have been too traumatic for the little bottle cap to say directly.

Literature on the Couch

Of course you noticed that the explanation of a rebus can take up a lot more space than the rebus itself. All that condensing, associating, and code switching can really cram a lot of material into a concise illustration. The same is true for jokes, which Freud also spent a lot of time analyzing. A joke might take seconds to hear and appreciate, but the explanation for the joke can take much, much longer. And as is well known, explaining a joke is simply not funny. Unless it is—see Mark Twain, or Freud himself in *Wit and its Relation to the Unconscious.*

The point is that this process—unpacking all the material that's been stuffed into a rebus or a joke and explaining how each piece fits—this process is like the task of literary critics, especially psychoanalytic critics. Freud argued that while everyone's mind operates in the way we've been discussing, it's writers and artists who seem to be better at packaging up unconscious impulses. Their psyches are better at sublimating, or transforming psychological energies into acceptable expressions.

When critics approach literature, therefore, they know they're in for a long but absorbing process of unpacking, sorting out, and rearranging the details of a text in order to explain how the text works and how it reveals psychological depths not visible to direct observation.

APPLY IT

As we saw in Chapter 9, Marxist critics stress that every work of literature should be seen from a materialist perspective. Similarly, psychoanalytic critics don't confine themselves to works that seem obviously psychological, and neither should you. Feel free to bring any work of art to the analyst's couch. Of course, there are still some works that have attracted attention because of their obvious psychological themes, including the following:

> *Hunger,* by Knut Hamsun (1890)
>
> "The Metamorphosis," by Franz Kafka (1915)
>
> *Steppenwolf,* by Hermann Hesse (1927)
>
> *Nightwood,* by Djuna Barnes (1936)
>
> *The Bell Jar,* by Sylvia Plath (1963)
>
> *Fight Club,* by Chuck Palahniuk (1996)

Psychological approaches to literature have been around as long as literature itself. Precedents to Freud's theories can be seen in Romanticism, for example, which explores the relationship between a poet's inner life and outer works (see Chapter 8).

Freud's legacy for literary criticism has seen critics branch out into hundreds of areas, so it may be helpful to organize their approaches, and your own, into three main objects of analysis. That is, what's being psychoanalyzed—the author, the characters, or the reader? Are you investigating the psyche of the creator of the text—the manifest content—in front of you? Are you looking for evidence in the text for the way certain characters indirectly reveal their unconscious impulses, whether it's through their actions or words? Or do you subscribe to the idea that criticism tells you a lot more about the critic than the book? If so, the reader's psychological response to the text takes center stage.

In the following sampling of important early psychoanalytic critics who have considered each of these three orientations, I've limited the scope of interpretations to those reflecting what Freud saw as the human psyche's two most fundamental preoccupations, sex and death.

Must Be About Sex

Ernest Jones (1879–1958) was a British critic instrumental in bringing psychoanalytic approaches to the study of English literature. He also wrote interesting pieces on a variety of other subjects, from religion to ice-skating. Jones is most famous for his study *Hamlet and Oedipus* (1949), in which he applied Freud's Oedipus complex to Shakespeare's famous play.

As we saw in the discussion of Aristotelian plot in Chapter 6, the Oedipus story describes the tragedy of a man who, through a complicated series of events, ends up unknowingly killing his father and sleeping with his mother. Freud argued that this story reflects a fundamental stage in male psychological development—a young boy's desires *do* tend toward the mother, and the boy, seeing the father as an obstacle to gratification, wishes to kill him.

Don't worry (or do worry), we'll discuss other responses to this in Chapter 18, but for now the importance of the Oedipus complex is that Jones developed a convincing and influential case that Hamlet is troubled by Oedipal issues. Jones argued that Hamlet's ambivalence toward killing his uncle Claudius reflects Hamlet's ambivalence over his attraction to his mother. Moreover, Jones argued that the play itself reflects Shakespeare's own Oedipus complex and that the continued popularity of *Hamlet* is even due to our own Oedipal complexes and our deep psychological need to see it brought out of the unconscious and made manifest. Interestingly, Jones was consulted for Sir Laurence Olivier's 1948 movie version of *Hamlet*.

RELATIONS

Another important figure in psychoanalysis, Carl Jung, was also Freud's student, friend, and collaborator for several years. Jung moved away from Freud's focus on individual psychology and developed his own theories of the collective unconscious, which we'll cover in Chapter 16 as part of structuralist approaches to literature.

Otto Rank (1884–1939), elaborated on the Freudian concept of the double, or doppelganger. In his criticism, Rank showed how psychological and sexual issues are often worked out in literature through the creation of Jekyll/Hyde-like characters, love-hate relationships, and disorienting hybrids of self and other. Rank's work referenced writers such as Edgar Allan Poe, Guy de Maupassant, Oscar Wilde, Fyodor Dostoevsky, and E. T. A. Hoffmann. For your own analysis, you might check out Joseph Conrad's story, "The Secret Sharer."

Critics have also interpreted Mary Shelley's *Frankenstein* as a novel that reveals its author's psychological anxieties over sex, childbirth, and death. The novel itself, in these readings, is Shelley's double. Just as common are readings that analyze Victor Frankenstein and Robert Walton as doubles, or Victor and the creature as doubles. Each character represents an exaggerated or estranged aspect of a full personality.

And you'll recall that a New Critical view (see Chapter 3) emphasizes that a critic's primary job would be to discover and track the formal patterning that contributes to the organic unity of the Frankenstein/Walton/Creature mirroring. Psychoanalytic critics would then want to explain why the patterning is significant for revealing deep instinctual processes. In Chapter 12, we'll see how feminist critics elaborate on Shelley herself as part of the characters' psychological mirroring.

Similarly, Marie Bonaparte (1882–1962, and yes, related), was influential in elaborating on Poe as a writer whose work could clearly be seen as a form of psychological therapy for the writer. A later critic, Frederick Crews, helped popularize the argument that Nathaniel Hawthorne's work often dramatized the Freudian idea of the "return of the repressed," or the eventual release of suppressed sexuality, despite a character's attempts to ignore or hide sexual impulses. The fate of Young Goodman Brown, in Hawthorne's story of the same name, is a case in point. Crews himself later rejected the validity of this approach.

APPLY IT

As with fiction, any movie at all is fair game for psychoanalytic interpretations. But also like fiction, many movies have attracted attention specifically for psychological themes and techniques (some rather extreme), including the following:

The Cabinet of Dr. Caligari, directed by Robert Wiene (1920)

Un Chien Andalou, directed by Luis Buñuel and Salvador Dalí (1929)

Citizen Kane, directed by Orson Welles (1941)

Spellbound, directed by Alfred Hitchcock (1945)

Psycho, directed by Alfred Hitchcock (1960)

Solaris, directed by Andrei Tarkovsky (1972) or Steven Soderbergh (2002)

Steppenwolf, directed by Fred Haines (1974)

Love and Death, directed by Woody Allen (1975)

Unless It's About Death

In his book *Beyond the Pleasure Principle* (1920), Freud argued that there had to be another instinctual drive at work in the human psyche, a drive that could explain behavior that he thought could not be explained by his earlier theory. Turns out, according to Freud, that it's actually death you're worried about all the time. This death drive was explored by literary critic Peter Brooks, who argued that since we're all afraid to think about our own deaths, our own "conclusions," we create art with beginnings, middles, and especially endings as a way of rehearsing or preparing for the big inevitability.

Stories help us feel like there is some kind of order, logic, and even repetition to our lives and deaths. They may do this thematically, in their content, by relating stories of lives well lived or even life after death. But according to Brooks, the most powerful force for psychological support comes from the patterns of plot itself. That is, we don't just crave content; we want to physically and emotionally feel plots and their repetition. Repetition and patterns give us a sense that there is more to a fictional story—and to the human story—than simply its progress toward "the end." As part of his evidence, Brooks points to the repetitive structures of fairy tales in particular, as well as the refrains of poems and songs. All of these transmit the basic "pulsation" of literature to us at very deep levels. Another example Brooks offers of reading plot psychologically involves Charles Dickens's *Great Expectations,* in which "each of Pip's choices in the novel, while consciously life-furthering, forward oriented, in fact leads back, to the insoluble question of origins."

Speaking of origins, I did mention that some critics focus on analysis of the reader, rather than the author or the characters. Critic Norman N. Holland brought it all back home by arguing that reading is always a transaction between the text and your own psychological fantasies and defenses. You inevitably read, according to Holland, to suit and defend your ego. Your interpretation is based on your own anxieties and what you think consciously or feel unconsciously that the text is doing to you. You also use the text as justification for already existing principles at stake in your own character. This certainly recalls reader-response criticism (see Chapter 5), but Holland distinguishes his approach from many of the others by noting that he advocates tracking the responses of an actual, individual reader—really *you*—and not an abstract "you" created through an interpretive community or even in collaboration with the text. In exactly the same way, critics should pursue and acknowledge their own psychological motivations for their work, no matter how professionally their interpretations are presented.

I would love to do that myself, I really would. But look at the clock—I'm late for lunch.

The Least You Need to Know

- Psychoanalytic criticism is based on a universal view of the human mind, not just on literature itself.
- Your mind is divided and dynamic, and its operations are not all accessible through direct observation.
- Unconscious impulses are converted by dreams as well as by literature into images, symbols, and other indirect manifestations.
- Your task is to interpret backward, to understand the deep psychological origins and motivations for what you see in a text.
- Psychoanalytic criticism can focus on the psychology of the author, the characters, or the reader of the literary work.

Saussure and Science Settle Into a Good Read

In This Chapter

- Saussure's theory of the sign
- Seeing language as a system
- Relational, not essential meanings
- Saussure's incredible influence
- Biology, the mind, and literature

Language is really strange. Think about it. Why does the word *cow* make you think of a cow? The word itself doesn't look like a cow. It doesn't particularly sound like a cow. And if you're thinking of a French or a Chinese cow, you've got completely different words in mind, anyway.

Not only that, but understanding a language doesn't mean you've *memorized* every sentence that could possibly be spoken in that language. You hear or read totally new sentences all the time and, based on some mysterious language ability, you make sense of them. What makes language work must involve some incredibly complicated faculty of the human mind.

This chapter looks at two fields that consider just how language works. The first is linguistics, the scientific study of language, and the other is cognitive science, the study of the mind in general. Why are we getting in so deep? First, because the specific linguistic ideas we'll be discussing have fundamentally influenced virtually every approach to literary theory since the beginning of the twentieth century. It's practically impossible to separate theory and criticism from this linguistic base. And as for cognitive science—an exciting and provocative newcomer to literary studies—it might sound difficult, but don't worry, it's hardly brain surgery. Oh wait, sometimes it *really does* involve brain surgery. But we won't do that.

Must Be a Sign

Ferdinand de Saussure (1857–1913, pronounced *so-SOOR*), was the Swiss linguist who developed an approach to studying language that also changed the way people study all kinds of subjects, including literature, history, psychology, and anthropology. Saussure lived and worked primarily in Geneva, Switzerland, and he never actually wrote the book that made him famous. His *Course in General Linguistics* (1916) was assembled from students' notes taken during lectures (mostly free of doodles) and published three years after Saussure's death. In order to make our way around his discussion and come in for a landing at literary studies, we'll begin with how Saussure messed around with the traditional understanding of how words have meaning.

To begin with, Saussure argued that you can't just look at *words* and see them as naturally linked to *things*. The word *cow* doesn't spontaneously come from the cow itself, and it isn't even associated with a real cow because of some divine decree (unless it is: see St. Augustine in Chapter 7). Instead, the connection between any given word and its reference is arbitrary. You already know this, of course. It's clear when you look at the variety of words different languages have for the same things. It's even clear that if you wanted to, you could develop your own personal code words to use with friends or family, and, as long everyone knew the code, you could communicate.

"Arbitrary? What about onomatopoeia? You know, the way some words really do match what they describe? Isn't that a natural connection?"

Nope. Saussure's ready for that one. He points out that even animal sounds are different in different languages. Dogs and ducks, for example, run around the world making the same noises, but people not only spell those noises differently, they *hear* them differently. Ask around, you'll find *woof-woof, guao-guao, ouah-ouah, quack-quack, coin-coin,* and even *ga-ga.* Saussure's point? Meaning depends on our participation in a system, not in a link between word and thing. Any doubts? Look up what people think roosters sound like.

"Okay, but what about interjections? If you drop a brick on someone's foot, you know they're going to make the same noise in any language."

Nope again. Saussure says everything we do in language involves the system, and we just internalize all the arbitrary associations we've inherited, so they feel natural. And since we're on this topic, what is it with the English word *ouch?* Seems awfully complicated when other languages just let you yell things like *aie!* You really have to be taught, directly or subliminally, to say *ouch.* (*Yuck* is funny, too. The French say *berk* instead, which is just as funny. Oh, this could go on all day.)

Anyway, says Saussure, there is something in the very nature of words that makes all these arbitrary links not only necessary but turns them into the very apparatus behind thought itself.

IN THEORY

"There are no preexisting ideas, and nothing is distinct before the appearance of language." —Ferdinand de Saussure

Saussure argued that a word is really a sign. The word *cow*, for example, is the sign for cow. And signs always have two sides to them, completely inseparable, like the two sides of a sheet of paper. These two sides are called the signifier and the signified.

The signifier is that aspect of a sign that you see written down or hear spoken. In the case of that cow, the signifier is the word you see right there, and it's also the sound you hear when you read it silently and "sound it out" in your head. Saussure also calls this a sound-image, because of this (kind of eerie) quality.

So just as you see or think this sound-image, the other side of the sign is right there, as well. The signifier's partner is the signified. The signified is that aspect of a sign indicating the concept or thought provoked by the signifier. It's the concept you have of what *cow* means. In this way, any sign (such as a word) unites a sound-image with a concept.

Signifier (sound-image) ⇔ Signified (concept)

At this point, I imagine, Saussure would lean out into the lecture hall and emphasize that under no circumstances should anyone think this means you simply substitute *signifier* and *signified* for *word* and *thing*.

"Why not?" a student would ask.

Because the signified isn't a thing, it's a concept. It's literally psychological, in your mind, as the notion of whatever the sign points you to. The cow isn't in your mind or directly responsible for the sign; it's the concept of the cow that's being transacted in language. And as we saw, the signifier is also psychological. The sound-image of *cow* might appear written or you could hear it spoken, but its power lies in your being able to call it to mind, psychologically. Signs, therefore, are the psychosocial currency of meaning.

"Linguistic signs, though basically psychological, are not abstractions." Instead, these "associations which bear the stamp of collective approval—and which added together constitute language—are realities that have their seat in the brain." —Ferdinand de Saussure

In other words, any word, any sign, is really a dynamic mechanism that brings psychological features together and produces the meanings that we seem so instinctively to grasp. And while it might sound like Saussure is just talking about communicating in symbols rather than, say, having a conversation by passing around an actual cow, he's really getting at the heart of the language system, which, according to Saussure, is as deep socially as it is psychologically.

Adding Some Structure

Linguistics, up to the end of the 1800s, tended to concentrate its study of language on comparing languages with each other, looking for evidence of "family relationships." This got particularly interesting when Sanskrit, an Eastern language, was compared with Greek, Latin, German, and so on, and the results seemed to show all kinds of parallels. It's one thing to recognize variations of the word *three*, for example, in *tres* (Latin), *tres* (Spanish), *trois* (French), and even *drei* (German), but it was very interesting to discover that in ancient Sanskrit, three is *trayas*. These kinds of similarities suggested deep, global roots to language development and change.

What these kinds of similarities did not show, however, was what language was really all about. Comparative and historical linguists may be able to track how languages have changed, but *how does language work* in the first place? According to Saussure, the proper object of study ought to be the principles that structure the very life of language. While the structure of the sign offered an explanation for the principle behind the way individual words carried meaning, Saussure had much more to say about how signs work together in the system of language itself.

Just a Slice, Please

The first move, for Saussure, was to point out that the history of a language doesn't make any difference to an actual user of that language. It's interesting, and certainly scholarly, to know that the word *derivation* has its roots in the Latin term for channeling water from its source, but when you actually use the word, you don't need to know this at all.

RELATIONS

Of course, word derivations and other historical facts about words are important to some users of a language. Poets and writers, for example, often exploit the hidden sources of names and words as part of their art and as a way of reviving language. And as we'll see in Chapter 17, deconstruction argues for the importance of word derivations in creating echoes of meaning across time and cultures.

Studying the development or evolution of languages over time, as linguists had been doing before Saussure (and still do), is called the diachronic study of language. Saussure insisted on the synchronic study of language, which looked at language at a single moment of time. That is, rather than looking at the whole developing history of language, like a tree with its old roots and new growth, Saussure called for a cross-section through the tree to see exactly what language is doing at any given time.

This signals a major shift in perspective, because it turns you away from tracking "the story of language" and squarely asks, what's the language system doing for you—and to you—right now? How do you, and everything you say, fit into language as it exists right now? And it turns out that when you look at that slice of language as a system you've inherited and are using right now, it looks a bit like a chess game.

It's Your Move

Saussure divided the components of the language system into two parts, famously calling them *langue* and *parole*. You can also call them that—but be sure to pronounce the first word *long*, and the second word requires an "R" sound that takes a little work depending on the language you're used to speaking. I'm going to switch gears myself and refer to *langue* as the system of rules and *parole* as an utterance.

The logic of Saussure's argument is pretty straightforward. The system-of-rules side of a language is the social, shared aspect of language. You're born into a language created by many, many users, with all its grammatical features and vocabulary. And since you're not a grammarian (unless you are), you're like the rest of us and our reactions to this system of rules—we've internalized it. You can hear a sentence and "just know" whether it sounds right or not. You would see the phrase "that big, old, broken-down fence," and know that it's preferable to "that broken-down, old, big fence."

Who knows why? Well, some people do, and Saussure could talk your ear off with such linguistic details. But the point he wants to make with the idea of a system of rules is that it exists before you speak, and you're predominantly affected by it without understanding it. "The linguistic faculty," as critic Jonathan Culler put it, "includes knowledge of how to combine elements, rules of combination."

As for utterances, they form the other side of language. Utterances are the actual things you say and write. Saussure wants you to see utterances as enactments or realizations of the system of rules. In this way, language is like a chess game, since the rules are set out for you in advance, and your activity consists in moving the pieces (or signs) around in accordance with those rules. You literally take what you have been given and, in making sensible moves, make sense. You're certainly free to make the game your own and move the pieces wherever you want, but in order to play the game correctly, you follow the limited, or finite, set of rules that both enables and restricts your activity.

One other point about that chess game analogy. You know how it's possible to replace a lost pawn with pretty much anything else and still keep playing? You just say that a piece of cheese is a pawn. And it works as long as you move that cheese just like you would move a pawn. It isn't the shape, size, or anything physical about a pawn or a rook that makes it a pawn or rook, it's how those pieces are moved.

Not only that, but if you take a pawn out of a chess game, you could use it for a doorstop, or a paperweight. Objects are objects, and it's only when they are used according to the rules of the chess game that they become "chess pieces." A pawn is a pawn because it can be distinguished from a rook and all the other pieces. And this difference isn't based on what the pieces are made of, it's based on what they do in the system. Saussure theorized that it's the same way with language. And by the way, if you keep moving that piece of cheese diagonally, you're going to have to call it a bishop.

Saussure argued that a sign does not have a *positive* value, but a *relational* value—it only gains meaning because of its difference from other signs. Musical notes are like this as well. Any single note in isolation has existence, but really no meaning, until another note—or a whole series of notes—is heard along with it. Same with daubs of paint in a painting. Any single brushstroke (or point, if you're looking at one of Georges Seurat's paintings) gains its effect by sitting alongside some other daub. And of course the same musical note or daub of paint could be dropped into another work of art, another system, and its meaning would change.

DEFINITION

Relational meaning describes the type of signification that Saussure sees in language. One thing only gains meaning through its relation to other things. This is in contrast to **positive (or essential) meaning,** which sees any single entity as having positive value, or a self-sufficient meaning.

Now, once you start down this road of relational meaning, you recognize that if every sign gains meaning only because of its difference from other signs, and from its role or function in a system, then what we traditionally think of as the quality or value of any sign really comes from the system. Signs don't give the system meaning, the system gives the signs meaning, and, as we'll see, value.

Stop in for Great Values

Always ready with analogies, Saussure also compared the language system with the system that makes money valuable. It isn't, he reminded his students, the actual value of the metal in a coin that makes the coin valuable, it's what the coin means in the system.

Colors and color words are obvious examples of relational values as well. How much of the color spectrum do you choose to call blue or red? Looking at any color, and naming it, is always a matter of contrasting it with what it is not. And you also have to abide by the vocabulary available to you. For example, if a system of language only gave you broad categories so that every color you see must either be blue, red, or yellow, then those words, or signs, become huge buckets of content. That is, whatever colors you see, no matter how various, must be divided into one of those three big categories.

Of course, languages have many more words for colors. But as specific as any color terms get, they only gain their particular values by *not* being some other term. Or let's consider that cow again. What kind of cow is it? *Cow* carries a different value than Guernsey, for example (which I hear is a kind of cow). Put another way, in some of the chess games you play with language, *cow* has enough value for what you want to do, such as distinguish between a cow and a horse. But for other games, or systems, you need the value created by the more specific term, such as when you're planning a farm.

IN THEORY

"Each language articulates or organizes the world differently. Languages do not simply name existing categories, they articulate their own." —Jonathan Culler

Speaking of animals, people have also created distinct linguistic value systems for describing animals as food. Saussure would emphasize the different values involved in calling something either *cattle* or *beef.* Is it because we don't want the system of animal names to get in the way of eating meat, so we develop another system of "food words" that we can switch to instead? Whatever the reason, Saussure argued that this fact of language use supports the principle that values only emerge from language systems, not from words or things themselves.

Put another way—and this is one of Saussure's most influential points—our ideas themselves develop out of the system. You are able to think of a certain cow because you have a word for it. Sure, you and a friend could both be looking at the same cow, but to you it's a Guernsey and to your friend it's a cow. The whole arrangement of thoughts about reality you are both looking at is shaped differently in your heads. "Language has neither ideas nor sounds that existed before the linguistic system," argued Saussure. Language only operates because of differences that result from the system.

APPLY IT

When you read *Frankenstein* or see any of the movie versions, notice how differences work to help define each character. For example, humanity is opposed to monstrousness, or masculinity is opposed to femininity, and in each case, definitions become possible. Can you also spot evidence that those definitions are vulnerable, because they are based on relational value? That is, do you ever see the monstrous becoming human, the feminine becoming masculine, and vice versa?

So does that mean everything we see is really an illusion of some kind? Not for Saussure, since the result of the system's interactions—just like the result of the signifier and signified working together—creates the only reality we know. And these signs in their language systems are not imaginary or abstract, they actually do things. Signs may be psychological but they are also *real.* We have to deal with them, we can manipulate them, handle them, and we come to internalize them as our own.

RELATIONS

At this point you just might be thinking of Immanuel Kant's ideas of how important the operation of your mind is for creating the world you see (see Chapter 8). Keep in mind, however, that Saussure's system isn't based on the kinds of hard-wired categories that Kant describes, but on social conventions and rules.

Another interesting example of relational value comes from the movies. In the 1920s, a Soviet filmmaker named Lev Kuleshov showed how the system of editing separate film shots can effortlessly provoke certain ideas in viewers' minds. In one of his experiments (you can see it online), Kuleshov showed a brief film featuring a man alone in the frame, looking at something, then the shot changes to a bowl of soup, then back the guy looking. Then the shot changes to a baby sleeping, then back to the guy looking. Then a shot of a scantily clad woman, then back to the guy looking.

When he asked the audience to describe the man's acting, most people said things like, "Oh my, very sensitive. First he looks so hungry, and then he's calm when he sees the baby, and finally he looks rather interested when he sees the lady." Turns out, however, that Kuleshov had used exactly the same shot of the man each time, so there was no difference at all in his expression. Any ideas the audience had regarding the connection between one shot and another was due to what's now known as the "Kuleshov effect," or the result of an internalized system with a rule that's roughly stated as "there's got to be a connection here somewhere."

Everybody Gets in On the Act

Language, literature, film—each of these is a sign system for Saussure. And Saussure called the science for studying sign systems semiology (pronounced *semmy-ology*, and from *semeion*, the Greek word for "sign"). It's no exaggeration to say that semiological studies transformed dozens of fields in the twentieth century. This is because, simply put, when you look out at the world, you don't see things, you see signs. Any social system, any kind of meaning-making can be seen as semiological, as a system of signs. And this has meant, since Saussure's work exploded onto the scene, that the products of social systems can be read as texts.

In later chapters, we'll see evidence of Saussure's influence time and time again. One field in particular that Saussure himself recognized as an important area of systematic thinking was anthropology, the study of human culture. Saussure suggested that "by studying rites, customs, etc. as signs, I believe that we shall throw new light on the facts and point up the need for including them in a science of semiology and explaining them by its laws." And it's those laws—the system of rules (or *langue*) of human society—that become the center of attention for structuralist critics of the later twentieth century, as we'll see in Chapter 16.

> **IN THEORY**
>
> Charles Sanders Peirce (1839–1914, pronounced *purse*) was an American philosopher whose work on linguistics is often compared to Saussure's. Peirce's writings are notoriously dense in their arguments yet often surprisingly vibrant in their tone. A contemporary of Mark Twain, Peirce sometimes sounds like he's got that writer's sense of humor figured out, such as when he writes, "The word *symbol* has so many meanings that it would be an injury to the language to add a new one."

In literary studies, a fairly direct application of Saussure's theory has been called structuralist criticism, which we'll also discuss in Chapter 16. One example of that approach is to consider any literary work an utterance (or *parole*) and investigate the underlying system of rules supporting it.

In the field of psychology, as we'll see in Chapter 18, Saussure's theories are blended with Freud's. The result is a range of psychoanalytic approaches to literature in which structures and relations are emphasized and language itself is seen as a cause, rather than a result, of the human psyche.

Social questions reflecting Saussure's clear influence are discussed in virtually every chapter to come. The consequences for seeing social institutions like schools, religions, and governments as texts becomes clear if you recall how important it was to Freud or Marx that you try to raise your awareness of what often seem like "natural" situations or conditions. That is, Marxist critics (see Chapter 9) want you to consider the ways ideology lulls you into thinking that economic and social exploitation "just happen." These critics call attention to what they see as the system of rules that define the social games we play. Similarly, psychoanalytic critics (see Chapter 10) advocate analysis of the unconscious system of rules that give rise to what you think of as your own rational behavior.

Both Marxist and psychoanalytic approaches, therefore, argue that the seemingly natural and individual character of human behavior is overestimated. The real focus, they suggest, should be on the rules of the systems we inhabit, in our minds and through our actions. It sounds familiar, then, to hear Saussure explain that "the distinguishing characteristic of the sign—but the one that is least apparent at first sight—is that in some way it always eludes the individual or social will." In fact, that last part—about the sign escaping even the *social* will—indicates how far Saussure was willing to go in arguing that language itself really calls the shots. Chapter 17's discussion of deconstruction will look into this more closely.

IN THEORY

"Linguistics, like psychology and a sociology of collective representations, will explain my actions by setting out in detail the implicit knowledge that I myself have not brought to consciousness." —Jonathan Culler

In the 1950s, the American linguist Noam Chomsky began developing his theories, following Saussure's general lead, of the importance of grammar. Grammar, as the system of rules that governs language, was generative because a finite set of rules can generate infinite instances of language. And grammar rules are transformative because they can explain how the same meaning can emerge in different forms, such as "There is a cow!" and "A cow is there!"

Chomsky described your internalized understanding of grammatical structures as competence, and your ability to form all kinds of new and unique sentences as performance. Together, these faculties enable the "rule-governed creativity" of everyday language. And for Chomsky, these rules go pretty deep; in fact, he called them deep structures and argued that they are the basis of all human language.

Recently, critics have turned their attention to deep issues as well, searching for the physiological basis for language and blending literary theory with biology.

It's All in Your Head

The field of cognitive literary studies, or cognitive cultural studies, has precedents that extend back for centuries in one form or another, but the form we're interested in is really a twenty-first-century creature. New discoveries in the biological processes that contribute to cognition, or thinking, are being brought into dialogue with literary and cultural studies.

IN THEORY

Some say "'look into our hearts and write.' But that is not looking deep enough; Racine or Donne looked into a good deal more than the heart. One must look into the cerebral cortex, the nervous system, and the digestive tracts." —T. S. Eliot

Critics such as Lisa Zunshine, Mark Turner, and Brian Boyd consider language and even literary skills to be parts of the "cognitive architecture" humans (and possibly others) have evolved as a species. Such a perspective puts a new spin on many of the older issues raised by literary theory. For example, Mark Turner takes a different approach to the imagination than the Romantic poet-critics did (see Chapter 8). Turner argued that the kind of imagination responsible for metaphors and allegories isn't actually all that original. In fact, the most effective metaphors, because they are more easily understood, can be ones that are the most unoriginal.

Think of it this way: for the allegory of the cave, all Plato has to do to be original is to switch the terms of the source (the cave situation) so that the target (Plato's point) follows along. Turner has explained that writers inherit such source stories all the time, then perform what often turns out to be rather unoriginal work. Unoriginality doesn't matter, though, because our brains love this kind of thing. We seem to be designed to appreciate what Turner called constraints, or the demands that certain stories make, and we like seeing these demands met. As Turner put it, "There is a system to imagination. Although infinitely variable and unpredictable, imagination is grounded in structures of invention."

Another striking aspect of cognitive literary studies is its interest in mind reading. Yes, mind reading. Lisa Zunshine has argued that it goes on all the time, and it can also be called theory of mind. "Mind reading is a term," Zunshine explained, "used by cognitive psychologists to describe our ability to explain people's behavior in terms of their thoughts, feelings, beliefs, and desires." In other words, when you watch people looking up at a fireworks display and you can imagine what they're thinking or feeling, that's mind reading. And for cognitive literary critics, it's also what enables you to make a certain kind of sense of the world around you.

For one thing, as Zunshine has noted, your biological ability to "explain observed behavior in terms of underlying mental states" helps you eliminate, without even thinking about it consciously, some of the "false options" for explaining why people are doing what they are doing. When you see people hailing taxicabs, for example, your theory of mind quickly eliminates the possibility that they're just waving their hands to say "Hi!"

 IN THEORY

It's "our ability to invest the flimsy verbal constructions that we generously call 'characters' with a potential for a variety of thoughts, feelings, and desires, and then to look for the 'cues' that allow us to guess at their feelings and thus to predict their actions." —Lisa Zunshine

Moreover, as Zunshine argued, "literature pervasively capitalizes on" mind reading. Stories are filled with descriptions of characters doing things as subtle as wrinkling their noses, trembling, or turning their heads, and because of the context of the story and your theory of mind, you rush to fill in the emotional and cognitive details that are not spelled out explicitly in words. Ultimately, then, what links literary studies with studies of the human brain is the argument that literature, according to Zunshine, "calls for the same kind of mind reading as is necessary in regular human communication."

The Least You Need to Know

- Signs don't just point to real things; signs are psychological and social.
- Signs only have value and meaning in relation to other signs.
- Ideas emerge from language use.
- Saussure's systematic or structural theories have been applied in dozens of fields.
- Cognitive literary studies argues for a biological basis for understanding language and literature.

Hey, Whose Book Is This?

Communities of readers take over in this part of the book. In these chapters, we'll explore influential theories developed in the light of readers' own interests and even creative functions. Feminist criticism explains the central principles of presumption, expectation, and bias in literary history. Other approaches elaborate on the way reading reflects and even becomes a part of our identities. We'll see how our associations with gender, ethnicity, and the physical body itself emphasize the active, social dynamics of literature.

Feminist Theories Change the Game

In This Chapter

- Feminist theory's project of change
- Patriarchy's false normality
- Reflections on male-constructed images
- Rereading the self and other
- Women's writing

"Literature is political," wrote the feminist critic Judith Fetterley in 1978. Yep, literature sure was political in 1978. Oh the '70s, such times. Disco. Feminism.

But then again, literature was political in 1792 when Mary Wollstonecraft wrote, "Women are everywhere in this deplorable state; for, in order to preserve their innocence, as ignorance is courteously termed, truth is hidden from them, and they are made to assume an artificial character before their faculties have acquired any strength."

And literature was political in the nineteenth century for John Stuart Mill, who wrote that "what is now called the nature of women is an eminently artificial thing—the result of forced oppression"; and for Elizabeth Barrett Browning, who crafted poetry into a rejection of the rule that women were to "keep quiet by the fire and never say 'no' when the world said 'ay.'"

And then there's Virginia Woolf in 1929, who reproached literary critics for asserting things like, "This is an important book ... because it deals with war. This is an insignificant book because it deals with the feelings of women in a drawing-room."

In fact, whether you look back to past literary debates or at the most recently published novels, it's very clear that feminism has been around for a while—and it never stops being relevant to literary studies.

In the previous chapter we discussed how Saussure's theoretical orientation profoundly changed the way other theorists and critics approached their studies. With feminist theories, we'll explore historic influences not only on theory and not only on criticism, but also on everyday practices of reading and writing.

Is This Pedestal High Enough for You?

Feminist literary theory and criticism is one aspect of a political program whose goals include exposing the effects of patriarchy (or social rule by men) and advancing equal opportunities for women in all areas of life. What makes literary study so appropriate for the first of these goals, according to feminist critics, is the textual nature of much of patriarchy's power. That is, patriarchy often looks and works just like a story—a deceptive and manipulative story.

Particularly Universal

Judith Fetterley's comment about the political nature of literature is followed by a reminder familiar to feminist critics. It's the reminder that political and social forces can succeed best when they don't look like force at all. It's one thing to recognize and react to exploitation, but it's another to just go through life thinking, "That's just the way things are."

Literature, in particular, Fetterley explained, can be all the more powerful as an enabler of patriarchy because literature is so often depicted as universal, or applicable to everyone without regard for sexual or social differences. To many people, it's just entertainment, after all. But literature, Fetterley argued, "insists on its universality at the same time that it defines universality in specifically male terms." In this way, feminism recalls Marxism (see Chapter 9) in pointing out the mystification of social forces.

IN THEORY

"When a system of power is thoroughly in command, it has scarcely need to speak itself aloud; when its workings are exposed and questioned, it becomes not only subject to discussion, but even to change." —Kate Millett

In 1949, Simone de Beauvoir (1908–1986, pronounced *BO-vwah*) published *The Second Sex*, in which she elaborated on "the myth of woman." This myth perpetuates the idea of the "Eternal Feminine," a range of images of women that obscure women's actual lives and qualities. In place of real, individual women with their own human characteristics, the Eternal Feminine simply sets up woman as man's opposite.

And it's hardly an equal split. Man has put himself at the center of the universe as the only real *subject*, the only true thinking being, while woman is an object to be admired, feared, used, simply looked at, or ignored. From this androcentric (male-centered) view of things, women have no subjectivity of their own. What counts as universal, therefore, is entirely a male affair. When you speak of mankind, it isn't just the word that favors men, it's the concept itself as it has been used throughout history. Feminist critics have pointed out, for example, that a field defined with the universal-sounding name "American literature" has actual been comprised of "American literature written by men."

 IN THEORY

"Few myths have been more advantageous to the ruling caste than the myth of woman: it justifies all privileges and even authorizes their abuse." —Simone de Beauvoir

The role of the Eternal Feminine in an androcentric worldview also splits men and women into radically unequal categories. Since man is associated with universality, he is seen as the model of normality, as well as of reason and activity in the outside world. Woman, without subjectivity, becomes an object of particularity, of exception, and is associated with the body, the emotions, passivity, and the home. One indication of this unequal split between universals and particulars is the way language still sometimes reverts to expectations about who usually works in an occupation. Unnecessary terms like *female construction worker* or *male nurse* puts the marked term of a particularity in front of the assumed universal term.

One of the first moves of feminist theory, then, is to expose the false universality of patriarchy and reveal its actual motivations and effects—to reread, in other words, the myth of woman. But don't think that this is only to set the record straight, or even to develop a more accurate myth. According to feminists, it isn't just the way that the myth of woman works to benefit patriarchal privilege that's the problem—it's how the myth becomes internalized by women themselves.

Betty Friedan's bestselling book, *The Feminine Mystique*, published in 1963, reread the myth of woman in the context of midcentury American culture. While the suburban housewife, Friedan explained, was mythologized as "the dream image of the young American woman and the envy, it was said, of women all over the world," Freidan revealed story after story of women recognizing that the dream didn't match reality, and that their own lives were at stake as they participated in the myth.

Literary studies and practices of everyday reading, therefore, have become central to feminist criticism. Critic Florence Howe wrote in the early 1970s that "we read to change ourselves and others." The critic and poet Adrienne Rich advocated "the act of looking back, of seeing with fresh eyes, of entering an old text from a new critical direction." And as Annette Kolodny explained, consciousness raising of this sort is a matter of an "attentiveness to the ways in which primarily male structures of power are inscribed (or encoded) within our literary inheritance."

APPLY IT

Consider the novel you're reading now, or a movie you've seen lately. Do you see any evidence that male characters are depicted in a universalist way and the female characters are objectified? Which characters seem to abide by the myth that men must be associated with reason and action, while women seem to emphasize the emotions and the body? And—just to add my two cents—how often do we see "guy movies" with female characters whose only real job seems to be to look pretty and laugh or shake their heads in (loving) dismay at what the male characters do?

One particularly insidious way of masking patriarchy as universal is to make something seem natural. And not just natural, as in normal, but biologically necessary.

It's Only Natural, Isn't It?

Simone de Beauvoir's *The Second Sex* made the famous argument, "One is not born, but rather becomes, a woman … it is civilization as a whole that produces this creature," based on the conventions, laws, and expectations of a patriarchal society.

It's a very old and also an always new question: are you "born that way"? Essentialist views answer yes, while constructivist approaches say no. Feminist literary theory has productively elaborated on both positions, and as we'll see in the next chapter, gender theories consider even more answers to the question of nature versus nurture.

In support of the idea that females are formed by patriarchal society into "women," Juliet Mitchell argued in 1966 that there was much more to the myth of woman than an abstraction or a culture of misunderstanding. Instead, Mitchell explored how the story of patriarchy is literally "written" into such socioeconomic structures as the control over women's reproductive functions. In this way, patriarchy claims to be supported by unchanging biological difference when it has in fact written the importance of those differences into the existing male-centered narrative.

APPLY IT

Feminist literary theory, like Marxist literary theory, is one facet of a broader political orientation with social change as its goal. For further background into feminism's history and scope, take a look at Estelle Freedman's *No Turning Back: The History of Feminism and the Future of Women* (2002), as well as any of the invaluable anthologies edited by Miriam Schneir.

Anthropologist Gayle Rubin used the phrase "transforming moral law into natural law" to describe the strategy of taking what is really just your own point of view and claiming that it has unchallengeable biological support. In this case, the point of view is patriarchal society, and the biological support is supposed to be the natural differences between the sexes.

However, as Rubin pointed out, while biological differences obviously exist between females and males, the actual *meaning* of those differences is not inevitable. "Sex as we know it," Rubin argued, is a social product better thought of as *gender*, or the transformation of sexual differences into cultural conventions. Simply put, "Gender is a socially imposed division of the sexes."

This is another example, by the way, of the kind of relational meaning that Saussure emphasized (see Chapter 11), since human differences only gain their real, active meaning by being part of a system—in this case, a patriarchal system. According to Rubin, it's "the system of relationships by which women become the prey of men." Women are women, but they become oppressed because of how they are made to function in society.

So why does a patriarchal society bother to transform sexual differences into cultural conventions maintaining that women are naturally inferior? Is it simply to make men feel better about themselves? Rubin and other feminist critics have pointed to more concrete reasons. For one, male society can more easily mystify the way it uses women and women's labor for its own ends. Labor is divided into work that produces capitalist profit—historically identified with men—and the domestic activities that support this work—historically associated with women. Rubin argued that child rearing and housework, for example, serve as essential prerequisites for the labor performed by capitalist workers. Domestic work by women, which allowed men to leave the home for work, has therefore been an integral part of labor, but it hasn't always been recognized as such. Instead, the division of labor was carried over to a division of the sexes in a way that made it seem natural for men, and not women, to be at the heart of labor and economic issues. While circumstances may be changing in many societies, feminists point out that the legacy of this unequal system is still potent.

In fact, one example of the sleight of hand motivated by economic interests is the way patriarchal societies label as "tradition" the kinds of activities that actually serve to preserve male dominance. From arranged marriages to male bonding over sexual conquests, what Rubin called the patriarchal "traffic in women" mystifies motivations of dominance and control as natural or traditional: "At the most general level, the social organization of sex rests upon gender, obligatory heterosexuality, and the constraint of female sexuality."

Girl, That Rochester Is Bad News

As we saw above, the Eternal Feminine functions in a patriarchal society by restricting woman to function as a male-dominated abstraction or object without a subjectivity of its own. Feminist criticism has paid particular attention to how this myth often breaks down into two main story lines: the woman is either an angel or she's a monster.

On the one side is the "angel in the house," which was also the name of the bestselling book-length poem published in 1854 by the Victorian poet, Coventry Patmore (a man). In this poem you'll find all the classic Western stereotypes of the perfect wife, a woman who, while set upon the highest pedestal of admiration possible, lives entirely for her husband. She's devoted, submissive, pretty, and pure. This poem (and it wasn't the only one of its type) clearly set the conditions for the wife whose value lies in staying home to ensure that the house is a "refuge" for her man when he returns from a challenging day "out in the world."

Critics Sandra Gilbert and Susan Gubar, in *The Madwoman in the Attic* (1979), focused on the role that literature written by men played in the promotion of such myths as the angel in the house, as well as her relatives, the saintly mother and the pure virginal girl.

Gilbert and Gubar argued that many male writers, including Dante (a poet of the early Italian renaissance), Milton (an English poet of the seventeenth century and the writer of *Paradise Lost*), and Goethe (the German Romanticist; see Chapter 8), were psychologically compelled to perpetuate images of the Eternal Feminine in order to soothe their own anxieties over actual women.

For these male writers, according to Gilbert and Gubar, real women represent mortality and a kind of control—particularly regarding the giving of life through childbirth—that men would like to believe only they possess. As a way of taming that power, which is in fact uncontrollable in real life, men perpetuate the imaginary masks of ideal women. Women characters are therefore denied any true ability to act, but only serve as man's "other," a literally selfless image employed in male fantasies. Again, Gilbert and Gubar pointed out, what may look like a harmless or even complimentary representation of women by men ("But I simply idolize you, baby") functions instead as a mechanism for control. And this control has two sides, as well, since "those mythic masks male artists have fastened over her human face" actually put women into two imaginary categories, not just one.

That would be the monster we're talking about now. Gilbert and Gubar point out that the same psychological issues that lead male writers to create idealized masks for women also prompt the creation of the angel's monstrous opposite. If men are frightened over a woman's ability to give life, they get positively hysterical (pun intended) over a woman's potential to take life away. Gilbert and Gubar, citing the feminist critic Dorothy Dinnerstein, explained that male anxiety over women's independence goes as psychologically deep as "everyone's mother-dominated infancy," and that "patriarchal texts have traditionally suggested that every angelically selfless Snow White must be hunted, if not haunted, by a wickedly assertive Stepmother."

Every "good" female image in literature, in other words, is likely to be accompanied by an explicitly negative image that inverts the idealized stereotypes and perpetuates images of women who are monstrous, unfeminine, dangerous, and out of control.

But why should it matter? People know the difference between real life and false representations in literature. Well, this isn't the first time we've seen literary critics point out how effectively mystified social forces can be and how deeply people can identify with false images. Feminist critics argue that when women look into the mirror, what they see is the product of a cultural construction.

Moreover, Gilbert and Gubar emphasized that for a woman writer, the mirror is literature itself; it's all those male-constructed masks that have served as literary models. The "female imagination," according to Gilbert and Gubar, has perceived its masked self in the literary mirror for a long, long time, and it's not a matter of simply wishing these false models away.

IN THEORY

"A woman writer must examine, assimilate, and transcend the extreme images of 'angel' and 'monster' which male authors have generated for her. Before we women can write, declared Virginia Woolf, we must 'kill' the 'angel in the house.' In other words, women must kill the aesthetic ideal through which they themselves have been 'killed' into art." —Sandra Gilbert and Susan Gubar

As you may have guessed, one case in point for seeing a female author struggling with patriarchal masks is, for Gilbert and Gubar, Charlotte Brontë's 1847 novel, *Jane Eyre.* That novel, with Rochester as its strong central male character and two opposing female characters—one pure and virtuous, the other seemingly mad and dangerous—offers a view of how one nineteenth-century female writer tried to exorcize the demons of patriarchy. "Pure Jane," for instance, may serve as an angelic figure, yet Brontë also twists the stereotype in order to shock Victorian readers with Jane's assertiveness and sexual energy. On the other hand, Bertha, "the madwoman in the attic," more clearly reflects the patriarchal Victorian stereotype of the monster, as internalized by a female author.

Diving Into the Stereotypists' Pool

Between the 1960s and the 1980s feminist theory saw a remarkable expansion in critical readings of literature to explore the varieties of myths created under patriarchy. In this section, we'll consider what has been classified as "woman as reader" criticism of male-authored texts, and in the next section we'll discuss approaches to "woman as writer."

Feminist critique of male-authored texts has moved far beyond simple "images of women" criticism. This type of criticism centered on identifying and condemning negative images of women and calling for more positive role models for women in literature. As Toril Moi has pointed out, despite its simplicity and generalizations, this type of criticism was instrumental in moving literary theory beyond the formalist emphasis of the New Critics (see Chapter 3) and for raising the political consciousness of a whole generation of readers in the early 1970s.

Other critics, however, were less interested in a style of prescriptive theory that told people what they should be reading, and more focused on skeptically rereading texts that had long been the object of traditional analysis by androcentric critics. Feminist criticism argued for an approach to male-authored literature that was, according to Elaine Showalter, "essentially political and polemical."

IN THEORY

"Insofar as literature is itself a social institution, so, too, reading is a highly socialized—or learned—activity. What makes it so exciting, of course, is that it can be constantly relearned and refined, so as to provide either an individual or an entire reading community, over time, with infinite variations of the same text." —Annette Kolodny

Feminist readings, explained Annette Kolodny, proved that reading was not something everyone did the same way. Reading strategies and habits were not universal, and feminist readings proved that "we appropriate different meanings, or report different gleanings, at different times—even from the same text—according to our changed assumptions, circumstances, and requirements."

If you studied literature in the middle of the twentieth century, you would be faced with an accepted collection of works considered "great literature." This canon of literature might even seem to have formed itself naturally, since only the best literature should survive the test of time, rise to the top, and so on. Of course, you're well aware now that whatever seems natural may need some looking into, and the literary canon is no exception.

In a patriarchal society, books favor men and male experience. Elaine Showalter noted that for decades, the typical college year for a female student of literature would conclude with "the favorite book of all freshman English courses, the classic of adolescent rebellion, *A Portrait of the Artist as a Young Man.*" Ultimately, Showalter explained, "by the end of her freshman year, a woman student would have learned something about intellectual neutrality; she would be learning, in fact, how to think like a man."

Making the connection between what is offered as neutral but what is actually masculinist is what Judith Fetterley addressed in her important book, *The Resisting Reader: A Feminist Approach to American Fiction* (1978). Fetterley takes up Kate Millett's groundbreaking approach in *Sexual Politics* (1969) to explore the literary sexual politics of the American literary canon. For Fetterley, the concern was not with male-authored "female masks" being fixed on female readers, but with women being forced to read like men and to identify with male characters and points of view. Fetterley argued that in fictions such as Washington Irving's "Rip van Winkle" or F. Scott Fitzgerald's *The Great Gatsby,* "the female reader is co-opted." In these works, women readers are faced with female characters that symbolize male fantasies and fears, yet in order to arrive at "correct" interpretations, women must identify with the male characters and reflect their responses to the female constructions.

Over time, this identification contributes to women's self-hatred and self-doubt. Therefore, according to Fetterley, the first move a feminist critic makes is to become a "resisting reader," one that begins to become aware of and eliminate "the male mind that has been implanted in us."

Writing Circles Around You

But enough about men. Showalter and other critics were well aware that concentrating on rereading male-authored texts was only one aspect of feminist literary criticism. Another aspect, "woman as writer," investigates the very nature of female creativity, language, and linguistics. Showalter called this critical activity *gynocriticism*.

Critical approaches to *Frankenstein* offer a particularly interesting variety of examples of gynocriticism. Shelley's novel has been read as a specifically female-centered birth myth by several critics. Ellen Moers combined biographical details of Shelley's life with a New Critical approach (see Chapter 3) to show how the novel is unified by overlapping layers of birth, death, and guilt. This reading makes much of the fact that Mary Wollstonecraft (yes, the same early feminist writer) died shortly after giving birth to her daughter, the author of *Frankenstein*.

Gilbert and Gubar also argued that Mary Shelley herself is one of the layers that merge with the identities of the creature, Victor, and Walton. In turn, these characters reflect the main characters of Milton's *Paradise Lost*—Eve, Adam, the serpent, and God. In their complex and informative reading, Gilbert and Gubar showed how patriarchal features of *Paradise Lost* find their way into Shelley's novel and how *Frankenstein* transforms them into "radically revised" images.

APPLY IT

So do you remember what all the female characters do in that male-centered novel, *Frankenstein*? Not many people do. Take a look at Elizabeth's letters to Victor, or the speech Elizabeth gives at Justine's trial. Then there's Safie. Who? Don't worry, we'll discuss her in Chapter 21. And there's Victor's mother, and Agatha, and even the "young Russian lady" that Walton mentions. Once you start reading differently—and yes, even with an agenda, as naysayers will charge—you'll find you're actually positioned to see more of what the text is really doing, culturally speaking.

Barbara Johnson (1947–2009) explained how *Frankenstein* functions like an autobiography for Mary Shelley. The novel, Johnson argued, illustrates the writer's "struggle for female authorship" because the very concept of writing autobiographies (and other literary works) was generally based on masculine models. *Frankenstein*, therefore, is a "textual dramatization" of Shelley's recognition that, at the time she was writing, a woman writer was likely to be seen as a "monstrous creator" of something only God (men) should do. As Johnson explained, Shelley knew she would seem monstrous in daring to answer "two of the most fundamental questions one can ask: where do babies come from? and where do stories come from?"

Evolving Phases

Elaine Showalter described three developmental phases in women's writing since the nineteenth century. These phases aren't marked by strict boundaries, since much of what is described for any one phase can occur at any other time. Yet, as Showalter described them, these phases have become (despite strong disagreements over details) enormously helpful for beginning to think not only about women's literature emerging from patriarchy, but about any art form developing in the context of a dominant social force (as we'll see in the discussion of postcolonial literature in Chapter 21).

The first phase, or "feminine phase," Showalter argued, occurred between 1840 and 1880. During this period, women wrote with an eye to matching men's achievements. Works written in this phase show women internalizing male assumptions about female culture. Male pseudonyms were a symptom of this: Mary Ann Evans wrote as George Eliot, Charlotte Brontë published as Currer Bell, and the French novelist Aurore Dupin Dudevant became George Sand. As Virginia Woolf wrote regarding the same period, a woman writer at the time "was admitting that she was 'only a woman,' or protesting that she was 'as good as a man.'"

During the "feminist phase," from 1880 to 1920, according to Showalter, "women are historically enabled to reject the accommodating postures of femininity and to use literature to dramatize the ordeals of wronged womanhood." That is, women writers directly confronted the negative effects of patriarchy. Consider the works of Elizabeth Gaskell (*Mary Barton, North and South, Cranford*) involving factory and home life, as well as class struggle. Charlotte Perkins Gilman ("The Yellow Wallpaper") and Kate Chopin (*The Awakening*) also belong to this phase.

In the third, "female phase" beginning in the 1920s and continuing through the century, "women reject both imitation and protest—two forms of dependency—and turn instead to female experience." Writers in this period, such as Virginia Woolf

(*Mrs. Dalloway, To the Lighthouse*) and Dorothy Richardson (*Pointed Roofs*) sought to create worlds in which a woman's identity, however linked to other characters, can be seen as autonomous and reflective of actual female experience.

Another important development of feminist literary scholarship involving all three phases has been the recovery of literature written by women but traditionally ignored by critics, school reading lists, and ordinary readers. The author and critic Alice Walker, for example (see Chapter 14), brought Zora Neale Hurston's valuable work back to the public's attention after years of neglect.

Body Works

If Showalter's model seems to privilege the influence of male writing, suggesting that women's writing is more strongly influenced through nurture rather than nature, another approach to women's writing seeks to identify the essentialist aspects of that writing. This is generally seen as a development of the later twentieth century and influenced by deconstruction and post-Freudian theories (as we'll see in Chapters 17 and 18), but you can actually see the idea at work in Virginia Woolf's view of female writing.

Woolf argued in the 1920s that there could be such a thing as a "man's sentence." The grammar and style that had developed in men's writing, according to Woolf, revealed signs and accents of the patriarchy surrounding that writing. For Woolf, such sentences were "unsuited for a woman's use," and she speculated on a future in which women would mold and shape entirely new forms of writing that did not reflect a male predisposition.

IN THEORY

"'Success prompts to exertion; and habit facilitates success.' That is a man's sentence; behind it one can see Johnson, Gibbon and the rest. It was a sentence that was unsuited for a woman's use. Charlotte Brontë, with all her splendid gift for prose, stumbled and fell with that clumsy weapon in her hands. George Eliot committed atrocities with it that beggar description. Jane Austen looked at it and laughed at it and devised a perfectly natural, shapely sentence proper for her own use and never departed from it." —Virginia Woolf

What Do You Mean, "We"?

Controversy has always been part of feminist literary theory, both in its relationship to patriarchal social structures and within its own multifaceted field. And in both cases, the controversies have led to progress.

It became clear in the 1970s, for example, that feminism was being defined in ways that were offered as universal, yet actually reflected a particular group's interest. Yes, irony is like that. Minority voices called on mainstream feminism to acknowledge and correct its biases, since "mainstream" was really dependent on white, middle class, heterosexual, and Western perspectives.

Barbara Smith took many of the influential 1970s feminists directly to task for their "racist flaws." She called for a "redefinition of the goals and strategies" of feminism such that other voices would become part of that project. If woman was supposed to be man's other, some women found themselves as the other's other by feminist critique itself.

 IN THEORY

"By and large within the women's movement today [1984], white women focus upon their oppression as women and ignore differences of race, sexual preference, class, and age. There is a pretense to homogeneity of experience covered by the word *sisterhood* that does not in fact exist." —Audre Lorde

As we'll see in virtually every subsequent chapter, feminist theory and criticism responded to these concerns, and it did so in two powerful ways. First, through transforming feminist theory itself by making it more inclusive, diverse, and self-aware. Second, principles of feminist theory became adapted as fundamental and intrinsic features of many other approaches to literature.

The Least You Need to Know

- Feminist theory emphasizes the always-political nature of literature in society.
- Patriarchy privileges male interests and masks those interests behind a universal image.
- Feminist readings offer resistance to oppressive male-centered worlds created in literature.
- Writing by women can be seen as an evolving response to, and distancing from, male styles of writing.

Gender and Queer Theories Read Desire

In This Chapter

- Nature and culture in theories of gender
- Gay and lesbian literary criticism
- Performing your gender
- Queer theory's challenge to identity

"Well, nobody's perfect!" replies Osgood, happy as could be, at the very end of Billy Wilder's 1959 movie, *Some Like it Hot*. Jerry (played by Jack Lemmon) has just told Osgood (Joe E. Brown) that they can't get married, as Osgood has proposed, because Jerry is a man and has only been pretending to be a woman throughout their relationship. Jerry's own response to Osgood's line is to look confused, but not that confused. After all, the masquerade has kind of grown on him.

If you've seen it, you know the whole movie is built around the complicated borders of male and female identity—the playacting, intentional and forced, that goes into appearing to be a man or a woman. Strict gender identities—whereby a man is a man, a woman is a woman, and that's the end of the story—have, in fact, never been the whole story for most people throughout history. Other fairly recent movies come to mind—*Tootsie; The Adventures of Priscilla, Queen of the Desert; The Crying Game*; and *Boys Don't Cry* —but there is also a centuries-old literary tradition that reflects an interest in how sexuality affects our sense and presentation of self.

There are all those Shakespeare plays, like *The Two Gentlemen of Verona* or *Twelfth Night*, where romance depends on the subterfuge of women dressing as men. This was particularly fun, since when Shakespeare's plays were first performed, boys would play all the female roles, so what you had was a boy playing a woman playing a man.

Then there's Shakespeare's famous Sonnet 20, in which the male poet swoons over the "master-mistress" of his passion who has all the charms of a woman—and then some.

And why not bring up Virginia Woolf's 1928 novel, *Orlando*, whose main character not only lives for 400 years, but changes from male to female gender during the course of the story? Or consider Christopher Isherwood's 1939 novel, *Goodbye to Berlin*, which codes the very active homosexuality of the story so carefully as to create a practically sexless text.

In this chapter, we'll survey several of the most important and interesting critical approaches to gender issues. At times these critical approaches take the form of theoretical investigations into sexual identity, others seek direct involvement in social issues, and several do both. And like the other chapters in this part, we find a history filled with tragedy, pain, and political oppression, but also much joy, discovery, and progress.

Tending Gender

The basic concept at the center of these approaches is the idea that sexual identities are—and always have been—complex social constructions. There is no direct relationship between sex, seen as biological difference, and gender, seen as a social category.

IN THEORY

"The charting of a space between something called 'sex' and something called 'gender' has been one of the most influential and successful undertakings of feminist thought." —Eve Kosofsky Sedgwick

The anthropologist Gayle Rubin has defined gender as a "socially imposed division of the sexes," which emphasizes the way social structures, such as those that privilege male power, strategically turn biological differences into "genders" that become working parts of the capitalist system. The literary critic Judith Butler has defined gender as "the cultural significance that the sexed body assumes." Butler's definition highlights both the reality of differences—we all have "sexed bodies"—and the way culture gives those differences their significance. Here you can see the influence of Saussure's linguistic theories (see Chapter 11), which emphasize that the meaning of a concept comes from the system it belongs to, not from itself as an isolated entity.

Under different circumstances, of course, all those biological differences and so-called sexual urges can be radically redefined. What is considered normal in one period or place is not normal everywhere. It's clear from the work of anthropologists such as Rubin that what people consider appropriate sexual behavior depends on social, cultural, and religious systems rather than simple biology.

And as we'll see, social systems, according to some gender critics, not only determine your views toward appropriate behavior, but lead to your sense of self and even instill specific sexual desires in the first place.

But really, sex is sex, isn't it? People don't think about sexual organization the way they think about other social regulations, like speed limits. Sex, whatever it means to a particular person, sure seems natural, and sexual restrictions have been justified on the basis of nature as well.

In fact, it's because of this seemingly natural basis that gender studies takes a critical look at Western views of sexuality. In particular, gender criticism offers various challenges to what Adrienne Rich labeled *compulsory heterosexuality*, which is the idea that while much of Western culture has employed sexuality as a universal term, it has really meant heterosexuality. Heterosexuality becomes the norm we are compelled to support, and anything else is seen as a deviation or a perversion.

For literary theory and criticism, gender studies follows feminism in emphasizing two main projects. One is exploring how our sexual identities are written for us and into us. That is, like the oppressive narratives of patriarchy written into women's lives (see Chapter 12), the demands of compulsory heterosexuality become aspects of our lives in need of critical examination.

Literary form itself can indicate one example of the normalizing of heterosexuality. Consider all those nineteenth-century marriage plots, for example. Once again, think of *Pride and Prejudice* or *Jane Eyre* and how the main action of those novels leads toward getting someone married. Critics have suggested that the order and closure of the literary marriage plot reinforces the presumption of order and closure in a heterosexual marriage. It worked out in the novel; why shouldn't it work out in life?

Gender critics, also following feminist theory, investigate reading habits as well. Feminist critics emphasized that there is no "universal reader" out there, responsible for a literary work's interpretation. What often passes for a universal reader is the white, male, English or American reader. Gender critics similarly question the way reader-response approaches (see Chapter 5) may hide their heteronormativity (another useful term, popularized by Lauren Berlant and Michael Warner) behind a so-called universal mask. Simple questions lead to a variety of insightful responses: How do people with different sexual orientations read the same text? How might an author be intentionally coding the sexuality of a text? How might sexuality be reinterpreted in a text regardless of the author's intention?

Does this mean you're expected to read into texts to uncover hidden aspects of gender, sexuality, and identity? Yes! Gender criticism, like several other approaches we've seen in this book, actively supports the idea that since you read with an agenda anyway, the best things you can do are, first, become more aware of that agenda (on account of it usually being hidden from your consciousness), and second, work to change your agenda, since even your most personal reading and cultural practices have an effect on society at large.

Typecasting Sexuality

One of the most influential theorists for gender theory has been Michel Foucault (1926–1984, pronounced *foo-KOH*), a French philosopher and historian, whose three-volume *History of Sexuality* explained, quite frankly, that sexuality *has* a history. Specifically, the idea that there are "types" of sexual people is relatively new.

Of course, people have always engaged in homosexual activities, and at various times, as Gayle Rubin explains, these activities have been "rewarded or punished, required or forbidden, a temporary experience or a life-long vocation." But the idea that these activities actually defined your identity is, according to Foucault, largely a development of the nineteenth century. The word *homosexual* itself most likely originates sometime in the 1850s, and the word *heterosexual* is even more recent.

Foucault's main point is that sexual acts went from being seen as practices to being seen as markers of a person's very nature. You can steal something and be punished as a thief, for example, or you can steal something and be labeled as a kleptomaniac, a person whose very identity is tied up with the action of stealing. In fact, Foucault emphasizes the medical terminology and legal structures that support this view, since it was during the rise of scientific and technological ways of maintaining social control and power that "the homosexual" became labeled as such.

IN THEORY

"The nineteenth-century homosexual became a personage, a past, a case history, and a childhood, in addition to being a type of life, a life form. ... Nothing went into his total composition that was unaffected by his sexuality. ... the homosexual was now a species." —Michel Foucault

Your physical actions, therefore, acquire their true legal meanings through a system that distinguishes right from wrong. Not only that, but this system of right and wrong hides its real motivations behind the screen of medical and biological truth.

And what are the real motivations for distinguishing proper from improper types of people? According to Foucault, it's all part of modern society's increasing need to manage all the various things that people do by associating them with categories. When your actions belong to a category, you're easier to control. Systems of power and social control, according to Foucault, turned from putting people away (or executing them) for what they did, to punishing them for what they were.

Or worse ... by labeling homosexual acts as evidence of a type of biological being, the law gets to then label that type of being as pathological, or sick. When that happens, and it did, you no longer find "people" punished for homosexual acts, you find "homosexuals" being hauled away to asylums or even executed "for the good of a healthy society." In fact, right up until 1973, the American Psychiatric Association classified homosexuality as a mental disorder.

RELATIONS

In fact, Foucault also had much to say about the creation of "normality" and "madness" for reasons of social power and the usefulness of categorizing humans into types. We'll consider his arguments further in Chapter 15.

Another important term involving the creation of a whole new way of setting out the boundaries for talking about people and issues is *discourse*. In this case, Foucault is focused on the discourse of sexuality. As this discourse is developed and employed in the legal and social systems, you would think you'd see a very devious and successful means of controlling those who are not in power. And you'd be right.

But Foucault also pointed out that there's another side to discourse. Look at it this way. The powers that be have begun to elaborate on what "you" are, and they develop very specific ways of talking about you, with all kinds of categories, subcategories, and precise words for what they see as perversions. Foucault argued that this process always leaves room for reverse discourses (or counter discourses), which allow you to claim any title given to you, form alliances with others similarly labeled, and then "talk back" as a group. Of course, there are significant difficulties to be worked out, since you're speaking, in a very real sense, the language of your oppressor. But since the possibilities for turning the tables on any current power structure are always there, ironically created by the very system that was intended to maintain power, you never know what new discourses might emerge. We might look, for example, at what happened to the concepts of "gay" and "queer."

Pride Fest

Anyone who spent significant time in the twentieth century (and you know who you are) can appreciate the remarkable successes, not only of feminism and the civil rights movement (see Chapter 14), but of gay and lesbian struggles for acceptance. These struggles for acceptance, respect, and political equality brought about changes that are now integral parts of the world we live in. Literature and literary critics have not only reflected on these changes, but served as agents of change in gay and lesbian liberation struggles.

APPLY IT

Highly recommended viewing: *The Celluloid Closet* (1995, directed by Rob Epstein and Jeffrey Friedman). This entertaining and informative documentary explores the central role that gay and lesbian artists played throughout the history of Hollywood filmmaking.

Gay and lesbian studies are both deeply indebted to feminist studies, and the influence is visible in the various critical approaches that have developed since the 1970s. In particular, gay and lesbian literary studies feature identity-based theories of both reading and writing. Critics focus on the ways in which gay and lesbian identities circulate in literature and film, and, crucially, what they do to individuals and to culture.

Beyond Stonewall

The path to gay liberation is often said to begin in 1969 with the police raid on the Stonewall Inn, a gay bar in New York City. What made this event so momentous, given that raids on gay bars were not unusual, was the response of patrons and community members in fighting back, not just against the raids, but for the rights of homosexuals in general.

Since that time, the consequences of the gay liberation movement have created space for critics to valuably explore gay literary traditions that predate Stonewall, as well as those that followed. Reclaiming a gay male literary tradition from the past has been a project of Richard Dellamora, for example. Dellamora examined issues of desire between men in Victorian writing, drawing on works by, among others, Tennyson, Gerard Manley Hopkins, Walter Pater, and A. C. Swinburne.

IN THEORY

"In attempting to recover the traces of shifts in masculine self-identification from the beginning of the century to the 1890s, I have had recourse to Foucault's suggestion that discourse formation provides a site at which individuals and groups can be isolated and subordinated, but at which they can also begin to shape strategies of resistance." —Richard Dellamora

Christopher Isherwood's *Goodbye to Berlin*, as I mentioned earlier, artfully kept the author's homosexuality obscured. Still, many readers knew what Isherwood was really saying (the novel would eventually be adapted into the musical *Cabaret*), but everyone recognized in his novel the even broader counter discourse, which was a critique of Nazi Germany's persecution of Jews, homosexuals, and other groups deemed undesirable.

APPLY IT

Once again (and it won't be the last time), Mary Shelley's *Frankenstein* offers an opportunity for critical analysis. Can you find passages of the novel that suggest the creature represents Victor's hidden or repressed homosexuality? As we've seen with a psychoanalytic approach to the novel's motif of doubling (see Chapter 10), the creature has often been seen as either a force that Victor cannot control, or one that he or his family cannot bear to acknowledge. What, for example, might you make of Victor and Elizabeth's wedding-night scene?

Critic Lee Edelman offered an interesting and convincing argument for "reading into" gaps and omissions in a literary text. Edelman suggested that while it's essential to recognize the value of homosexuality as an identity because of the way such a classification enables social activism and solidarity for gay men, there is a danger as well. The danger, as Edelman pointed out (following Foucault), is the possibility of simply echoing the "homophobic insistence" that distinct sexualities be regulated.

Edelman argued, therefore, that both the discourse and the counter discourse of homosexuality is at work in literary texts. That is, there is often a kind of unspoken quality to homosexuality in general that is also reflected in literature. This unspoken quality can take the form of extreme homophobia and intolerance, such as when legal or religious condemnations of homosexuality refuse to even name it because of its "unspeakable" nature. But the other side is the kind of ambiguous language that can and should be read as homosexual.

Edelman's analysis of such works as Oscar Wilde's *The Picture of Dorian Gray* reveals how homosexuality is a very real thing, but its reality does not consist of a single discourse or designation; it emerges in the act of reading itself. Edelman compared this to the meaning that emerges from homographs, or words that look the same but have different meanings, depending on the context. The word *rose*, for example, is undeniably real, but its meaning only becomes real when its context is clear—when it's recognized as either a noun or a past-tense verb. Wilde's novel, for Edelman, illustrates the way sexuality depends on being "written into" a text that is then read in a particular way.

Lesbian Revisions

The title of a book written by Judith Butler in 1990 gives you an idea of the relationship between feminism and the kinds of issues we're considering in this chapter. The book is called *Gender Trouble: Feminism and the Subversion of Identity*. From this you know, first, that feminism *subverts* identity. As we saw in the last chapter, identity created under patriarchal conditions is not simply natural, but constructed by social and cultural interests. Yet what happens when feminism itself tries to claim an identity for women? According to Butler, what happens is "gender trouble," a set of useful complications that prevent overly simplistic definitions of woman, definitions which may repeat the problems of defining woman under patriarchy. Instead, lesbian criticism seeks to move beyond an analysis of woman's relationship with man.

Then there's the direct approach. Back in 1973, author and critic Jill Johnston (1929–2010) simply wrote, "Feminism at heart is a massive complaint. Lesbianism is the solution." Now that's how you get things moving in theory and criticism. Still, the relationship between feminist theory and feminist critique has many aspects, from total estrangement to close partnerships, and many lesbian critics have no problem with identifying as feminist as well.

Literary studies has benefitted from lesbian criticism in ways that recall some of the feminist approaches we've discussed. For example, in the recovery and popularizing of a lesbian tradition in literature, critics have brought lesbian literature out of the closet and into the open, or at least into college reading lists. Authors such as Emily Dickinson, Radclyffe Hall, Willa Cather, Gertrude Stein, and Virginia Woolf were either introduced to readers for the first time or read in ways that made their lesbianism an important dimension of their works.

The poet and critic Adrienne Rich (1929–2012) coined the term *lesbian continuum* to describe the range of same-sex female relationships, some sexual but most not, that bind women's lives together. These connections are genuine, supportive, and powerful, and bypass the oppressive demands of heterosexual relationships.

In her reading of *Jane Eyre*, for example, Rich explained that Jane's story illustrates a resistance to traditional gender roles and a heroic insistence on mutually supportive relationships.

IN THEORY

"It is clear that Charlotte Brontë believes that human relations require something quite different: a transaction between people which is 'without painful shame or damping humiliation' and in which nobody is made into an object for the use of anybody else. … In *Jane Eyre,* moreover, we find an alternative to the stereotypical rivalry of women; we see women in real and supportive relationship to each other, not simply as points on a triangle or as temporary substitutes for men." —Adrienne Rich

Jane's life story, according to Rich, is filled with loving and supportive relationships with women, as well as rejections of anything but an equal role with the men who want her. In fact, even Jane's eventual marriage does not conform to the traditional "marriage plot" that assures social stability in a male-dominated heterosexual pairing. Instead, Rich argued, "coming to her husband in economic independence and by her free choice, Jane can become a wife without sacrificing a grain of her Jane Eyre-ity."

Similarly, critic Barbara Smith has read Toni Morrison's novel, *Sula*, as a lesbian story. Smith explained that this is not simply because of the passionate relationship between the two main female characters, but because of "Morrison's consistently critical stance toward the heterosexual institutions of male/female relationships, marriage, and the family."

IN THEORY

"Consciously or not, Morrison's work poses both lesbian and feminist questions about Black women's autonomy and their impact on each other's lives." —Barbara Smith

It's Showtime!

You'll recall Simone de Beauvoir's famous argument that "one is not born, but rather becomes, a woman" (see Chapter 12). Some gender theorists suggest that no matter what you're born with, you become your gender through performance.

Judith Butler, in particular, argued that gender is a purely performative act. As you've seen with Saussure's influence on seeing identity as relational, gender theories often reflect theories of language use. Butler's approach to gender adapts a linguistic theory developed by J. L. Austin. Austin distinguished between language that simply represents something and language that makes things happen.

For example, when someone says something like, "You are a veterinarian," that person is making a statement. You can test the truth or falsity of that statement—are you a veterinarian? On the other hand, if someone says something like "You're under arrest," something else is going on. For one, as long as it's spoken under the right conditions (legal conditions, in this case), then by golly you are under arrest. Second, this kind of utterance itself can't exactly be tested for truth or falsity. It either works—the person saying it is a police officer and abiding by the rules of the legal system—or it doesn't—it's a friend of yours making a joke. A statement doesn't change the state of things. A performative utterance enacts something in reality.

Butler argued that your gender is enacted and created by the performative actions you make every day. What you wear, how you move, the way you talk and gesture—all of these contribute to giving you a gender. Each performative act is neither true nor false. Instead, what you become either works or doesn't work based on the conditions you're in.

Take drag, for example. Drag is often assumed to be an example of cross-dressing, or wearing the "other" look for your particular sex. Butler, however, has insisted that "drag is not the putting on of a gender that belongs properly to some other group." Instead, drag is really a condition that creates anyone's gender.

All of your actions are involved in what Butler called "necessary drag." We typically internalize social and legal conventions, the "regulatory fictions" of gender, yet even when we think we are being purely ourselves, we are participating in the gendering that emerges from performance. And there's no way out, according to Butler. Even though performative utterances cannot be tested for truth or falsity, they really do *do* things. And one of the most profound things that performance does is create your own deepest sense of self.

Think of it like having to hold up a mask before speaking to someone. Or even like having to speak in a certain way, no matter how awkward it might first seem—"Yes, tell me what's on your mind, but do it in rhyme." This all seems so contrived, yet Butler's point is that you are never in a position to be without a mask or without a way of speaking. Not only that, but if you start early enough, you can learn how to "express yourself" in virtually any style, no matter how unusual, and if you do it long enough you'll forget how odd it was at first. Social interaction is impossible without these prerequisites and the conventions they employ.

Of course, society often wants to restrict gender to a true-or-false choice. Conventions and laws insist on taking what should be seen as performative acts and converts them into statements of fact. Why? Because statements of fact can be tested, and the answers to these tests form the basis of social control—and even psychological comfort. As Butler put it, "Performing one's gender wrong initiates a set of punishments both obvious and indirect, and performing it well provides the reassurance that there is an essentialism of gender identity after all."

So, any hope for change or relief from this constant state of drag? No, not from the overall system, since, according to Butler, the "actors are always already on the stage, within the terms of the performance." But remember—it's individual acts that give the system its strength in the first place. And this means the system is always vulnerable to being modified through other individual acts of subversion, rebellion, and play.

Beyond Gay and Straight

Queer theory is a term coined in 1991 by Teresa de Lauretis. Like a coin, the term has been passed around, exchanged for all kinds of other terms, and generally become mixed up in the literary critical till. Nevertheless, the term still carries a very high value, and that value is based on queer theory's challenge to categorization.

The term *queer*, of course, began as a way of signifying, in a negative way, the "strangeness" of homosexuals and homosexual activity. In one of those successful moves in reverse discourse, *queer* was reclaimed by those it had been designed to stigmatize. The result is both a celebration of identity and a wide-ranging critique of identity, worked out in literature, culture, and politics.

One area of interest is the simple notion that the categories of gay and straight are too limiting. We've already seen such categories as "woman" called into question because of the way any label obscures differences within a category. And Adrienne

Rich, as discussed previously, pointed to a "lesbian continuum" to designate the range, rather than the category of female same-sex relationships.

Queer theories go even further with the logic at work here. In questioning categories, queer theory not only questions gay and lesbian as stable identities, but reveals the queerness of any form of sexuality, particularly heterosexuality.

The fascinating work of Eve Kosofsky Sedgwick (1950–2009) is central to queer theory. In one of her most important books, *Between Men: English Literature and Male Homosocial Desire* (1985), Sedgwick argued that a "homosocial continuum" has existed at least since the nineteenth century in men's relationships with each other.

Like Rich's lesbian continuum, this homosocial continuum consists of a range of relationships, some but not all involving homosexuality (hence the term homo*social*). Sedgwick's point is that Western society has twisted, defined, and limited this range so that men are forced to feel that there are only two choices for male relationships—"manly men" friendships and gay relationships. What's left out, according to Sedgwick, is the wide range of very real feelings of intimacy, closeness, support, and even physical appeal that men have for each other. Social codes simply partition the whole continuum into two sides, and the resulting either/or choice becomes part of men's psyches.

IN THEORY

"To be a man's man is separated only by an invisible, carefully blurred, always-already crossed line from being 'interested in men.'" —Eve Kosofsky Sedgwick

Since patriarchy generally oppresses both women and gay men, the system of patriarchy needs to police the borders of what "real men" are, do, and feel about each other. Sedgwick showed, by looking at examples in literature and culture, that the possibility of "border checks" on male identity has produced social as well as psychological responses.

Take, for example, places such as the locker room, men's clubs, the (traditional) board room, and the more recent "man cave." Each is a setting that is set up to emphasize and reinforce patriarchal "not gay" bonding, and yet, as Sedgwick pointed out, these are also exactly the places where men are most likely to be faced with that part of the continuum of feelings and attractions that are not socially coded for "real men."

The psychological response to all those inevitable clashes between what you think you are and what you believe you feel is, according to Sedgwick, panic. Specifically,

Sedgwick called the reaction *homosexual panic*, the feeling that someone who does not identify as gay will be outed as gay, not because he desires sex with men (although he may), but because he exhibits an interest in any of the qualities on the continuum that don't belong to the "not gay" side.

APPLY IT

Speaking of homosexual panic, check out *Gods and Monsters* (1998, directed by Bill Condon, starring Ian McKellen and Brendan Fraser). It's a beautiful movie about James Whale, the openly gay director of the only somewhat openly gay *Bride of Frankenstein* (1935). Life, art, and memory collide while Brendan Fraser's character comes to terms with his homosocial continuum.

What's particularly interesting is Sedgwick's point that you only feel homosexual panic if you have (or think you have) a stake in "male heterosexual entitlement" in the first place. That is, if you want to retain the so-called privileges of patriarchy, you've got to be the man. On the other hand, if you identify as gay, there's no threat to having your "normal" heterosexuality questioned. Most men, according to Sedgwick, are somewhere in the middle and entirely vulnerable to "homophobic blackmail" to one degree or another. It's blackmail because you're reacting to the threat that someone will take away any power you have in the patriarchal system.

Sedgwick's approach has been called antihomophobic because it seeks to reveal and reverse the physical and psychological violence committed because of homosexual panic. In literary studies, this can lead to readings of texts that highlight characters' struggles with gender identities called into question by the actual continuum of desire. "Queering the text," as it has been called, can examine gay and lesbian texts just as critically as heterosexual ones. Any gender category, to Sedgwick and other queer theorists, both enables your identity and leaves you wondering what to do with the parts that "don't fit."

You might examine one response to homosexual panic, for example, in Dickens's *David Copperfield*, in which the close feelings between Copperfield and his friend Steerforth are never faced directly by those characters. Instead, the two male characters mediate their desires through their triangular relationship with Little Em'ly. In this way, a female presence becomes the "proper" partner for male desire, and there's no longer any need for the boys to work it out on their own.

APPLY IT

Time for *Frankenstein* again. Sedgwick pointed out that a particular type of nineteenth-century novel, which she called "paranoid gothic," revolves around male characters who are haunted by "evil doubles." These doubles, for Sedgwick, represent those aspects of the male character that don't fit into the character's male identity. That is, the main character attempts to live by a male patriarchal gender role, while the double stands for excluded desires.

Sedgwick argued that *Frankenstein* was just such a paranoid gothic, and that Victor clearly exhibits homosexual panic. Do you agree? Notice, for example, when Victor and the creature speak to each other. What do they say and how might the conversation support Sedgwick's point?

The ongoing legacy of queer theory also brings us back to the first point we considered in this chapter. Queer theory seeks to highlight the fact that homosexuality is not simply heterosexuality's "other." Queer theory doesn't oppose homosexuality to heterosexuality, but shows how each is relied on to construct the other. The result is a better understanding of the arbitrary nature of any sexual designation.

And once again, theory and criticism seem to confirm what many people have long recognized. In this case it's not just my friend's mother's affirmation that "we're all a little gay." It's that our desires, needs, and sexual identities develop out of our interactions with people whose own sexual identities can't just be ignored after we've benefited from them.

The Least You Need to Know

- Gender comes from the social organization of sexual differences.
- The idea of sexual identity is a development of the modern administrative system.
- Gay and lesbian criticism seeks to reclaim lost and ignored literary traditions and to revise modes of reading.
- Gender is not only performed by social actions, but created by them, too.
- Queer theory seeks to expose the fluidity and interdependence of sexual identities.

Ethnic Studies Changes the Key

In This Chapter

- Ethnicity and the literary canon
- Double consciousness and identity
- Writing yourself into the social narrative
- The psychological function of "others"
- Figurative language's centrality
- Border identities

"That's funny, I hear it like this," says one musician to another, before beginning to play. You could say that writers create or perform after getting a sense of what they want to say—I hear it like this in my head, now let's get it on paper. Writers, as well as readers and critics, often improvise with texts, emphasizing what they see in them and filling in what they don't see but know to be true. The field of ethnic studies offers a look at how literature itself reads, revises, and creates. The widely varying critics in this field share a view of texts, cultural traditions, identity, and community as dynamic compositions filled with the challenges and opportunities of interpretation.

Are You What You Read?

One of the most important consequences of ethnic theory and criticism has been the transformation of the literary canon. When you look at bookstores, classrooms, and reading groups these days, you see things that didn't exist for earlier generations— and not just because some of the bookstores are now electronic.

Who chooses what you read? Why, you do, of course; but you also get a lot of help in choosing. There are the books you're supposed to read in school, there may be books you need to read for work, and there are books you might want to read to keep up with what's popular. Then there's access—what's easy to get? You'd think these days you can find anything, and you can—but only if you go looking for it. Otherwise, what you find easily accessible is what someone else has decided is worth putting in your way, or what someone simply wants to sell you.

In both cases, you can thank literary theory and criticism for much of the positive change that has occurred over the past few decades. And thank Oprah, too. Students are still assigned works by many of the "dead white European males" that used to monopolize reading lists, but those students are now likely to be assigned books by Toni Morrison, Ralph Ellison, or Amy Tan alongside those by Charles Dickens or John Milton. Similarly, publishers recognize the value and popularity of books published by writers who, taken together, look a lot more like actual society than used to be the case.

What all this means is that the canon—the stated or implied collection of texts you're "supposed" to read—is now radically changed. In previous chapters of this book we've seen how intimately connected reading is to cultural, political, and personal identity. For most literary critics, change in the canon means change in the way we see ourselves and our societies. Literature both represents the world's exploration of itself and contributes to it.

In addition, when the canon changes, everything in it looks slightly—or even significantly—different. That is, any single work gathers its full meaning through its relationship with the other works. You think of what you've read before; you make comparisons; you discover precedents to works you once thought of as totally unique. Those dead white European males, for example (many of whom really did write tremendous works), get reread in new ways, not only when new readers get to them, but when they are considered in the light of other readings. Likewise, all those new or rediscovered works previously absent from the canon spur writers to think and create in new ways as well.

National Sensations

In whatever shape, a literary canon is often seen as a reflection of national culture. The logic, of course, is that each nation should have its own culture. The problem (as we'll see in Chapters 19 and 21) is that people do not always agree on what national culture means. Many people see a nation's culture as the broad collection of a country's actual cultural practices. Some, however, see culture as a kind of goal or ideal. Culture is seen to reflect the best of a nation's cultural products, often drawn from the past.

Ethnic studies has influenced both of these views in recent decades, and one measure of these changes can be seen in literary anthologies. Current anthologies of national literature have both expanded the range of included items, which changes the "family portrait" view of a country's culture, and confirmed the value of previously noncanonical works as part of the nation's high culture.

APPLY IT

Consider your own view of multiethnic nationality. Do you prefer the metaphor of the melting pot to describe the way various ethnicities all contribute to one national character? Or do you see the country more like a salad bowl, with ethnic characteristics standing out individually? Do your views influence your reading choices?

There are dozens of other issues at stake, and we're not going to cover them all, but consider some of the questions that anthology editors have to ask. As people keep writing (and they never stop), which authors get included in new anthologies and which are left out? Does the "national" literature all have to be written in the same language? Works of American, Canadian, or French literature, for example, have always been written in multiple languages. What about those national boundaries, anyway? Does French literature stop with the borders of France, or should it include works written in French by writers from other countries? And what's with English literature? Does that mean literature in English, or literature from England? Should it be "British" literature, in order to include works from the other countries of the United Kingdom in addition to England?

Our discussion in this chapter focuses mainly on responses to questions about national identity in American literature. Chapter 21's discussion of colonial literature expands the discussion to a more global scale. And in the American context, of course, questions about national identity have been played out, in life as in literature, largely in the context of race.

Please Check One of the Boxes

Literary and cultural critics point out that while it's clear that the category of race has no actual biological basis, it's still one of the most potent forces in culture and politics. That is, viewing race as a biologically determined quality that divides the human species is unsupportable. Yet recognizing race as ideological—as a social interpretation of difference—reminds us of the enormous power that social fictions wield. As the title of an important book by Cornel West puts it, *Race Matters*.

You may know the feeling of looking at the choices on a census form or a college application, asking you to check one of the boxes for race or ethnicity. You look at the choices and you know that they're "just categories," while you're a whole person. Still, you have to choose a box. And besides, there's power in those boxes as well, since decisions are made based on the categories offered. Changes to census forms, for example, are fiercely debated, since they affect the representation and funding that communities receive.

IN THEORY

"Race must be viewed as a social construction." —Ian F. Haney-López

Checking a box, therefore, is a weird combination of self-identification, ethnic solidarity, and economic involvement. It's personal and political at the same time. And what's particularly remarkable about literature is the way it can explore the intersections between your own view of self, family, community, and nation, and the view provided by the social fictions about those same categories.

American Autograph

African American literature has been around as long as America has been around, but it certainly hasn't always been made to seem that way. In the twentieth century, African American literary theory drew on this very long history, and then, crucially, made that history visible.

The early history of African American literature illustrates how an individual's views of the self can be shaped and misshaped by social views and prejudices. Yet the same history shows how individual efforts of creating literature also became collective gestures that would ultimately change how American literature and society were defined.

During the long history of slavery in the United States, it was understood by most of white society that African Americans had no written voice at all. Slaves were generally denied literacy outright, and the question of African American participation in the written testament of national identity was, in the minds of most Americans, closed. But of course not everyone agreed.

Write Makes Might

Phillis Wheatley (c. 1753–1784), a slave born in West Africa and living in Boston during the period of the American Revolution, not only learned to read and write in English, but published a volume of poetry in 1773. Her remarkable achievement, according to Henry Louis Gates Jr. and Nellie Y. McKay, was not only to produce literature, but to "write her way into American literature." And despite Thomas Jefferson's infamous remark that her work was "below the dignity of criticism," Wheatley's volume stood as a clear signal of an African American literary presence even before the country declared its independence.

One literary genre that received enormous attention between independence and the end of the Civil War in 1865 was the genre of the slave narrative. During this period, over 100 accounts of slavery were published. By 1944, over 6,000 ex-slaves had woven their stories into what Gates calls "the very foundation upon which most subsequent Afro-American fictional and nonfictional narrative forms are based."

 APPLY IT

Check out the fascinating and convenient volume *The Classic Slave Narratives,* edited by Henry Louis Gates Jr. It marked a milestone of publishing when it first appeared in 1987, bringing four remarkable stories to the attention of a new generation of readers, and it continues to attract avid readers of all types. The narratives include those written by Olaudah Equiano, Frederick Douglass, Mary Prince, and Harriet Jacobs.

The most famous of the American slave narratives is that of Frederick Douglass (c. 1818–1895). First published in 1845, the book's full title is *Narrative of the Life of Frederick Douglass, an American Slave, Written by Himself.* This last part is important— "written by himself." Why put that in the title? Because at the time, many people simply could not accept that African Americans were capable of writing their own stories. They assumed or charged that the narratives were written by white authors, since, to their minds, the reality of black authorship would unsettle an entire worldview.

Beginning with Wheatley's volume, in fact, a tradition arose of having white publishers, writers, or abolitionists attest to a book's African American authorship. It was not enough for the African American writers themselves to simply claim authorship. Critics have pointed out that this "interracial literary etiquette," as Gates called it, was an important aspect of African American literary history. Basically, it highlights the fact that African American writing developed against the assumption that it shouldn't even exist.

Douglass's narrative, and other slave narratives, therefore, took the form of auto-biography, a form of literature typically associated with men of high standing (see Chapter 12's discussion of Mary Shelley's feminist appropriation of this genre as well). If Benjamin Franklin had something to offer readers by publishing an autobiography, then so did Frederick Douglass and Harriet Jacobs. In fact, autobiography has a way of showing how individual lives are part of national lives, and these American examples were no exceptions. Simply put, the story of American culture included the voices of slavery.

In their various ways, the slave narratives also offered lessons on how to hear the voices that comprised them. Like a literary critic, in fact, Douglass explained how songs, conversations, and writings had to be understood with respect to the specific context of slavery's oppression. For example, Douglass described his astonishment at hearing white people claim that since they heard slaves singing, this must be "evidence of their contentment and happiness." Douglass explained that there is much, much more to the story. A song's motivations may come from the deepest despair and yet sound "rapturous," while other songs might sound "pathetic" and yet be filled with a joyful message.

APPLY IT

James Baldwin's short story "Sonny's Blues" features characters who come to understand the power of music as an intimate means of communication. The challenge lies in learning how to hear and feel the music and realizing what it does for the musician.

Even "ordinary communication," for Douglass, was a complex process under the conditions of slavery. Using language to communicate means involving yourself in the written and unwritten rules of culture, politics, and even the human mind itself. In the context of slavery, conversation often demanded a coding system, so that slaves could understand each other while the slave owners were kept ignorant of what was really going on. Douglass's narrative describes how fatal "telling the simple truth" could be, and how slaves developed forms of speaking and writing whose codes, levels, and misdirections would shape the development of much African American literature to come.

Following the Civil War, the prolific sociologist and historian W. E. B. Du Bois (1868–1963, pronounced *doo-BOYZ*), wrote essays and articles about virtually everything concerned with America's struggles with racial identity. In 1903 he published *The Souls of Black Folk* and explained to anyone who would listen that race was a matter of culture, not nature or biology.

In particular, Du Bois argued that African Americans living in a racialized society developed a double consciousness. Du Bois explained that this double consciousness is "no true self-consciousness," but the experience of seeing yourself through the eyes of white America.

IN THEORY

"It is a peculiar sensation, this double-consciousness, this sense of always looking at one's self through the eyes of others, of measuring one's soul by the tape of a world that looks on in amused contempt and pity. One ever feels his twoness —an American, a Negro; two souls, two thoughts, two unreconciled strivings."
—W. E. B. Du Bois

For Du Bois, the goal was not the separatism that would be argued by some later critics, but a blending of the two struggling sides in order to "merge his double self into a better and truer self." Understanding the black American self, for Du Bois, was not simply a matter of clearing out the presence of white America, but of establishing the conditions for an entirely genuine black self that could freely emerge in American culture. It simply wasn't possible, Du Bois argued, for Americans, black or white, to understand themselves without "tearing away the veil" that separated their worlds. Du Bois explained that politically, culturally, and psychologically, he "simply wishes to make it possible for a man to be both a Negro and an American."

APPLY IT

Recommended reading: Take a look at the stories of Charles W. Chesnutt (1858–1932). Chesnutt, a contemporary of Du Bois, put his own stamp on the character of the American short story with such works as "The Passing of Grandison" and "The Goophered Grapevine." His stories blend hilarious dry wit, slapstick humor, and very clever incorporation of serious and, for his time, risky social concerns.

Literary theory and criticism will see this concept of double consciousness, or hybridity, emerge time and time again, in a variety of situations. Du Bois's linking of it to social development associates his critique with feminist approaches and sets the stage for much postcolonial theory to come (see Chapter 21). Yet despite the connection to feminist theory in principle, critics have pointed out that Du Bois's arguments tend, like many did throughout the twentieth century, to privilege men at the expense of women.

In discussions of race in America, questions of "black and white" have often been limited to matters of "black men and white men." We've seen this move before, whereby a so-called universal situation obscures a more specific actual focus. In the case of African American literary and cultural theory, critics have pointed out how important it is to recognize issues of race that were specific to women's experience. As we saw in our discussion of feminist criticism in Chapter 12, patriarchy can be an unwelcome aspect of even the most progressive struggles for social liberation.

Modern Subjects

As the black American canon began to emerge, it did not always reflect the women who had contributed to the changing terrain of American literature. Similarly, as the early feminist movement developed in the early 1900s, African American women were often overlooked in the process of creating an image of the so-called "new woman." Black women writers, therefore, sometimes found themselves fighting against resistance on two sides.

The critic Deborah E. McDowell has argued that writing about black female sexuality was complicated by "a literary era that often sensationalized it" in primitive and exotic stereotypes. On the other side, McDowell pointed out, African American women were excluded from literary images of the "cult of true womanhood," which set out the ideals of the modern domestic woman (rather like the "angel in the house").

In spite of these challenges, the 1920s and 1930s saw two women in particular who were instrumental in changing the image of American national identity through their literature, although they would both receive full recognition for their achievements only years after their deaths. That period was also known as the Harlem Renaissance, because of the flourishing of African American literature and arts in New York City's Harlem neighborhood.

Nella Larsen (1891–1964) was the author of two important novels. *Quicksand* was published in 1928 and reviewed very favorably by Du Bois. Larsen's second novel, *Passing*, appeared in 1929, after which her writing career quickly began to fade out.

Zora Neale Hurston (1891–1960) was an anthropologist, author, playwright, and co-founder of a literary magazine. Hurston's work in preserving African American folklore, including her book, *Mules and Men* (1935), has been invaluable for generations of scholars (and fascinating for any reader), but Hurston is probably most well known today for her novel *Their Eyes Were Watching God* (1937). In fact, it was Alice Walker, the author of *The Color Purple* (1982), who brought Hurston's work back from obscurity and in 1973 even tracked down Hurston's unmarked grave and provided it with a headstone. In many such instances, literary criticism has played an important role since the 1970s in recovering neglected African American texts, including those by Larsen and Hurston.

Several male African American writers from the Harlem Renaissance to the 1950s also established many of the terms for debate in literary criticism. The poet Langston Hughes (1902–1967) favored depictions of the working class and promoted the legitimacy of "racial art" that did not try to gloss over the realities of African American lives. Hughes wrote simply, "We know we are beautiful. And ugly too."

Richard Wright (1908–1960) wrote fiction and essays and is most famous for his novel *Native Son* (1940), his story collection *Uncle Tom's Children* (1938), and his autobiography *Black Boy*, the first part of which was published in 1945 and the second part published posthumously in 1977. Wright was a fierce advocate of Marxism, associated with the writers of the *negritude* movement, and was celebrated both during his life and by writers of the 1960s as a premier writer of protest fiction.

 DEFINITION

Negritude is a concept of pan-Africanism or an African-centered world view that aspires to unite all black people around a common identity. As first envisioned by French-speaking African writers such as Aimé Césaire and Léopold Sédar Senghor in the 1930s as a reaction against Western colonialism, negritude was and is an international political and artistic movement based on, as Césaire wrote, "the simple recognition of the fact that one is black, the acceptance of this fact and of our destiny as blacks, of our history and culture."

On the other hand, James Baldwin (1924–1987) argued that protest literature such as Wright's works—and even Harriet Beecher Stowe's classic *Uncle Tom's Cabin*—were actually doing more harm than good for African Americans. He argued that protest novels too often reduced black culture to images of simplistic degradation and victimization. Not only that, but they tended to elicit mere sympathy because of their sensationalism, while real change required more than provoking the reader's emotion.

For this reason, Baldwin's nonfiction essays tended to address protest themes and explore specific issues of race and politics, while his novels explored more personal and cultural issues, including his own homosexuality.

Novelist, critic, and essayist Ralph Ellison (1914–1994) famously asked, "Why is it that so many of those who would tell us the meaning of Negro life never bother to learn how varied it really is?" Ellison's classic novel *Invisible Man* (1952), as well as his other works of fiction and nonfiction, explored the diverse facets of African American experience, from the very good to the deeply troubling. Some critics claimed Ellison's *Invisible Man* was a betrayal of its African American origins, since it did not promote the Marxist agenda promoted by other writers, and it viewed black nationalism with skepticism. Most critics, however, have come to see this remarkable novel as a quintessentially American exploration of double consciousness and the nature of identity in a multiethnic nation. Critic Theodore O. Mason Jr. said that Ellison's philosophy of the novel form was that it "refuses to provide specific answers but instead is an arena for speculation, for investigation, for a complex meditation on the informing social conflict of the day."

APPLY IT

Consider *Invisible Man* with both African American criticism and New Criticism (see Chapter 3) in mind. As you read it, begin tracking any of the following key images and concepts. These images and concepts appear over and over again in order to develop the novel's theme of identity and self-understanding: invisibility, light, the boomerang, spirals, cycles, and hibernation.

In the 1960s, writers, artists, and critics of the Black Arts Movement emphasized the instrumental nature of art. That is, they saw art as a tool for social change. Literary criticism of this period tended to be evaluative and concerned with promoting works seen as most useful for African American interests. This is also the period that saw significant changes in colleges and universities, particularly in the addition of departments of African and African American Studies. Key figures in the Black Arts Movement included Amiri Baraka (formerly known as LeRoi Jones), Malcolm X (1925–1965), the feminist critic Audre Lorde (1934–1992), Ishmael Reed, and Nikki Giovanni.

Theory Turns

Beginning in the 1980s, along with the general emphasis on theory that characterized literary study, African American theory developed into a fascinating and complex field. The critic bell hooks (and yes, her name is spelled in lowercase), emphasized that theory was not just a set of abstractions about literature, nor was it rule book for writers. Instead, she argued that theory was an essential aspect of social practice. hooks showed, for example, that lives and institutions can be forced to change when theory reveals the flawed logic and ulterior motives behind racism and patriarchy.

Reading Like a Writer

You are probably familiar with Toni Morrison, the author of such novels as *Sula* (1974), *Song of Solomon* (1977), and *Beloved* (1987). In 1992, Morrison, who in addition to being a novelist is also a playwright and essayist, published a very influential book (based on a series of lectures) called *Playing in the Dark.* Among the interesting points that Morrison made in these lectures, one in particular has seemed to resonate with critics, novelists, and ordinary readers alike. It's Morrison's discussion of how the presence of Africa and African Americanism can be felt throughout all American literature.

Morrison begins by explaining how common it used to be (and still can be) to ignore African American voices in American literature, particularly by professors who claimed not to specialize in African American literature. What's black about Edgar Allan Poe, for example, or Henry James, Willa Cather, or Ernest Hemingway? For black America, you go to African American literature, so goes the argument. Morrison explained that even she felt this way, until she began to "read like a writer."

What Morrison meant is that when writers create their fictional worlds, these worlds will always reflect the writer's consciousness, and for most American writers, white or black, that consciousness is shaped by "its encounter with racial ideology." So any time an African or African American character or issue arises in a "white text," Morrison sees it as integral to the consciousness of the story, not just local color or incidental detail that merely provides a sense of realism. As Morrison put it, "As a writer reading, I came to realize the obvious: the subject of the dream is the dreamer."

IN THEORY

"I am interested in what prompts and makes possible this process of entering what one is estranged from—and in what disables the foray, for purposes of fiction, into corners of the consciousness held off and away from the reach of the writer's imagination." —Toni Morrison

As a critical reader, Morrison wanted to examine the function of what she called the "Africanist presence" in much of American literature. And this function, according to Morrison, is often deeply psychological—writers use or struggle with the Africanist presence in their works in order to work out psychological issues (see Chapter 10 for more on the Freudian basis of this).

As an example, Morrison considered Willa Cather's novel, *Sapphira and the Slave Girl*. Morrison pointed out that critics have viewed this novel as flawed and uneven, yet Morrison's own reading shows that the so-called flaws are evidence of Cather struggling with telling a story about a white woman and a slave, yet being unable to clearly separate the two characters' dependence on each other. Cather's novel sets out to tell "two stories," yet reveals Sapphira's psychological use of "the slave girl" to construct Sapphira's own identity *and* the novelist's own use of the story to meditate on the ironic "moral equivalence" of slave and slave owner.

Another major critic, Hortense Spillers, wrote in 1987, "My country needs me, and if I were not here, I would have to be invented." By this Spillers meant something similar to Morrison's point, which is that the Africanist presence is essential to understanding American literature as such—and understanding American literary criticism as well.

Other critics also pushed the boundaries of existing theory, often by bringing feminist theory into contact with African American interests. Hazel Carby, for example, suggested that it's better to think of the very category of black feminist criticism "as a problem, not a solution." And she meant this in a productive way, since just calling something "black feminist criticism" won't solve conflicts between black and feminist interests. Instead, such a field should explore the varied nature of actual writing and reading experiences.

Barbara Smith in 1979, and later Deborah McDowell, both called on critics to turn their attention to the specifically black writing practices of women, rather than the lives of women writers themselves. Investigating black women's distinctive use of literary techniques would lead to a better understanding of how these writers have created a specific literary language and tradition.

Well, That Figures

And speaking of the creation of a specific literary language and tradition brings us again to Henry Louis Gates Jr.

Gates's groundbreaking study, *The Signifying Monkey: A Theory of African American Literary Criticism*, appeared in 1988. This book brought anthropology and structuralism (see Chapter 16) along with deconstruction (see Chapter 17) into a dialogue with African American studies. Gates's central interest was to trace a literary tradition, specific to black writers, which forms the basis of African American writing. And it isn't a tradition that spins off from the Western tradition; it's a true alternative or parallel literary tradition, derived from the unique experiences of African and African American people.

This tradition is based in the idea of signifying, which Gates spelled Signifyin(g), in order to (1) distinguish the word from its use in white signification, and (2) indicate that "this word is, more often than not, spoken by black people without the final *g* as 'signifyin'."

So what's white signification? It's the process we've generally discussed in this book (such as in Chapter 11's survey of Saussure), whereby meaning is created through your use of signs. You simply get your point across by using language. Gates argued that an alternative African and African American tradition has always emphasized that "simply" getting your point across is not what language is always about. Instead, Signifyin(g) language use is all about interruption, playful ambiguity, and "talking around a subject," often to confuse someone.

Why do this? Gates explained that language use, in the Signifyin(g) tradition, is a process of both protection and of artistic creativity. Protection, because in a situation where you are at a disadvantage, talking indirectly and with misdirection as your goal might help you survive. In fact, the image of the "Signifying Monkey" comes from African folk tales of a monkey staying one step ahead of much stronger animals by virtue of his clever use of language.

And creativity, because the very tools that white signifying sees as extras or add-ons to "regular language," Signifyin(g) recognizes as the very heart of human literary creation. That is, in the white signifying tradition, tropes like metaphor, rhyme, hyperbole, and irony—what Gates called the "master's tropes"—are set to the side of real, instrumental language. These tropes are examples of figurative language, not literal language.

As Jacques Derrida has shown, however (see Chapter 17), even the most literal of literal language is essentially figurative. Gates argued that the Africanist Signifiyin(g) tradition has long recognized this, so his theory gives tropes a central, rather than a marginal, role in language use.

Gates's study showed how Signifyin(g), which is "a rhetorical act that is not engaged in the game of information giving," has historically ranged from the childishly humorous to the profoundly sophisticated. For example, a word game like "the dozens," with its insults (particularly directed at someone's mother), is a ritual of Signifyin(g). Here, the creation and escalation of "insults" tests a kid's creativity as well as his (or her) ability to remain above it all and treat the utterances as part of a game.

Much jazz music also offers opportunities for Signifyin(g). Gates called attention to this as "formal parody," meaning that the musicians exploit the form of whatever music they are playing in ways that "repeat with a difference." The music may be set out one way (as white signification would have it), but the musicians hear it another way, and play a new form into existence.

In his reading of Hurston's *Their Eyes Were Watching God,* Gates sees Hurston's text Signifyin(g) on earlier African American works by claiming an oral quality to the written text and a textual quality to the dialogue spoken by characters. That is, Hurston's novel, according to Gates, weaves together the direct speech of the African American vernacular and the presumably authoritative "narrator's voice" in a way that doesn't privilege either side, but instead shows that a specifically Signifyin(g) African American voice controls the whole show.

> **APPLY IT**
>
> As you read *Their Eyes Were Watching God,* think about the importance placed on speaking, telling stories, captivating an audience, or participating in conversation. It seems clear in scene after scene that language use is never entirely neutral, but instead serves some purpose. In some cases, language is used to bring characters together; in other cases, a power struggle seems to be at stake.
>
> *Frankenstein* bonus item! Do you think the creature Signifies on Victor? Are there scenes in which the creature's language use shows up Victor's character or reveals his hypocrisy? Also, which characters in the novel seem to depend on literal language and which emphasize using language figuratively?

Borders and Belongings

Borders interrupt, complicate, and create ethnic identity everywhere in the world. From his perspective, critic Ramón Saldívar explains that "positioned between cultures, living on borderlines, Chicanos and their narratives have assumed a unique borderland quality, reflecting in no uncertain terms the forms and styles of their folk-based origins."

Latino and Latina (sometimes written as Latino/a) critics and writers have developed literary approaches that often emphasize the maintenance of folk or indigenous cultures. The broad collection of voices ranging throughout the ethnicities of the New World also includes critics who embrace the creation of new identities fashioned by and against borders.

Gloria Anzaldúa (1942–2004) explored a remarkable mode of self-construction in her book, *Borderlands/La Frontera: The New Mestiza* (1987). This fascinating book filled with poetry, prose sketches, criticism, songs, and sayings also combines several different languages, including English, several distinct dialects of Spanish, Spanglish, and Nahuatl.

The form of Anzaldúa's book reflects the book's theme. Identity for Anzaldúa is always prompted by existing identities and traditions, yet the result is entirely new. Anzaldúa described the various identities that had been imposed on her, and showed how she transformed such impositions into an identity reflecting her "own intrinsic nature." What's particularly interesting about her book and has made it so influential, not only to people living on American borders, but on borders around the world, is that Anzaldúa sensitively linked the lived reality of her identity to language and literature. Anzaldúa did not view writing as merely a means of representation or even expression. Instead, she saw writing as active agent in the creation of new composite (*mestiza*) identity, and, more importantly, new forms of solidarity as well.

IN THEORY

"The switching of 'codes' in this book from English to Castillian Spanish to the North Mexican dialect to Tex-Mex to a sprinkling of Nahuatl to a mixture of all of these, reflects my language, a new language—the language of the Borderlands. There, at the juncture of cultures, languages cross-pollinate and are revitalized; they die and are born. Presently this infant language, this bastard language, Chicano Spanish, is not approved by any society. But we Chicanos no longer feel that we need to beg entrance, that we need always to make the first overture—to translate to Anglos, Mexicans and Latinos, apology blurting out of our mouths with every step. Today we ask to be met halfway. This book is our invitation to you—from the new mestizas." —Gloria Anzaldúa

Meanwhile, in many Asian American novels, according to critic Lisa Lowe, "the question of the loss or transmission of the 'original' culture is frequently represented in a family narrative, figured as generational conflict between the Chinese-born first generation and the American-born second generation."

In this regard, you might be familiar with such novels as Louis Chu's *Eat a Bowl of Tea* (1961), Maxine Hong Kingston's *The Woman Warrior* (1975), and Amy Tan's *The Joy Luck Club* (1989). If not, check them out. Then keep in mind that Lowe actually argued for a somewhat different approach to reading them. According to Lowe, focusing only on generational issues in these novels leads to an essentialist view of Asian Americans and the issues they face; problems and themes simply seem to be handed down "naturally" from one generation to the next.

Lowe advocated focusing on the "horizontal" relationships between friends or siblings instead of "vertical" relationships between the generations. In any of the preceding novels mentioned, this critical approach would reveal, according to Lowe, a more extensive view of actual ethnic issues, since you're looking into how people in the same ethnic group (and of the same age) feel about and define themselves.

The development of the American literary canon has also been expanded to include Native American texts, such as the bestsellers *House Made of Dawn* by N. Scott Momaday (1968) and *Ceremony* by Leslie Marmon Silko (1977).

Critics of Native American literature, including Gerald Vizenor, Arnold Krupat, Robert Dale Parker, and Carlton Smith, have emphasized the importance of oral storytelling and the spiritual importance of the earth for indigenous writers. In fact, Arnold Krupat has emphasized that critics of indigenous literature should be grounded in "the animate and sentient earth." In Chapter 22, we'll see how ecocriticism even moves beyond the borders of human society emphasized by ethnic studies.

The Least You Need to Know

- Ethnicity both shapes and challenges national identity.
- Du Bois's concept of double consciousness set many of the terms of debate for African American literary history.
- Literature has the power to shape individual and national identity.
- An Africanist presence functions in significant ways in most American literature.
- Signifyin(g) is language use that emphasizes figurative language and literary parody.
- Ethnic studies recognizes the importance of physical and cultural borders in the development of literary criticism.

Disability Studies Gets Physical

In This Chapter

- Disability studies and the social model
- What's normal, and who decides?
- Gender and disability
- Literary representations of disability
- Deaf culture, social history, and languages

This chapter is about disability studies and literature. But wait, you might say, isn't disability all about the physical body and medical things? And isn't literature, you know, all about the mind? Didn't Shakespeare say something about poetry being "airy nothings"? And don't we settle into a good book and just let our minds soar? Really, what does literature have to do with the body?

Well, keep reading, because literature has everything to do with the body, since bodies are involved with everything. From literature's creation and content to its consumption and criticism, bodies are right there along for the ride. There's no mind without a body of some kind or another.

So Shakespeare was wrong? No, Shakespeare was never wrong. Theseus in Shakespeare's *Midsummer Night's Dream* actually tells us that a poet takes "forms of things unknown" from the imagination, shapes them, and "gives to airy nothing a *local habitation* and a *name*." Your body itself is one such "local habitation," and as for the name your body is given—that's part of what disability studies investigates. Why? Because the names that society gives to bodies—particularly "able-bodied" and "disabled"—form the foundations for how we read both literature and people. And they even influence how we tell our own stories.

Social Ills

Disability studies considers the life experiences of people living with a wide range of physical and mental disabilities. As a multidisciplinary field, disabilities studies includes work in medicine, political science, sociology, anthropology, philosophy, and history, among others. When it comes to literature, critics in disability studies emphasize an important distinction between medical and social approaches to disability.

The medical model of disability focuses on intervention, treatment, and "cures." As critic Nicole Markotić (pronounced *MAR-ko-titch*) has explained, the medical model sees disabled people as "perpetually ill and in need of cure."

IN THEORY

"Nearly every culture views disability as a problem in need of a solution. ... the perception of a 'crisis' or a 'special situation' has made disabled people the subject of not only governmental policies and social programs but also a primary object of literary representation." —David Mitchell and Sharon Snyder

The social model, on the other hand, investigates disability in its social dimensions. *Social* dimensions? Isn't a disability a disability? That wheelchair seems pretty personal (and medical) to me; what's so social about it? Well, think about what we've been discussing in many of the previous chapters. Literary theories often examine the way physical differences are given value, yet if you could look at them objectively, they'd just be just differences, without value.

But objectivity is hard to come by, so differences end up being worked into values, based on how society judges and treats those differences. You'll recall how individual differences turn into social values in our discussions of feminism (Chapter 12), gender (Chapter 13), ethnicity (Chapter 14), and language itself (Chapter 11). For each of these approaches, physical (and linguistic) differences exist, but they attain the meaning and values they have only in socially coded systems. Similarly, critics in disability studies explore how politics and culture work physical differences into the social codes we all live by.

Consider the distinction between *impairment* and *disability*. Impairment means the loss or abnormality of a body part, structure, or a function. Disability, on the other hand, describes what happens when impairment meets social expectations.

As an example, the United Nations notes that it isn't physical impairment itself that makes someone in a wheelchair "handicapped" or disadvantaged when it comes to certain kinds of work and mobility; it's access, particularly the kind of access that many people take for granted, like the environmental barriers of inaccessible buses or staircases.

Just as we saw with social constructions of sexuality and race, the social model of disability allows critics to create new approaches to reading and understanding literature based on what society does with real, lived experiences.

Critic Tom Shakespeare has emphasized, however, that while "a social approach to disability is indispensable" and "the medicalization of disability is inappropriate and an obstacle to effective analysis and policy," disability studies demands multiple levels of analysis, at times including both medical and social levels.

Similarly, Michael Oliver has argued that just as theory investigates race, class, and gender as sociopolitical categories, the same is happening to disability studies. In his own life, Oliver pointed to the most important aspect of this, which is a fundamental transition "from personal struggle to political understanding."

Marked Bodies

So how do physical differences get coded by society? How does society even create difference in the first place? In Chapter 13 we discussed Michel Foucault's argument that social power was responsible for organizing sexual activities into "types" of people in the nineteenth century. Well, Foucault is back to explain the rise of categorizing body types as well.

Quick digression, though. Think of this as the elevator-speech version of what's to come. The American literary critic Leslie Fiedler (1917–2003) has explained that the "tyranny of the normal" is what society wields over those it defines as abnormal. The effect of this in literature and culture is to make the "normal" fade into the background, while those who don't match up become alienated, ridiculed, exiled, and sometimes even glorified as exotic. At the same time, the tyranny of the normal also sets out unattainable ideals of normality that nobody can actually maintain, so everyone is vulnerable to exclusion. Okay, now let's move on to some of the details.

Foucault's 1975 study, *Discipline and Punish: The Birth of the Prison*, explored the "binary branding" of the eighteenth and nineteenth centuries that began to divide people into opposing categories: mad/sane, dangerous/harmless, normal/abnormal.

Foucault called these "coercive assignments" since they were assigned to people by others, and they were, well, coercive.

These categories, according to Foucault, support society's "literary fiction" of control and organization. Without categories, ordinary life in all its pesky variety seems like chaos and threatens to move in unexpected directions. And that frightens anyone in power. The development of categories actually replaces individuals with the larger groups they are put into, and those larger groups are much easier to move around, politically speaking. Foucault's historical example involved plague and how the authorities attempted to handle outbreaks of sickness by creating categories for sick and healthy individuals. Yet Foucault emphasized that the logic of social categorization went well beyond public health and became a "political dream" for handling any kind of social or ideological "outbreak."

IN THEORY

All too often, the disabled body has been "a repository for social anxieties, such troubling concerns as vulnerability, control, and identity." —Rosemary Garland-Thomson

The novelist and critic Susan Sontag (1933–2004) wrote two books relevant to this as well. *Illness as Metaphor* (1978) explored Sontag's own experience with cancer and its social stigma, while *AIDS and Its Metaphors* (1989) continued her exploration of the social construction and exploitation of illness.

Foucault's main point is that those in power don't stay in power by eliminating others, they do it by breaking human actions into ever more specific categories, or disciplines, and making the organization of those disciplines serve the interests of existing power. Crucially, as we saw in Chapter 9's discussion of ideology, this organization of disciplines is always offered to us as natural, scientific, and in service of the common good. And by the way, we all usually go along with it.

So just as sexual acts were organized into categories or types of people, so too were the unlimited differences in human ability, appearance, temperament, and intellect organized into categories of healthy/sick. Variations from the norm were not eliminated, but "disciplined" so that they could be brought into a system that individuals did not seem to control.

So the next time you hear the word *discipline*, you can remind yourself of its two meanings, and consider that what might be much worse than the discipline of a "smack from a ruler" is the control you lose by being installed into a system of "analysis, categorization, and knowledge-gathering."

IN THEORY

"The body is also directly involved in a political field; power relations have an immediate hold upon it; they invest it, mark it, train it, torture it, force it to carry out tasks, to perform ceremonies, to emit signs." —Julie Rivkin and Michael Ryan, summarizing the main argument of Foucault's *Discipline and Punish*

Stormin' Normin'

One of the most influential critics in disabilities studies, Lennard J. Davis, has explained that while categories of abnormality have a history, the whole concept of normality has a history as well. Davis pointed out that like the term *homosexuality*, *normality* is a term that has arrived on the scene only since the nineteenth century. As Davis reminds us, "The idea of a norm is less a condition of human nature than it is a feature of a certain kind of society."

So how did it develop? One aspect of the turn to the "norming" of society is the shift from ideal to normal. According to Davis, the concept of the ideal body, as represented in ancient Greek art, for example, was not supposed to be attainable by actual people. It was an ideal, after all, and represented the best that could be imagined. In fact, paintings and sculptures would combine the best features from different models, and the result would be an unrealistic, ideal hybrid.

Davis explained that in most people's minds, this kind of ideal stood apart from ordinary expectations. That is, people knew there were gods with their ideal bodies, and then there was everybody else. This idea, in fact, suggested a kind of egalitarian sense that all bodies are in some way disabled.

However, over time, the ideal came to be replaced as an abstract representation of what humans could aspire to but never reach. Or, put another way, the ideal as a model for inspiration (rather than actual emulation) was replaced with the idea of the normal, a concept that emerged through scientific principles and statistics. And, you guessed it, this shift was linked to social control, national identity, and economics—and it was presented in the guise of scientific fact.

The new normal, according to Davis, played rather fast and loose with what was statistically average for people and what was imagined as the best of all human characteristics. As Davis put it, "The concept of the norm, unlike that of an ideal, implies that the majority of the population must or should somehow be part of that norm." The consequences of falling outside the norm have been tragic in many ways, especially with regard to eugenics. Eugenics, the project of genetically manipulating human beings in order to "improve the species" by breeding certain types of people and eliminating others, offers a particularly graphic illustration of the power of norming.

APPLY IT

You may want to see Andrew Niccol's 1997 movie *Gattaca,* starring Ethan Hawke and Uma Thurman. Critic Roger Ebert has called it "one of the smartest and most provocative of science fiction films, a thriller with ideas." The film deals with issues of genetic superiority, social organization, and personal identity.

Davis emphasized that the creation of a superior race through eugenics was not only the dream of mad scientists and Hitler, but a goal shared by mainstream scientists, politicians, and philosophers as well. In fact, Alexander Graham Bell (the inventor of the telephone) warned very publically and emphatically that deaf-mutes should not marry other deaf-mutes, since an entire race of deaf people might result. Davis has compared Bell's fear to the fear Victor Frankenstein feels when the creature asks for a mate. Victor agrees at first, then relents as his mind is filled with the horrible thought of the "race of devils" that would result from the monstrous union. Later in this chapter we'll see how real the threat of eugenics remains to the Deaf community.

IN THEORY

"As the president of the University of Wisconsin declared after World War One, 'we know enough about eugenics so that if the knowledge were applied, the defective classes would disappear within a generation.'" —Lennard J. Davis

Another important consequence of viewing normality as a socially constructed and reinforced standard is recognizing how often the standard is challenged. Davis and other disability studies critics have argued that issues of disability are hardly limited to literature about disability, but that any work of literature, since it relies in some way on ideas of the normal, also relies on the concept of the abnormal. "One can find in almost any novel," Davis argues, "a kind of surveying of the terrain of the body; an attention to difference—physical, mental, and national." With disability studies in mind, you can see how texts make use of disability and the abnormal, usually in ways that shore up or support the idea of the normal.

IN THEORY

"To borrow Toni Morrison's notion that blackness is an idea that permeates American culture, disability too is a pervasive, often unarticulated, ideology informing our cultural notions of self and other. Disability—like gender—is a concept that pervades all aspects of culture: its structuring institutions, social identities, cultural practices, political positions, historical communities, and the shared human experience of embodiment." —Rosemarie Garland-Thomson

Davis's rereadings of texts that illustrate the "tyranny of the normal" include novels by Joseph Conrad, Émile Zola, Gustave Flaubert, and Shelley's *Frankenstein*, among others. Davis has also made the point that the traditional novel form itself subtly contributes to norming the physical body. After all, even Plato and Aristotle emphasized that art should be organic and "whole," like the human body with all its parts included and matching. You might also recall how the Victorian marriage plot serves to normalize heterosexuality (see Chapter 13).

Posing Gender

Critics have also explored the intersections between disability studies, feminist criticism, and queer theory. For Rosemarie Garland-Thomson, it's a matter of seeing how valuable feminist critique can be for disability studies. Garland-Thomson has pointed out, for example, that "Western thought has long conflated femaleness with disability" and defined "female bodies as non-normative."

The history of feminist theory is a history of exposing the oppression of being labeled "not normal," so the connection should be clear—follow the feminist theory model. In fact, says Garland-Thomson, "All too often the pronouncements in disability studies of what we need to start addressing are precisely issues that feminist theory has been grappling with for years." Susan Wendell has also pointed out the productive logical connection between the basic feminist reminder that "the world has been designed for men" and the disability studies examination of a world designed for the able-bodied.

Wendell and other critics, such as Jenny Morris, have also called attention to matters of experience. As we've seen (Chapter 12), one of patriarchy's go-to tactics is the devaluing of women's experience. Wendell has pointed out that "like women's particular knowledge, which comes from access to experiences most men do not have, disabled people's knowledge is dismissed as trivial, complaining, mundane (or bizarre), *less than* that of the dominant group." In fact, defining what is normal experience and what isn't is inevitably abusive and oppressive. As Jenny Morris has argued, disability studies allows you to be receptive to the social and personal aspects of disabled experience without first demanding medical "improvements" to normalize the disabled.

Queer theorist and disability studies critic Robert McRuer has drawn a parallel between Adrienne Rich's term *compulsory heterosexuality* and the oppression of *compulsory able-bodiedness*. McRuer's argument is that while compulsory heterosexuality creates a system in which a select set of desires is normalized, compulsory able-bodiedness sets a standard that both excludes anything "dis-abled," and frustrates the so-called able-bodied with an ideal that's impossible to live up to.

As an example of how his argument influences interpretation, McRuer has shown that the disabled and gay characters in the 1997 movie *As Good as It Gets* primarily serve "to effect the consolidation of heterosexual and able-bodied norms." That is—and we've seen this before—the minority characters simply shore up the dominant ideology.

IN THEORY

"A system of compulsory able-bodiedness repeatedly demands that people with disabilities embody for the others an affirmative answer to the unspoken question, Yes, but in the end, wouldn't you rather be more like me?" —Robert McRuer

Of course, when you see this kind of exploitation going on—in novels, on the screen, or in life—you know that it says more about the anxiety of the dominant ideology than it does about the minority voices. In this case, it's the anxiety of the able-bodied at stake, not disabled identity as such.

With this in mind, McRuer recalled Judith Butler and her theory of performance (see Chapter 13). McRuer's approach revises Butler's "gender trouble" in the context of both queer and disability studies and points to "ability trouble." Ability trouble, clearly stated, is "not the so-called problem of disability but the inevitable impossibility, even as it is made compulsory, of an able-bodied identity." According to McRuer, people are always anxious about "performing" their able-bodiedness correctly, just as they are worried about performing their ideal sexualities. And because we're all, in fact, only temporarily able-bodied, our performances will eventually change, whether we like it or not. As Susan Wendell thoughtfully reminds us, "Unless we die suddenly, we are all disabled eventually."

Book It

When it comes to representations of disability in literature, you might think that a key issue is the presence of derogatory, stigmatizing, and patronizing depictions of disability. And you'd be right. Yet there is more to the story, as usual.

Leslie Fiedler famously discussed images of the abnormal in literature and popular culture in his 1978 book, *Freaks: Myths and Images of the Secret Self.* Fiedler also discussed disability directly in several essays, exploring in one of them the idea that disability often represents the deep psychological traumas suffered by those who see themselves as able-bodied. According to Fiedler, disability has been used as a sign of the inward malignity or moral failing that we all are said to fear. Fiedler's list of works projecting "what we cannot bear into the 'other,'" include Shakespeare's *Richard III*, Melville's *Moby Dick*, Hawthorne's *The Scarlet Letter,* and Hugo's *The Hunchback of Notre Dame*, as well as Charles Dickens's *The Old Curiosity Shop* and the archetypal image of Tiny Tim in *A Christmas Carol.* In such texts, Fiedler argued, the disabled characters—as psychological projections of authors as well as readers—stand as troubling reminders of human vulnerability.

Lean on Me

David Mitchell and Sharon Snyder have offered an alternative approach to depictions of disability. In their 2001 book *Narrative Prosthesis*, Mitchell and Snyder agreed that disabled bodies are exploited in literature and movies, but they wanted to show how this exploitation does more than simply project pity and fear. They explained how texts rely on disability to illustrate the human dependence on the materiality of the body, in contrast to society's emphasis that the mind is really in control.

IN THEORY

"Our phrase *narrative prosthesis* is meant to indicate that disability has been used throughout history as a crutch upon which literary narratives lean for their representational power, disruptive potentiality, and analytical insight." —David Mitchell and Sharon Snyder

What's particularly important in Mitchell and Snyder's argument are the references to disruptive potential and analytical power. For Mitchell and Snyder, disabled characters *do things* in texts. Specifically, these bodies "show up in stories as dynamic entities that resist or refuse the cultural scripts assigned to them." These cultural scripts include all those standards of behavior and morality that perpetuate ideals of the body as whole or normal. In many texts, physical differences lead to a heightened sense of dependence on physicality itself, and that leads to a view of social conventions with the attitude, "No, I won't play it that way."

Mitchell and Snyder's examples include *Richard III*, William Faulkner's *The Sound and the Fury*, and Ken Kesey's 1962 novel *One Flew Over the Cuckoo's Nest* (and the 1975 movie of the same name). In these and other examples, Mitchell and Snyder see disabled bodies called on to do the "heavy lifting" of exposing everyone's dependence on the "shifting values and norms imposed on the body" in a world where ideas are typically thought to have all the clout.

APPLY IT

Many critics have interpreted the creature in *Frankenstein* as an image of disability and abnormality. Mitchell and Snyder, for example, have argued that while the creature was useful in getting the entire story going, he must be exterminated at the end by a novel that actually feels guilty for exploiting him. How do you interpret the novel from the perspective of disability studies? Which details of the story suggest that the creature embodies pity, fear, heroic resistance, or exploitation?

I See What You Mean

Of all the variations of human disability, one has tended to stand out as so "metaphorical" that its place in literature seems unrivaled. Blindness, as many critics have pointed out, is the metaphor of all metaphors.

Naomi Schor (1943–2001) explained that what makes blindness so powerful as a metaphor is that it's a particular type of metaphor, called a catachresis (pronounced *katta-KREE-sis*). Schor defined catachresis as an "obligatory metaphor," because there seems to be no alternative to using it. Examples include the *leg* of a table or the *arm* of a windmill. Saying someone is "morally blind," therefore, means using a metaphor that's so naturalized by culture that it doesn't even seem like a metaphor.

In one of her influential essays, Schor elaborated on blindness as a catachresis of "the moral superiority of the physically blind over the sighted." That is, characters with impaired sight are often depicted as attaining a higher form of insight that usually serves to teach a lesson to the sighted characters and readers. As examples—and there are many—Schor mentions the blind man in *Frankenstein* who accepts the creature as a fellow being because he is not restricted to judging the creature by his visual appearance. In *Jane Eyre*, Rochester's whole attitude is improved by his temporary blindness (and, it should be noted, by his dependence). And, Schor added, the moral blindness often remarked on in *Pride and Prejudice* serves to emphasize how the sighted characters need to be taught a lesson in how to "see" past their preconceptions.

As for disability studies critic Georgina Kleege, she would like to see literature and pop culture simply "abandon the clichés that use the word 'blindness' as a synonym for inattention, ignorance, or prejudice." Kleege has called attention to what she calls the longstanding image of the "Hypothetical Blind Man," or, simply, the Hypothetical. In countless instances, the Hypothetical stands for either lack of physical or moral sight, or for a realm of imagination to be explored for the benefit of sighted people. The Hypothetical, in other words, is sight's "other."

IN THEORY

The Hypothetical Blind Man is a "prop for theories of consciousness. He is the patient subject of endless thought experiments where the experience of the world through four senses can be compared to the experience of the world through five. … His primary function is to highlight the importance of sight and to elicit a frisson of awe and pity which promotes gratitude among the sighted theorists for the vision they possess." —Georgina Kleege

In contrast to this, Kleege has advocated for a deeper and broader understanding of texts actually created by blind writers. Following the model we've seen so successfully employed by feminist critics, Kleege looks not only to a greater awareness of contemporary blind writers, but also the recovery of memoirs, essays, and other works from the past.

In one of her essays, Kleege described the work of the nineteenth-century French activist Thérèse-Adèle Husson, who wrote from the position, rare for her time, that her first-hand experience with blindness meant that she should be telling institutions for the blind how to run their businesses, rather than the other way around. Kleege also mentions Helen Keller's important 1908 book, *The World I Live In*. Kleege's central point is that while images of the Hypothetical perpetuate an oppressive and constricting view of blindness, reading works by blind authors reveals their "urgent desire to represent their blindness as something besides the absence of sight." And the reason is simple—the writers "do not feel themselves to be deficient or partial—sighted people minus sight—but whole human beings who have learned to attend to their nonvisual senses in different ways."

Thinking Otherwise

Medical and social models of disability have clashed most recently on the issue of autism. Music and disability studies theorist Joseph N. Straus has explained, reflecting other critics we've discussed in this chapter, that the characteristics currently classified as autistic are not unified by science but by culture. Autistic categories, according to Straus, are really "clusters of behavior, abilities, and attitudes, that, under the right cultural conditions, get grouped together and provided with a label. The label appears to confer coherence on the category, but this is a fiction, or rather, a contingent cultural construction."

In fact, Straus has suggested that the same traits typically associated with autism—feelings of aloneness, desire for sameness, lack of big-picture thinking or attention to others, unusual imaginative skills, impaired traditional communication skills, and intense attention to minute details—all look different if you change the social context. Why? Because autism has to be seen as a "relational phenomenon, a function of the interaction between people." The concept of *neurodiversity*—different ways of thinking—describes the same kind of relational context that we've seen with disability studies in general.

IN THEORY

"The autistic world and the normate world are distinct—but the boundary between them permits people on both sides to see through (it's not an impermeable wall), and possibly to move through as well. Autism culture is distinct, but it's still a human culture." —Joseph N. Straus

Straus has shown that the medical model of autism and the social model are also reflected in the literature about autism. He noted that works written *about* autistic people, often by researchers or even parents, often include images of walls, aliens, and concealment. Works written *by* autistic people, on the other hand, actually feature metaphors of doors, windows, and other images of separation—but it's separation with the possibility of some kind of contact.

Straus notes, for example, the work of Temple Grandin, whose book, *Emergence: Labeled Autistic* was adapted into the 2010 film, *Temple Grandin*, directed by Mick Jackson. Grandin, a doctor of animal science, has become the most public voice of autism, publishing several books in addition to *Emergence* and speaking out on a variety of subjects, from psychology and education to animal rights.

As we discussed in Chapter 11, some literary critics have identified theory of mind, or the ability of people to interpret other people's internal states of mind, as central to the experience of reading fiction. Now, since people with autism lack this "mind reading" ability to one degree or another, the question becomes one of whether autistic people are simply left out when it comes to fiction. Straus and others have argued that this isn't the case, particularly since people with autism have written works reflecting their own and others' states of mind.

Grandin's own view emphasizes that there is more than one way to tell and appreciate a story. Since she does not "read" faces like most other people do, Grandin has built up a "library" of visual images through experience, and these images help her understand and predict what people are thinking. Her reading strategies may differ from the typical ones explored and even assumed in this book, but they become part of the human experience of literature.

IN THEORY

"Thinking in visual pictures and making associations is simply a different form of thinking from verbal-based linear thought. There are advantages and disadvantages to both kinds of thinking. Ask any artist or accountant." —Temple Grandin

In fact, despite the challenges of autism—challenges that can stem from personal frustrations and anxieties as much as social ones—Grandin, for her part, would not want to "cure" her "disability": "If I could snap my fingers and be nonautistic, I would not—because then I wouldn't be me. ... I have become fully aware that my visualization skills exceed those of most other people. I would never want to become so normal that I would lose these skills."

Aud, Isn't It?

"Disabled," according to the clear assertion by critics Carol Padden and Tom Humphries, "is a label that historically has not belonged to Deaf people."

Why? Because "it suggests political self-representations and goals unfamiliar to the group. When *Deaf* people discuss their deafness, they use terms deeply related to their language, their past, and their community." Yet, according to Padden and

Humphreys, because the general public understands the language of disability so readily, Deaf people will self-consciously employ such terms as *access* and *civil rights*. As we have seen throughout this book, identities are social realities, not personal or physical facts. So when society gives you a label, you can try to tear it off, but you can also wear it proudly, wear it subversively, transform it, or even revise it.

 DEFINITION

When spelled with a lowercase letter, *deaf* refers to the nonhearing (or partial hearing) impairment itself. Spelled with a capital letter, **Deaf** refers to people who identify as part of the Deaf community, shaped by shared culture and the linguistic difference of sign language.

Deaf culture, for literary theory and criticism, offers fascinating challenges to dominant approaches to language and communication. Deaf culture also reflects on the enormous challenges it has faced from a history of oppression.

The influential Deaf critic H-Dirksen L. Bauman has elaborated on the term *audism*, originally coined by Tom Humphries in 1975, as a term that links the treatment of Deaf people to the oppressive histories of racism, sexism, and classism. Audism, for Bauman, should be defined in three ways. First and foremost, audism is "the notion that one is superior based on one's ability to hear or behave in the manner of one who hears." Second, it is the "system of advantage based on hearing ability." And finally, audism describes the "metaphysical orientation that links human identity with speech."

Regarding the first definition, educational policies throughout much of the twentieth century were clearly biased against any system of communication that did not strive to emulate the speaking-hearing model. *Oralism* refers to such modes of deaf communication as reading lips, mimicking speech, and using actual speech, while *manualism* refers to the use of sign language.

R. A. R. Edwards has explained that while manualism was generally accepted and taught to deaf students in the nineteenth century, the rise of oralism in the twentieth century shifted the emphasis. According to Edwards, the change meant that "signed communication of any sort was generally forbidden" since "the goal of oral education was to make deaf people over in a hearing image." As we discussed previously, disability studies critics argue that there is a very fine line between wanting to "cure" a condition and calling for the elimination of a type of person. The struggle for Deaf people to sign and participate fully in the development of Deaf culture is a reaction to this threat.

Critic Nicole Markotić has shown that when signing is seen as a symptom or manifestation of a disease, people are inevitably led to think that a cure is in order. And if a cure can't be found, certain people must be isolated or eliminated. Such cures have included teaching only oralism, and, more recently, the surgical implantation of cochlear implants (high-tech hearing devices) in deaf infants. According to Kathryn Woodcock, "hearing people want to eradicate deafness [with cochlear implants] and, by implication, wish that they—Deaf people—didn't exist."

APPLY IT

The multiple-award-winning movie, *Children of a Lesser God,* directed by Randa Haines and starring Marlee Matlin and William Hurt (1986), may be one of the most well-known movies involving the Deaf community. After seeing it, take a look at Roger Ebert's review of the movie as well (it's online). Ebert clearly likes the movie, yet raises some very provocative points regarding interpretation, such as, "If a story is about the battle of two people over the common ground on which they will communicate, it's not fair to make the whole movie on the terms of only one of them." Another recommended film is *The Hammer* (directed by Oren Kaplan, 2010), about a deaf collegiate wrestling champion. Also, be sure to check out the PBS documentary *Through Deaf Eyes* (2007). And if you're interested in movies in ASL, head to DeafMovies.org for a growing list and commentary.

Educational policies have changed, however, and in North America many more schools today are either open to or entirely committed to manualist training. As Padden and Humphries have written, "'Oral' schools promote ideologies counter to those of Deaf people; 'manual' schools, which allow use of signed language in schools, are ideologically appealing to Deaf people."

Linguistically, it's important to keep in mind that American Sign Language (ASL) is not simply "signed English," but a separate language making use of gestures, facial expressions, and body orientation. This is why the choice between oralism and manualism as an educational goal is so important—it determines the culture that develops around the condition of deafness. Paddon and Humphries call for "beginning from a different center" when it comes to understanding deafness in literature, culture, and everyday life. That different center moves anyone—the deaf and the hearing alike—away from seeing Deaf people as trying to hear and communicate verbally but failing, and toward an understanding that Deaf means living with another dimension of experience, communication, and culture.

For Bauman, the nature of ASL as a coherent signifying system also illustrates the deconstructionist principle (see Chapter 17) that language is not the same as speech. What Bauman called the "metaphysical" aspect of audist oppression is based on the Western tradition of placing speech at the foundation of all language. And if language, argued Bauman, is held up as the quality that actually makes us human, then anyone who does not participate in speech must logically be seen as less than human.

In Bauman's case, therefore, as with the arguments of many of the critics we have discussed in this chapter, theory and criticism become tools for revealing the limitations of social narratives and indicating new directions for understanding, expression, and interpretation.

The Least You Need to Know

- Disability and normality are both social constructions.
- Feminist theory informs many of the critiques of disability studies.
- Literature has employed images of disability to both demean and romanticize people with disabilities.
- Blindness has served (and still does) as a particularly stubborn metaphor in literature and film.
- Critics have recently explored the opportunities as well as the challenges for understanding autistic thinking.
- Deaf culture does not view deafness as a disability, yet recognizes the productive dialogue between disability studies and the interests of the nonhearing community.

Try to Watch Your Language

There's some heavy lifting here, but you're ready for it. In this trio of chapters, we look at some of the most influential investigations into the relationships between literature, language, and thought. You'll see system and structure take center stage, and you'll find out that deconstructing a salad may not be what Jacques Derrida originally had in mind. You'll also get to revisit psychological approaches to see what's happened to Freud since we saw him last.

Structuralism Senses a Pattern Here

In This Chapter

- Structuralism and the rules of literary form
- Counting and sorting all those fairy tales
- The deep importance of storytelling
- Reading culture like a book

Once upon a time, as you'll recall from Chapter 11, Ferdinand de Saussure changed everything by calling attention to the importance that systems play in your understanding of anything. And as you may recall, Charles S. Peirce also developed a study of signs—semiotics—although he's never received the same credit that Saussure did, maybe because Saussure's book included little drawings of horses and trees and people with dotted lines running through their ears and out of their mouths. In any case, Saussure's central argument that language is just one example of a system of interrelated signs really caught on.

You make sense of language, Saussure explained, not because you've seen every exact sentence before, but because you know how the system works—you know how grammar works. You may not be a grammarian, but you know what "sounds right" and you can make sense of all kinds of entirely new sentences. You've internalized many of the structures or rules of grammar and it just seems natural to make sense of practically any sentence you see.

So then Saussure said somebody ought to study how everything, not just language, is made up of signs. After all, he said, when you look out at the world and see clothing, facial expressions, eating habits, ceremonies, and all kinds of cultural traditions, you're seeing sign systems in action. You actually make sense of what you see because of the codes that you've internalized, like a grammar. You have an internalized under-standing of social structures. Writers write and readers read without consciously knowing or intending much of what they're doing. By golly, someone should study these structures, Saussure said, since that will lead to understanding the laws that actually provide the meaning that most people incorrectly believe comes from the signs themselves.

So one day, and in fact through the first half of the twentieth century until the late '60s, all kinds of critics took up this challenge and began to track down the structural laws that organized meanings for such fields as anthropology, psychology, history, art, sociology, and philosophy, as well as linguistics and literature. These critics were called structuralists, and they believed that we spend too much time in our daily lives relying on internalized codes and grammar without thinking about them. They wanted us to think about them.

Let's see how it worked out.

Patterns and Rules

Saussure's argument that when we look at the world we don't just see things, we see signs, was taken very seriously by the Russian linguist Roman Jakobson (1896–1982, pronounced *YAH-cubb-son*). Jakobson, by the way, directly links the Russian for-malists (see Chapter 4) with Saussure and all later developments in structuralism and post-structuralism. Inaugurating the term *structuralist* itself in 1929, Jakobson explained that anything you would want to study should be seen as a structural whole, not just a bunch of data. The point of this new approach was not to focus on the data itself, but the internal processes that make the data meaningful.

IN THEORY

Another important figure in the early history of structuralism is Paul Valéry (1871–1945), a French symbolist poet who also wrote literary criticism and essays on all kinds of topics. Valéry saw literature as operating like language and emphasized that the poet and the reader both belong to a structured system of artistic and interpretive conventions.

Structuralists, in fact, tend not to be too concerned about content, but with the processes that create meaning. Jakobson would study anything with regard to its poetic function, or the ways in which a text emphasizes form and pattern. This led to analyses of everything from Shakespeare and Baudelaire to an "I Like Ike" campaign button.

In practice, Jakobson's approach to the "poetry of grammar and the grammar of poetry" meant looking for patterns in poems. The result was typically a reading that looked very scientific, and to many other critics, rather dull. A sonnet, for example, might be broken down into patterns of adjectives or verbs, or, if he was feeling adventurous, verbs that turn into adjectives. The process was detailed, long, exhaustive, and intended to produce what Jonathan Culler called a kind of "algorithm" of poetic description.

Not *What* It Means, but *How* Does It Mean?

When Jakobson moved to New York in the 1940s he began collaborating with the anthropologist Claude Lévi-Strauss (1908–2009, pronounced to rhyme with "heavy mouse," rather than with the jeans maker). Lévi-Strauss refined and expanded the structuralist approach into the study of society, culture, and literature.

As an ethnographer, or researcher of cultures, Lévi-Strauss first became notable for showing how kinship systems operate like languages. The rules for marriages, for example, and the exchange of women among families through marriages in particular, were not just natural developments or even neutral traditions, according to Lévi-Strauss, but aspects of communicating culture by responding to internalized rules. Feminist critics have developed this idea as well, highlighting the predicament of women's objectification, as we saw in Chapter 12.

When it came to literature, Lévi-Strauss's structuralist approach, like Jakobson's, reflected a scientific character. The goal was to take a literary work and find out how it really works—how its internal structure produced what you see and feel. What were the laws and patterns, Lévi-Strauss wanted to know, that were operating behind the scenes to make the literary work happen?

And like Jakobson's method, this meant creating literary "readings" that can seem rather bizarre. Instead of laying out what the Oedipus story means, for example, Lévi-Strauss would turn the work into a diagram or chart and show you the skeleton that the story was built around. Running down the first column of the chart would be one set of patterns he discovered, such as recurring instances of family intimacy. Running down the next column would be instances of family violence. Other columns would include repeated instances of certain actions or images. If you read the columns downward, you see all the evidence for the patterns the critic had discovered, like the pillars supporting a building. If you read across, you get the story as it's usually told. Lévi-Strauss liked focusing on the columns best. Why just *read* the story (left to right) when you can *understand* the story by studying its inner patterns?

Lévi-Strauss explained that after studying hundreds of myths from various cultures, he could show that the underlying structures—the skeletons or pillars of all the myths—were remarkably similar and consistent, no matter how various the final products looked. Rather like people and buildings.

Oh That Old Chestnut (or, Why So Grimm?)

This wasn't the first time linguists had investigated patterns in folktales and myths. Vladimir Propp (1895–1970), one of the Russian formalists (see Chapter 4), studied thousands of Russian fairy tales and determined that they were all based on 31 story elements. His 1928 book, *Morphology of the Folktale* (*morphology* means the study of changes in the shape of things), explained how a basic pattern or model can produce endless variations. Any given story may not have all 31 elements, Propp argued, but it will reproduce the basic pattern he discovered.

The basic pattern comes down to a template for fairy tales. Put another way, fairy tales follow a pattern and order—a syntax like the structuring of a sentence. The example, "Prince Charming breaks the spell and awakens Sleeping Beauty," has the skeletal form, "The blank blanks the blank and blanks the blank." So fill in the blanks any other way you like and you've got a story. "The hero kills the dragon and saves the town." "Grandma adds the salt and rescues the soup."

And even before Propp, the famous brothers Grimm—linguists by training—also collected fairy tales. Their fairy tale collections published in the early 1800s served as the basis for much further study. Propp's work, along with the cataloguing of fairy tales by the Grimms, also led to identifying and naming all kinds of fairy tale categories with great specificity.

You'll want to know, for example, that the basic skeleton plot of the Cinderella story is classified as type #510 in the Aarne index of folktales—and it's #510A if you ask a later guy who added subtypes. According to one study published in 1893, in fact, various cultures had produced at least 345 variations of the basic Cinderella story structure. The variations follow the same basic structure—unappreciated girl gets magical help and eventually wins the hand of the prince after the shoe fits—but differ in exact details. By 1951, another scholar had counted about 700 Cinderella variations. As for the present count, you're on your own.

IN THEORY

"Cinderella story. Outta nowhere. A former greens keeper, now, about to become the Masters champion. It looks like a miracle—It's in the hole!" —Bill Murray in *Caddyshack* (1980, directed by Harold Ramis)

Really, though, what was the effect of structuralist approaches to literary study, other than reminding writers of proven standard plots to repeat over and over? Well, one effect was to turn literary criticism away from looking at the laws that governed single works, like the New Critics did with their notion of organic unity (see Chapter 3), and toward the search for the laws that govern all narratives.

Working the Story

So then, structuralist critics asked why it is that certain stories keep getting repeated. Why are myths shared across cultures? Why do we like to hear "the same story" over and over again? Well, in the spirit of structuralism, we can break down the responses into three categories.

Logical Tools

For Claude Lévi-Strauss, the myths that we tell ourselves over and over help us deal with paradoxes in life. According to Lévi-Strauss, you're faced with paradoxes and contradictions all the time. How can you really distinguish between people and animals? What's with life and death? That sort of thing. The contradictions depend on binary oppositions, or the pairing up of two things so that each can define the other. People are people because they're "not animals." Life is "not death," and vice versa—and so on. Binary oppositions, by the way, will feature prominently in the next chapter's discussion of deconstruction.

In his reading of the Oedipus story, for example, Lévi-Strauss argued that the story really involves the contradiction between ancient myths that say human beings sprang up from the ground (or are created by a divine force) and the knowledge that people come from the union of other people. All the dynamics of the Oedipus story, with its mistaken identities, family violence, and tragic sexual issues, serve to exorcise the paradox of how people are created. Lévi-Strauss explained that myths don't actually resolve the deeply troubling binary oppositions they address, but they let you move beyond the paradoxes by following a story that's structured around a traumatic situation. A myth is a kind of logical tool used to examine a cultural contradiction, and as long as the contradiction stands, the myth will keep being retold, in one form or another.

APPLY IT

Frankenstein has been read as a modern myth. In fact, you might see the binary opposition that structures the story as forcing an unsolvable question: do you create new things from your own will and imagination, or do you create something new simply by manipulating already existing (even dead) things? The novel seems to raise this issue regarding art and literature as much as human life. What do you think?

And what about all those variations and updates of the Frankenstein story? How have so many people made the structuring issues of this myth reflect their own concerns?

Jung at Art (or, Swingin' a Myth)

The Swiss psychiatrist Carl Jung (1875–1961, pronounced *yoong*) began as a partner of Sigmund Freud but moved into his own area of specialization. While Freud studied the unconscious as a feature of individual minds (see Chapter 10), Jung was focused on what he called the collective unconscious. The collective unconscious, according to Jung, is made up of humanity's psychic memories and deep primordial images. And while Freud saw all art as a symptom of individual psychological issues, Jung saw myth, literature, and art as a collective "venting" of humanity's psyche. That is, we keep telling the same stories because they relate to fundamental parts of our minds.

IN THEORY

"The primordial image, or archetype, is a figure—be it a demon, a human being, or a process—that constantly recurs in the course of history and appears wherever creative fantasy is freely expressed." —Carl Jung

Archetypes, or universal symbols, therefore, will inevitably end up in the stories that people tell, whether they intend it or not. Critics have sometimes gone to great lengths to catalogue these archetypes (you saw what happened to Cinderella), yet despite some critics overdoing it, you can still spot some pretty genuine examples of the classic images that Jung and others argued will always pop up: the sea as an image of life, the river or road as the continuity of life, water standing for rebirth, the color red for trouble and green for growth; and then there are archetypal characters such as the good mother, the wise old man, and the trickster. Feminist critics have also pointed out the prevalence of images of the angel and the monster to reflect female identity (see Chapter 12).

IN THEORY

It seems like people have always wanted to collect stories from around the world in order to produce a kind of matrix or spreadsheet revealing the unseen universal principles that unify all cultures. One example from real life is Joseph Campbell (1904–1987), whose multivolume study *The Masks of God* connected religious myths throughout history. In literature, one of the best novels ever written, George Eliot's *Middlemarch* (1874), features a character who has given himself the task to compile a *Key to All Mythologies*.

Now, with all these deep psychological issues at work, you might be wondering, what about the author's own creativity and intentions? Jung was ready for that question, and he made his point clear: "The poet's conviction that he is creating in absolute freedom would then be an illusion: he fancies he is swimming, but in reality an unseen current sweeps him along." That is, for Jung the "unseen current" of the collective unconscious is in large part responsible for getting the words on the page. Sounds pretty spiritual, and it is, but keep in mind that even the linguistic structuralists argued that it's the codes and "grammar" of myths that sweep you along when you write a story.

It's the Economy

So if Lévi-Strauss said your reading and retelling of stories is based on your need to deal with cultural contradictions, and Jung said it's humanity's collective unconscious that sweeps you along, what's left? What else could be the moving force behind structures of meaning?

Marketing!

The Marxist critic Fredric Jameson has reminded us that any talk about structure or system must always mean a *particular* structure or system. Even when theorists claim universality, Jameson argued, they can only produce evidence that reflects a particular sociocultural situation—especially the situation that surrounds the theorists when they write. In this way, structuralism is a way of investigating ideology (see Chapter 9). And it's the ideology of dominant economic interests, Jameson emphasized, that we're caught up in as we read and write all those stories. Stories, therefore, don't reflect universal psychological preoccupations, but particular social ones.

APPLY IT

Ever find yourself thinking in book group that every book is ultimately about the same thing? Or maybe that some people, no matter what the book of the month is, will always say the same things? Without getting into a fight, discuss how such habits might reflect on ideology or deep psychology. And good luck with that.

So you might consider the story so far in this way: some critics are looking for the laws that govern single works (New Critics), some are looking at literary works for the laws that govern all literature (formalists and structuralists), and some are looking at literature for the way it reveals the ideological laws that govern a specific society or period (materialist approaches to structuralism).

Then there's the more specific issue of marketing, pure and simple. We've seen critics typically talk about myths as deeply human and seemingly uninvolved with current events, but what if the myth you want to consider isn't one of saving the princess or "birth-death-rebirth," but the myth of "this vitamin supplement will change your life" or "lather-rinse-repeat"? What one critic calls the unconscious influence of myth, another calls the unconscious influence of advertising.

Who is this other critic?

Does This Tie Match My Signifying System?

Well, he's not the only other critic to read popular culture like literature (see Chapter 20), but let's focus on the French literary and cultural critic Roland Barthes (1915–1980, pronounced *bart*). In his wide-ranging essays and books, Barthes showed that popular culture creates "everyday myths" that can be read like literature, if you're careful about it.

Clothing, for example, involves the same two dimensions of organization that sentences do. That is, sentences and outfits both depend on horizontal and vertical choices. Your horizontal choices organize your overall outfit, like the syntax of a sentence organizes the order of the words. A vertical choice is when you choose between different synonymous words that you could drop into the places you've organized. In clothing, this means choosing a particular tie, hat, or skirt. Identifying the "grammar" behind clothing choices—and Barthes gives the same treatment to dinner parties—should also remind you of the structuralist habit of filling in the blanks.

Barthes also revisits Saussure's theory of the sign by pointing out how everyday myths require careful interpretation in order to see what's really going on. In fashion, for example, the whole system of choices described earlier becomes, not the end of the story, but just the beginning. Things we see that Saussure argued are signs—hats, shoes, entire outfits—Barthes saw as signifiers governed by the system of fashion itself.

In other words, the things we see in the world are not just signs, but the raw material that gets woven into everyday cultural myths. So the meaning of that tie may actually be shaped by the signifying system of corporate power. Or that bowl of macaroni and cheese is imbued with meaning because it belongs to a signified system, created through advertising, of a happy home life. Barthes demystified all kinds of things by redirecting our attention to context in this way—travel guides, laundry soap ("foam can even be the sign of a certain spirituality"), toys, professional wrestling, Garbo.

Great Expectations

When it comes to literary analysis as such, Jonathan Culler has emphasized the importance of systems as well. In his study *Structuralist Poetics* (1975), Culler argued that the real object of study for literary criticism "is not the work itself but its intelligibility." According to Culler, much of what makes a literary work intelligible is your awareness that it's a literary work in the first place. That is, you come to any piece of writing with expectations—is it a stop sign, a menu, a poem, or a novel?

Culler pointed out that we unconsciously assimilate the rules of various forms of writing, so our very perception of literature is guided by the expectations these rules create. If you think you're looking at a poem, for example, you'll read a text differently than you do when you think you're reading a novel or an instruction manual. The conventions of reading enable you to read, but they also might lock you into a single way of reading. Culler suggested shaking things up by imagining how differently you would read prose if it were set out like poetry.

Try the following, for example. I've arranged the opening sentence of *Pride and Prejudice* so that it "looks poetic."

It is a	truth
	universally acknowledged,
That a	single man
In	possession
of a	good fortune,
Must be in	want
Of a	wife.

Or, try this sentence, from the beginning of *David Copperfield:*

Whether I shall turn

       out

  To be the hero of my own

        life,

    Or whether that station will be held by anybody

          else,

These
Pages

Must
Show.

Culler's point is that your response to literature—and your interpretations—don't just come from a novel's words themselves, but from your internalized expectations regarding how to read novels. He called this your literary competence and compared it with Noam Chomsky's theory of linguistic competence (see Chapter 11). However, when you modify your approach you find that your equally internalized competence for reading poetry can reveal features, tones, and interpretations that may go unnoticed in a prose passage.

RELATIONS

Structuralism was instrumental in the development of narratology, or the scientific study of narrative. Tzvetan Todorov, who named the field, has written on the internal structures of detective fiction. He also helped bring Russian formalists back into wide circulation with his translations of their work in 1965. Gérard Genette (pronounced with a *t* at the end) has developed theories of plot that elaborate on the details of the plot/story-stuff distinction. See Chapter 4 for more on the Russian formalists and plot.

So You Say

Structuralism's detractors have protested that the approach puts too much distance between literature and actual readers. The American literary critic and education specialist Gerald Graff, for example, once pointed out "the fact that literature possesses an internal grammar of forms does not mean that this grammar cannot or ought not be answerable to anything outside itself." And as we'll see in subsequent chapters, structuralism has responded to this charge by exploring various approaches to the "outside."

Critics, including many of the key structuralists themselves, have continued to challenge and modify structuralist insights. Sometimes this leads away from strict adherence to the scientific aspirations of structuralism, and sometimes this leads to productive new paradoxes. For example, Jonathan Culler has shown that the exact same patterns that Claude Lévi-Strauss and Roman Jakobson were counting on in one study to prove that a particular poem was "poetic" could also be found in those critics' own prose.

Some have argued, therefore, that the quest for stable underlying principles of literature actually ends with the discovery that the quest itself may be the only underlying principle in town.

And so, structuralism lives happily and paradoxically ever after.

The Least You Need to Know

- Structuralists look for underlying principles that govern literary creation and interpretation.
- Through scientific study of folktales, linguists have developed theories of core story structures common to many cultures.
- Myths and folktales play an important role in social organization and reflect humanity's collective unconscious.
- Everyday cultural activities can be seen as modern myths that can be read and analyzed like literature.
- Your interpretation of any literary work is influenced by the conventions for reading that you have internalized.

Deconstruction Says It's Not What You Think

In This Chapter

- Deconstruction and philosophy's aversion to language
- Speech as internalized writing
- Collapsing the binaries
- No limits to the text
- Words are real

The term *deconstruction* is all over the place now, especially in food. Deconstructed chocolate cake, deconstructed club sandwich, deconstructed stuffed cabbage. For recipes, deconstructed means rearranging the dish's ingredients so that the result looks kind of like the original, but inside-out, with all its parts exposed. A deconstructed dish may also end up emphasizing ingredients that are overlooked or underappreciated in the original by bringing them out into the open.

In literary theory, deconstruction describes a critical approach that, according to the *Oxford English Dictionary*, is "directed towards exposing unquestioned metaphysical assumptions and internal contradictions in philosophical and literary language." Sounds complicated, but stay with me, because once you've got a handle on the meaning of "metaphysical assumptions and internal contradictions," you can get back to the chocolate cake.

The whole process starts by asking this question: what's more real and true, your thoughts or the way you manage to get those thoughts into words?

Philosophy's Low Opinion of Language

Generally, Western philosophy has put thinking in a privileged place over speaking and writing. We saw how Plato did this (see Chapter 7), and he even warned against poetry because it would get in the way of pure thought. Ideas come first, the argument goes, and expression is secondary, extra, and even optional.

The French philosopher Jacques Derrida (1930–2004, pronounced *DAIRY-dah*) said this approach of philosophers trying to get to ideal meanings behind all that "clutter" of expression is hopeless. Instead, ideas and expression have to be considered inseparable.

Plato had set things up, however, to favor a separation. Writing, in particular, was singled out as dangerous, because it led to ambiguity. If you're having a conversation with someone, Plato argued, you're engaged in a one-to-one exchange in which each person literally stands behind what he or she is saying. The *presence* of each person's thoughts guarantees the reliability and stability of the knowledge passed around. Writing, on the other hand, signals the *absence* of the real source of meaning.

That is, if you write something down and just send it out, there would be no way for the note itself to answer for any ambiguities or questions raised by the words you've chosen. In fact, since words take on a life of their own once they "get out," your note could be wildly misinterpreted. Not only that, but all kinds of people could read your note, even if it isn't intended for them. Imagine finding a postcard that begins "Dear Sweetheart" and is filled with all kinds of nice compliments, but the card wasn't written for you. How terrible—language has gone astray! Truth is lost and all that's left is a kind of literary eavesdropping! This possibility, which most writers and readers don't mind at all, drove Plato crazy. So he emphasized that philosophy (literally, "love of knowledge") needs to be philosophy, darn it, and rhetoric—the art of using language, and the stock-in-trade of the *sophists*—needs to know its place.

Derrida set out to show that despite the dream of keeping philosophy and rhetoric separate, the two always interact. Of course, similar points have been made by plenty of other critics, poets, and artists throughout history. Emily Dickinson (1830–1886) wrote this poem in 1861, for example:

> THE THOUGHT beneath so slight a film
> Is more distinctly seen,—
> As laces just reveal the surge,
> Or mists the Apennine.

DEFINITION

Plato had competition as a philosopher. These folks were called **sophists,** and they made their living by teaching people how to be clever with language. They taught methods of persuasion, fancy figures of speech, and various strategies for selling whatever ideas you wanted to sell as truth. They also backed up what they did philosophically by arguing that it's impossible to know absolute truth directly.

The sophists argued that the only kind of knowledge humans can really have is provisional and fleeting. For them, knowledge was always a matter of context and limited by everyone's different circumstances and perceptions. All the rhetoric the sophists taught (like grammar, figures, and word derivations) might have been a challenge to Plato's idea of pure ideas, but it supported the sophists' view that humans had to rely on such things just to make sense of the world. This aspect of the sophists' approach is reflected in Derrida's deconstruction.

Dickinson's poem describes the way that any "slight film" will bring out the shape of a thought better than the bare thought itself. Likewise, lace draped on a woman's neckline and mists around the Apennine mountain range in Italy suggest the power of the screen to provide a better appreciation of, rather than to obscure, the image beyond.

In theory and criticism, we've also seen formalists (see Chapters 3 and 4) as well as the Romantic poet-critics (see Chapter 8) respond to Plato by emphasizing the necessary fusion of form and content. Still, Derrida went much further in his critique of the distinction between thought and language. You'll notice in Dickinson's poem, for example, that despite the film, lace, and mists, there still exist real and objective thoughts, surges, and Apennines. Deconstruction's central argument, however, challenges the very concept that thoughts exist without some kind of language.

The result of Derrida's work, in fact, has been to unsettle all kinds of traditional understandings of philosophy, art, politics, psychology, and religion. Why all the fuss? Because the fact seems to be that people really, *really* like the idea that ideas come first. Much of the Western worldview depends on placing ideas in a pure realm, separated from material things.

Truth First

Take, for example, the presence-versus-absence issue regarding thought and speech. The notion that someone's presence guarantees the truth of what is spoken is the same notion that sees a nice stable thought standing behind any utterance. Derrida calls this logic the traditional Western metaphysics of presence. Metaphysical means something is being explained by linking it to an idea of truth. In this case, Derrida explains, Western philosophy places ideas as the basis for truth.

Going back to the original definition at the start of this chapter, then, one of the "unquestioned metaphysical assumptions" at work in Western history is your belief that the presence of ideas is more stable and more truthful than materiality. It's like the presence of the internal, formless "breath of inspiration" that supports the Romantic poet's written creations. It's also like the presence of the soul that animates the body.

Deconstruction actually questions this logic, so you can imagine the backlash: "What, no soul? No truth? No reality?" Well, no; that's not exactly the case. What deconstruction does instead is investigate how these concepts have relied on paradoxical and contradictory logic in order to stay privileged. These concepts still exist for deconstructionist critics, but they're explained differently.

With Writing in Mind

Consider the relationship between speech and writing again. The traditional view holds that writing is "recorded speech." Put another way, speech is prior to writing. That's certainly the way Plato saw it. Derrida explained, however, that all of the rules we typically want to confine to writing are also at work in speech. Speakers, in fact, have internalized the rules that just seem to be exclusive to writing. This was true even before the invention of writing, and it's true for any speakers who *cannot* write, since even they rely on grammar rules and conventions to make sense of spoken language. Speech, therefore, which is supposed to be so present and immediate as an expression of your thoughts, only feels natural because you have internalized the rules (some of which are very complicated) that have developed through society over time. In a sense, the hard work of getting the system of language in place has been done for you, and you just adopt language as "your own."

APPLY IT

In Shelley's *Frankenstein,* notice how the creature's consciousness, including his sense of self, are clearly linked to the language that he learns. You'll find details of this in the creature's first discussion with Victor. It's almost as if Shelley wants to illustrate the deconstructionist principle that consciousness doesn't come before language, but develops along with language.

But Derrida pointed out another reversal involving speech and writing as well. As we saw, Plato had worried that writing can "go astray" since it's vulnerable to being read by anyone, even those for whom the writing is not intended. The traditional logic behind this is that writing is an *external* representation of internal thoughts and the speech that seems to flow effortlessly from those thoughts. The problem with this logic, Derrida explained, is that writing is no more external than speech is.

Derrida showed that if the internal character of speech just comes from getting used to all those social rules and conventions that have developed over time, then speech itself—and the thoughts that develop with it—are actually filled with external features. All those things that Plato wanted to keep out of the realm of pure ideas—rules of grammar, figures of speech (especially metaphors), dictionary definitions, and the intervention of other people's styles of communicating—they're always part of your innermost processes of thinking and speaking.

According to Derrida, one of the biggest problems with the "faulty logic" of separating the internal and the external is that it forces you to rely on binary oppositions and to privilege one side over the other. That is, Plato could only hold up the "pure realm of ideas" by condemning language as an external impurity. Derrida saw this happening all the time in Western philosophy—a pair of concepts exists only so that one can be negatively compared to the one that gets privileged status. Much of Derrida's work demonstrates how you critically view this logic at work.

IN THEORY

"All ideality and all ideal notions of truth are plagued by a necessity they cannot expel." —Julie Rivkin and Michael Ryan

Deconstruction, in a sense, does a close reading (see Chapter 3) of Western philosophy and shows how pairs of concepts are set up to be separate but are actually, when you just look at them very carefully, interrelated. Going back to the definition that began this chapter, it's the "internal contradiction" within Plato's philosophy that Derrida wanted to call your attention to.

Bye-Bye Binary

Speaking of internal contradictions—remember Claude Lévi-Strauss (see Chapter 16), the structural anthropologist who studied myths? Well, his work was the subject of one of Derrida's first deconstructions. In a 1966 essay, Derrida demonstrated how

Lévi-Strauss's scientific study of myths actually resulted in another myth, rather than a scientific study.

According to Derrida, Lévi-Strauss had relied on a pair of concepts that were supposed to be opposed—a binary opposition. On the one side was a structuralist study that sought to discover the principles underlying the surface features of myths. On the other side were the myths themselves. Which one is privileged? For structuralists, the fundamental principle is privileged over the actual myths themselves, since the principle shows you the stable idea or template behind any number of various myths—like all those Cinderella stories mentioned in Chapter 16.

The problem with this binary opposition is that it depends on the idea that you can stand outside whatever it is you're studying in order to comprehend the whole structure. If you can do that, you get to create something totally new—a view of the myths that couldn't be achieved by the myths themselves. If you're caught up in the myths themselves, all you can do is pick, choose, and rearrange the already existing parts of the basic story structure. Lévi-Strauss sought, like any structuralist, to distance himself and describe the big picture scientifically.

IN THEORY

"Language bears within itself the necessity of its own critique." —Jacques Derrida

But Derrida argued that you can't stand outside whatever it is you want to study, whether it's myth, philosophy, or language. He said you can only pick, choose, and rearrange the already existing parts of your object of study. As for Lévi-Strauss, Derrida not only showed how a structural study became yet another myth, but he explained that Lévi-Strauss himself was aware that this was happening. That is, Lévi-Strauss's *argument* kept insisting that something structural and big picture–like was going on, but the actual *language* of Lévi-Strauss's discussion couldn't be distinguished from the language of myth. At this point you may recall from Chapter 16 how Jonathan Culler argued that a deconstructionist reading of a structuralist essay on poetry actually revealed that poetic language was essential to its prose interpretation. Culler in general refers to the way deconstruction "undermines the philosophy it asserts, or the hierarchical oppositions on which it relies."

RELATIONS

I want to warn against two fairly common but rather misleading definitions of deconstruction. It's not entirely accurate to say that deconstructionist readings simply expose contradictions, ambiguities, gaps, or instances of disorganization and inconsistency. You can tell from our discussion of the New Critics (see Chapter 3), at least, that such features of literature have been commented on for a long time. Deconstructionist readings have instead tried to show what kind of work these contradictions and gaps actually do, such as luring you into uncritically accepting the hierarchy of a binary opposition. Also, you don't want to think that deconstruction boils down to something like "there's no meaning in anything," or "literature means anything you want it to mean." On the contrary, good deconstructionist readings actually consider texts very, very closely, pointing out how the meanings that are discovered or claimed by a text often get caught up in their own nets, so to speak.

In Derrida's literally *post*-structuralist reading of Lévi-Strauss, the point is not simply to condemn structuralism's "mistakes," but to show how any attempt at writing that seeks to downplay the reality of language in order to play up the value of ideas or system is doomed to collapse. But it's a good kind of doom, according to Derrida's own writings, because it shows you how diligently and sincerely people try to maintain binary oppositions, often against their own interests. And it shows that when these binaries are unsettled or destabilized, life and even truth go on, but perhaps more honestly.

Culturally speaking, binary oppositions can also cause a lot of trouble. As we've already seen in several chapters of this book (and we'll see more), binaries such as man/woman, soul/body, white/black, Western/non-Western, or straight/gay establish hierarchies dependent on dominant versus marginal values. And the social consequences of these binaries have always attracted critique. Deconstructionist readings of literature and philosophy, as well as texts in sociology, religion, psychology, and legal studies, have contributed to these critiques by deeply challenging the so-called natural logic they often rely on.

IN THEORY

Deconstruction reveals that "the distinguishing qualities of the marginal entity are in fact the defining qualities of the dominant .... As we consider the matter, it is no longer clear which is dominant and which is marginal." —David H. Richter

Texting from Work

One of the steps to deconstructing a binary opposition is recognizing how any two elements are hardly limited to being linked only to each other in binary opposition, but are actually linked to, well, as groovy as it sounds, to everything.

Think of any word, for example. If you aren't sure what a word means, you look it up in a dictionary, and there's the definition—another word. If you don't know what *that* word means, you look it up, and so on, and so on. Words endlessly relate to other words. And as Saussure explained (see Chapter 11), the meaning of any single word comes from its relation to others.

Derrida's approach to this aspect of language was to call attention to the potentially infinite postponement that occurs with meaning. That is, to really comprehend the fullness of meaning of any single term would take an understanding of the entire network of meaning-making that supports it. Instead, most of us get by through a process of "cutting off" just enough of the connections to give us a confident sense of truth. Meanwhile, though, actual truth (if it were possible to know it) remains suspended in a system where terms both *differ* from one another and *defer* (or put off) their meanings from one term to another. Derrida's famous term for the condition of all language and thought—*différance*—combines these two processes of differing and deferring.

IN THEORY

An important influence on Derrida's work was the German philosopher Friedrich Nietzsche (1844–1900, pronounced *NEET-sheh*). Nietzsche argued that people actually create the truths they mistakenly think exist in the objective world. People do this by acting like artists or poets and creating metaphors. Nietzsche's reason was that when you use a word, like *cow*, you are not naming a thing but a concept. The proof is that the word doesn't name a particular cow from your own experience, but a figure of speech for any number of cows with any number of individual differences. Every concept, for Nietzsche, is defined by linking *different* experiences and events together and referring to them by one word. Then you forget that this process of metaphor making (or lying, as he called it) has taken place, and you live, along with the rest of society, thinking that each concept names one truthful thing.

So does deconstruction mean language prevents us from ever getting to real reality, or that because of *différance* and relational meaning there is no truth? It depends on how you look at it. What some people react to with panic or anger is the sense that something is being taken away from them, philosophically speaking. But Derrida's point is that the traditional Western notion of truth has more to do with Plato's investment in idealism than in truth itself. To complicate matters, language itself tends to support Platonic idealism as well, unless it's read differently. Deconstruction wants you to read differently, and many critics (as well as ordinary readers) have found it very fulfilling to do just that.

Take Roland Barthes, for example. In Chapter 16, we discussed him as a structuralist, intent on reading culture to discover the underlying codes at work in creating "everyday myths." By the late 1960s, and influenced by Derrida's work, Barthes was in post-structuralist mode, investigating how meaning arises in literary works because of their suspension in infinitely interrelated networks, like words defined in dictionaries. A literary work's meaning, in other words, extends well beyond the work itself, and this should change the way you read. Instead of thinking that you're reading a single novel, for example, you should recognize and follow any lines that run through that novel, whether they come from other literary works, or from cultural codes or social texts like laws, traditions, and customs.

Barthes called attention to the difference between the traditional way of reading and his preferred way by using two terms, *work* and *text*. According to Barthes, you talk about reading a *work* when you see the book in your hand as a complete, self-contained entity (Derrida's term was *natural totality*). But for Barthes, you should really recognize that the novel in your hand is part of a *text*. Text, like the word *textile*, emphasizes all the woven aspects of meaning.

Knowing that you are reading a text means knowing that anything you get out of it is intimately related to metaphoric and symbolic connections that you may not even be aware of. There is no closure when you recognize a literary work as a text—its meanings and effects can be traced backward, forward, and sideways. And your own involvement as a reader is an active part of the whole process.

 IN THEORY

"A work conceived, perceived, and received in its integrally symbolic nature is a text." —Roland Barthes

"'Work' and 'text' are thus not two different kinds of object but two different ways of viewing the written word." —Barbara Johnson

In fact, because the text you are reading is part of an unending network, it can be read without the usual constraints of a "work." That is, you are free to recognize various starting and stopping points—does the meaning of *Frankenstein* really start with the novel's first page, or does it begin with images from movies you've already seen? Does *Pride and Prejudice* end with its final page or does it continue into the way you look at other novels or even real-life relationships?

APPLY IT

Consider that novel you're reading as a text and discuss how it forms part of the endless network made up of other texts, images, memories, cultural issues, and even scientific knowledge. You might also consider how, as just one portion of its author's own unending text, the novel is related to other books the author has written.

By the way, Barthes also argued that you're free to recognize that the so-called "author" of the work is only one facet of the text, just like you are, and not its ultimate source. Going so far as to pronounce the "death of the author," Barthes explained that what really got that novel written was not a writer, but writing itself. No matter where you go to pin down the creative presence of an author, Barthes said, you only find intertextuality and already existing images, words, references, and forms. Again, it's like tracking the endless meanings of words through the dictionary. And as we saw in Chapter 5, reader-response criticism looks at this situation and shows you how reading a novel actually becomes an exercise in writing a novel.

Living in the Material Word

Derrida liked to refer to the unending intertextual nature of writing as "writing." Really. But wait, it makes sense. Derrida's point is to use the same word you always use but nudge you toward seeing it differently, which is rather like deconstruction in general. In this case, it means recognizing that writing never really stops. Any written word, sentence, or literary work is not limited or tethered to any single idea. Instead of being the indicator of abstract ideas, writing is material and it does material things. Writing doesn't just *mean*, it *happens*.

American literary critic Barbara Johnson (1947–2009) emphasized the materiality of writing by calling attention to how writing surprises you, whether you're reading or writing. What Johnson meant by this is related to those binaries we've been talking about. When people set out to make a point with a binary opposition, they're hoping you'll just buy into the logic that they claim is tethered to the opposition. They're hoping that you'll simply see through the writing to get to their preferred meaning.

What often happens instead, especially when you "read against the grain," as Johnson put it, is that the writing calls attention to itself and to the various ways it can be radically reinterpreted.

Johnson herself, for example (see Chapter 12), demonstrated how the text of *Frankenstein* doesn't sit still for the traditional binary that forces a choice between being a woman and writing an autobiography. Instead, a careful reading of the novel reveals the text's own struggle with the "monstrousness" of female authorship. Similarly, Gloria Anzaldúa (see Chapter 14) highlighted the textual interweaving of different languages and cultures to show that identity doesn't stop at a single border, but emerges from a network of texts, histories, and cultures.

IN THEORY

Deconstruction involves "a reading strategy that goes beyond apparent intentions or surface meanings, a reading that takes full advantage of writing's capacity to preserve that which cannot, yet, be deciphered." —Barbara Johnson

Derrida's deconstruction of the speech/writing binary was also important to critiques of audism, or the prejudice toward hearing persons (see Chapter 15). As H-Dirksen L. Bauman explained, there is a metaphysical aspect of this prejudice, since the West has long defined personhood with speech: "Historically, we humans have identified ourselves as the speaking animal; if one cannot speak, then he or she is akin to human in body but to animal in mind. In this orientation, we see ourselves as becoming human through speech." Bauman pointed out that the word *language* deconstructs itself—it's based on the word for *tongue* yet is *not* dependent on speech. *Any* sign system can serve as the heart of language, and this point helps invalidate the philosophical basis for the prejudice of audism.

IN THEORY

"The writer writes *in* a language and *in* a logic whose proper system, laws, and life his discourse by definition cannot dominate absolutely. He uses them only by letting himself, after a fashion and up to a point, be governed by the system." —Jacques Derrida

Deconstruction and a focus on the materiality of writing have also been important for Henry Louis Gates Jr.'s theories of Signifyin(g) (see Chapter 14). In fact, Derrida's own writing often Signifies on the subjects he is addressing—which is one reason many people find Derrida's writing rather difficult.

That is, a reading by Derrida, as the Belgian-born critic Paul de Man (1919–1983) explained of deconstruction in general, is like the allegorical retelling of someone else's story. It reveals aspects of the "original" that have been oppressed or silenced in favor of maintaining the original's supposed intentions. The American critic J. Hillis Miller (also discussed in Chapter 5), along with de Man, Geoffrey Hartman, and others, formed part of the "Yale Deconstructionists" in the late 1970s. Miller's work in deconstruction has emphasized very active close readings of texts, often familiar ones such as *Wuthering Heights*, and the importance of remaining "aware of the strangeness of the language of literature." Deconstructionist readings can therefore be rather playful, and like Signifyin(g), they're characterized by an unapologetic manipulation of language, which, really, is always just begging to be manipulated.

Okay, now you can get back to that chocolate cake. Keep in mind, however, that since deconstruction demonstrates how any single term actually relies on and ultimately expresses its suppressed binary other, you may find that a "deconstructed chocolate cake" turns out to have been its own opposite all along. That's right, dessert is now creamed spinach. *Bon appétit!*

The Least You Need to Know

- Deconstruction challenges Western philosophy's downplaying of language.
- Thoughts are always dependent on language.
- Binary oppositions try but fail to assert the primacy of one element over another.
- Understanding a literary work as a text acknowledges that it has no boundaries and its meaning ranges through an endless network of textual relations.
- Writing is not a transparent window to ideas, but a real, physical system of signs that should be handled with a sense of play, curiosity, and even suspicion.

Psychology Brings Linguistics to the Couch

Chapter

18

In This Chapter

- Lacan's cocktail of Freud and Saussure
- The endless matrix of language identity
- Finding your spot in society
- Reconsidering the womb
- Psychology and ideology

Freud is back, and this time he brought Saussure. Or, think of it this way: psycho-analysis has teamed up with structuralism to deconstruct your unconscious.

Either way, it's interesting, adventurous, and very literary.

The work of several (generally) French theorists since the 1950s takes you through some familiar Freudian territory, but with new twists. For one, your unconscious isn't made up of wild and uncontrollable impulses, but language. And while that might sound like a good idea, it means that the language you think you're using is actually using you.

Then there's the fact that the day when you first recognized yourself in a mirror was the best day of your life and the beginning of all your worst days.

On the other hand, literature can still help you out, since it's like a visible uncon-scious, and it gets even more helpful when your thinking is interrupted by feminine writing, which may or may not require a female writer.

Like I said, Freud with some twists.

Post-Structuralist Mind

The French psychiatrist Jacques Lacan (1901–1981, pronounced *lah-KAHN*) brings together several strands of theory and criticism that we've been discussing so far. As we'll see, he started with Freud's views (see Chapter 10), brought in structural linguistics (see Chapter 16), and became part of the first wave of deconstruction (see Chapter 17). Lacan's work has been also adapted by critics in a variety of fields, including feminism (see Chapter 12) and postcolonial critique (see Chapter 21), among others. With all of those cross-references, it won't surprise you that Lacan's name (like Freud's and Marx's) has been adjectivized; you can refer to his approach as Lacanian (pronounced *lah-KANE-ian*).

What's at stake in Lacanian theories is the nature of human identity: how do you become "you," and what happens next?

Mirror, Mirror, Then the Wall

Lacan argued that your sense of identity began with the recognition of yourself, as an infant, in a mirror. There you were, a mass of babyness, with no sense of self, just looking around and seeing things happen—arms and legs moving about, some big faces appearing every once in a while, a breast or bottle when you cried. Anything you heard or saw was just part of a "big blob stage" of existence, since you had no concept of boundaries separating you from everything you encountered. Your needs were either met or not, but you had no way of knowing how anything worked, because you had no sense of "you."

Then, one day, everything changes. You catch sight of yourself in a mirror, and it hits you: "Wait a minute, I'm *something!* Seriously, look at that! There's coherence and unity to all those various moving parts I've seen! I'm *whole!* And if I'm whole, if I'm *me,* then I can make things happen! Let's go!"

Then you wiggle around and realize you can't really go anywhere yet. You don't yet have control over that image you have of yourself. But you'll learn, of course, so you're on your way, baby.

IN THEORY

"The infant in front of the mirror … unable as yet to walk, or even to stand up, and held tightly as he is by some support, human or artificial … he nevertheless overcomes, in a flutter of jubilant activity, the obstructions of his support and, fixing his attitude in a slightly leaning-forward position, in order to hold it in his gaze, brings back an instantaneous aspect of the image." —Jacques Lacan

Yes, that first recognition sure was a jubilant moment while it lasted, and, according to Lacan, that moment never leaves you. Your psyche always maintains, as part of your sense of self, that image of a unified "you." Lacan called it your "Ideal-I." And like any ideal, it leads to some problems in real life.

Let's start with the fact that when you looked at the mirror and thought, "That's me!," you were looking at an image that, by definition, wasn't you. The image was separate from you; it was, literally, over there. Lacan explained that your first attempt at understanding the relationship between you and the world (or, as he put it, "the organism and its reality") actually relies on a fictional "you" that is outside of you. How else could you see it as you, in its wholeness, unless it was outside of you?

By the way, it's at this point that Lacan can assure you that the whole mirror episode does not have to involve an actual mirror. That is, what's important in forming this image of yourself is that you *have* an image in mind, not where it came from. For example, your mirror-image "aha! moment" (the term is shared by Lacan and Oprah, among others) might have come from realizing that one of those big faces you've seen was looking at "you." One way or another, you developed a sense of self out of a reflection. You saw yourself as "out there," as something that others could see. Lacan referred to this aspect of your psyche as the imaginary order because it's based on this all-important image.

APPLY IT

We've already seen how the concept of the double runs throughout *Frankenstein* (see Chapters 3, 10, and 13). For a Lacanian reading, you might consider how both Victor and the creature seem to have similar mirror-stage moments. Specifically, because each character reflects on the other for identity, their reactions shift quickly from "Yay, I'm me!" to "Oh no, I'm me!" They both want to be individuals, but neither can accept how they must be defined by outside forces.

Lacan explained that your fictional Ideal-I, which is the basis of your ego, or self, is the result of a misrecognition. You inevitably identified with a fiction that was not you but that you took to be you—your image in a mirror or in the eyes of others. This means, among other things, that when you vowed to get control over that image you first saw, you bought into a lifelong struggle to get control over something that's really an *aesthetic* creation. You became a whole you, Lacanian theory states, because of that "armor of an alienating identity" which will always be with you.

And that's even before you run up against language.

Subjects of Significance

According to Lacan, you soon discover that your activity in the world isn't limited to just admiring your own paradoxical reflection. This happens when you realize you're involved in a system of language: you have to ask for things by using names, you have to respond to cues from other people using language skills, and you have to think in terms of, well, terms.

And remember, language was around before you were. For Lacan (and for Derrida as well; see Chapter 17), this is big. It means that you are born into a social world of signification, so the very building blocks of your identity—your subjectivity—come from a social system of meaning-making that you're not in control of. Lacan called this subjectivity your "Social I" and said it emerges from that aspect of human experience called the symbolic order. It isn't symbolic like big-time literary symbols exactly (see Chapters 2 and 8), but symbolic in the general sense that everything you perceive now has to go through the symbolic system of language—everything seems to stand for something else.

So it's no longer just a world of big faces, breasts, and bottles anymore, baby. Instead of experiencing images or impressions, you're now involved in a comprehensive system of language and social exchange. When you look at a face, for example, it's accompanied, whether you like it or not, with significance; it's literally part of the sign system that forms all of your thoughts. You may recall that the Romantic poets as well as Nietzsche argued for a similar connection between perception and language (see Chapters 8 and 17).

And then when you look for your own image, you can no longer find it in a single mirror or point of view. In the symbolic order, you see your "self" reflected back from the entire system. It's like a mosaic image made up of all the things that contribute to making you "you"—everything from proper names and family relationships to the clothes you wear and the chairs you sit in. Everything operates, as Claude Lévi-Strauss explained (see Chapter 16), as a big system of signification, and Lacan emphasized that it's this external system that your ego has to deal with, not just the inner rage of the id.

Getting Saussure Stuck in Your Head

So arguing that an external system of signification creates your internal self leads Lacan to famously state that your unconscious is "structured like a language." As we saw in Chapter 10, Freud argued that your unconscious was a seething field of primal urges and psychic traumas. Lacan always insisted that he wasn't opposing Freud's theories, but actually getting back to their original insights. So when it came to the unconscious, Lacan showed how Freud's own analysis highlighted the linguistic nature of the unconscious.

IN THEORY

"The unconscious is neither primordial nor instinctual; what it knows about the elementary is no more than the elements of the signifier." —Jacques Lacan

For example, Lacan called attention to all the literary examples in Freud's writing about the unconscious—all the stories, jokes, and even rebuses. (Remember the rebuses? More on them in a minute.) The point was to emphasize that the unconscious was not a hidden force, but a visible field or structure. At the heart of your ego is not a special place of balance, where the id and superego threaten your sense of self. For Lacan, your sense of self is inherently imaginary—it's based on that image of your Ideal-I. But you have to live most of your life trying to satisfy the demands of that Ideal-I with the resources of the Social-I. And those resources are all part of a big signifying system.

So Lacan liked to investigate how people use language and how language uses people. He said that psychoanalysts and literary critics need to get used to dealing with all the minute details of texts and communication, even and especially the so-called "marginal" matters of puns, jokes, and figurative language. If it is structured like a language, the best way to understand the unconscious is to watch it at work in the world. In praising Freud's own literary-critical approach, Lacan once said that "to interpret the unconscious as Freud did, one would have to be as he was, an encyclopedia of the arts and muses."

In fact, when you see language as something that uses you, reflects your unconscious, and determines your very identity, you can no longer treat language as a passive tool for your own purposes. For example, you can't "just write down what you're thinking," because each of the important concepts in that phrase—*write*, *you*, and *thinking*—all overlap. This is why Lacan's writing itself, like Derrida's, can seem so difficult to read. Typically, neither writer is simply explaining a point, but performing an example of a point. It's rather like poetry—you can reduce a poem to a summary, but you're well aware that the real meaning of the poem is not contained in the paraphrase but in the experience of the poem itself (see Chapter 3). Lacan, as well as the feminist critics we'll discuss at the end of this chapter, are actively trying to provoke a response from the reader that acknowledges the restless materiality of any text, even their own.

Chain Letters

Back to Saussure for a moment. Remember how he argued that the sign is made up of a signifier and a signified? The signified, according to Saussure, is supposed to be the concept that always accompanies the sound-image of the signifier (see Chapter 11). The two always go together, like the two sides of a sheet of paper, to form a sign such as a word or a gesture.

The problem, Lacan argued, is that the signified is an illusion. For Lacan, the so-called "concept" part of a sign is no more than another sound-image, another signifier. It's like he's taking that dictionary-definition black-hole example very seriously—all a signifier does is point to another signifier and says, "That's what I mean." Then that signifier points to another one who says the same thing, and so on. In other words, for Lacan, your mind just creates the concept of *concept* so that you'll feel you're getting somewhere when you think.

IN THEORY

"No signification can be sustained other than by reference to another signification. … The signifier, by its very nature, always anticipates meaning by unfolding its dimension before it." —Jacques Lacan

In fact, part of Lacan's proof was Freud's rebus analysis (see Chapter 10). For Freud, the various little pictures of a rebus puzzle have to be interpreted with regard to what they bring to the whole rebus sentence. Doing this, Lacan explained, means looking at the pictures only as signifiers. The pictures actually operate like letters, without unchanging concepts behind them. The only meaning letters and rebus pictures have is absorbed into the meaning of the whole sentence. And, of course, the same letter or picture may be interpreted totally differently in a different sentence.

Now take all of that and drop it into the idea that your unconscious is structured like a language. Go ahead, I'll wait.

Lacan argued that the signifying chain formed by always jumping from one signifier to another without actually landing on a signified was more evidence of your existence in the symbolic order. The idea of a signified is like your obsession with the Ideal-I; it doesn't exist, and what takes its place and covers up for its absence is an endless series of connections. Psychologically, this process involves a deep-seated sense of lack—you're missing the unity you feel that you must have once had. This leads to a perpetual desire to keep the signifying chain going, since doing so gives you the illusion that you're getting closer to that unity.

Of course, the endless connections have meaning and give you subjectivity, but like the meaning of a rebus or a sentence, the meaning of any single element is a product of the system it's a part of. Lacan argued that your subjectivity arises in the same way. Like a letter or a rebus picture, your psyche is formed by becoming part of an already existing linguistic structure.

Taking Your Place

Lacan argued that as you become part of this system you inhabit a subject position. And inhabiting a subject position, according to one of Lacan's examples, is as natural as walking into a restroom.

Lacan explained that when you see two identical restroom doors, one marked "ladies" and the other marked "gentlemen," you're faced with two signifiers without different signifieds. That is, the doors are identical and the rooms are (for the sake of Lacan's illustration) the same as well, since they both serve the same purpose. The only difference is the little sign on each door. When you walk through one of the doors you literally inhabit the signifier and then you assume the role of the signified. Why is a ladies' room a ladies' room? Because it calls ladies to it, not because it's functionally different from a men's room. All of sociolinguistic organization is like that, for Lacan. As you see signs and follow conventions, you occupy your various subject positions.

Now if you think about what other people see when they watch you walking into a restroom (hey, it's Lacan's illustration; I'm just going with it), you can start to see where this leads. To the observer, you complete the signifier-signified pairing and *become the sign* for "lady" or "gentleman." Even more importantly, you see *yourself* this way as well. Remember, for Lacan, your desire to see yourself as a coherent whole can only work through the sign systems you inhabit. Language, quite literally, pushes you around. Or, put another way, you willingly follow language around.

For a literary example, Lacan pointed to Edgar Allan Poe's 1844 short story, "The Purloined Letter." The story involves blackmail, carried out by a government minister who has purloined (stolen) a letter that proves the Queen's infidelity. As long as the letter is in the minister's possession—and the Queen knows he has it—he has power over her. The story's hero, Dupin (an early model for Sherlock Holmes), realizes what the police do not, which is that the minister has cleverly hidden the letter in plain sight so that it would seem perfectly normal, and therefore invisible, to someone looking for a hidden secret. Dupin then manages to steal the letter back and return power to the Queen.

Lacan explained that the story enacts the importance of "the letter," or the signifying system, in determining what people do and what subject positions they occupy. Lacan called it symbolic determination. As the letter moves around, that is, it reconfigures the power structure, first putting the Queen at a disadvantage, then returning her to dominance. It also leads everyone to act the way they do. In fact, it doesn't even matter if a character knows exactly what's in the letter—the characters all know what it *does*. They know it has the real power to move them around in their actions and social positions.

The detective, in fact, acts like a Lacanian literary critic in several ways. For one, he recognizes that the hiding place of the secret is right under everyone's noses, just as the materiality of language reveals the supposedly hidden unconscious. He also makes a point of reasoning from observed facts to interior causes, rather than the other way around. Dupin even suggests that by shaping his own expression to match someone else's face, he can determine what that person is thinking. For Lacan, this illustrates the way a person's interiority (the signified) is provoked by visible actions (the signifier). Like people lining up for the two restrooms, a signified is discovered, since it is created, by the movement of the signifier.

APPLY IT

In movies and fiction, a MacGuffin is anything serving as a central object of desire. It doesn't really matter what it is, as long as characters want it. A MacGuffin operates like Poe's purloined letter by making people do things and determining their characters. The most famous example of a MacGuffin is probably the Maltese Falcon in the movie by that name, but you can find MacGuffins in many works. The next time you read a novel or watch a movie, see if you can identify the central object of desire. How does it drive both desire and action? What does it make the characters do? And what does it make *you* do? Does it position you to favor a particular character or plot ending?

Baby Talk (Or, a Womb with a View)

For Lacan, anything that happened before language and before the imaginary order is, by definition, not accessible to you in any direct way. Lacan calls this unreachable dimension of existence the "real," although it isn't the same as reality. Instead, Lacan's real mysteriously stands as everything that's forever left out of subjectivity. There is simply no way of reaching it, but its effects can be detected in that nagging sense, mentioned previously, that you're missing something.

Some feminist critics, while not all specifically addressing Lacan's "difficult third term" of the real, have explored how subjectivity is interrupted and challenged by the body's prelinguistic history. For these critics, Lacan's map of the psyche reveals important issues of gender.

Like Freud, Lacan argued that language marks the end of your unity with your mother and the beginning of your immersion into a masculine field of discourse. That is, your mirror stage provoked both a sense of yourself and a sense of the other that you relied on—the image of a mother that served, in a sense, as the first mirror you needed to validate your own image.

But this imaginary order, which associates prelinguistic images with the maternal and with the body, gets superseded by the symbolic order, which pulls you away from direct contact and into that always mediated system of language. Lacan called this transition the result of the "father's 'no,'" which says "no" both to union with the mother (the incest taboo) and to living only in the imaginary order.

Lacan, again like Freud, recognized that psychosexual development was more a matter of culture than biology (see Chapters 10, 12, and 13). Nevertheless, the emphasis, even metaphorical, on language as masculinist has led several critics (sometimes referred to as the post-structuralist "French feminists") to elaborate on Lacanian theories in ways that shed new light on the intersections of sexuality, culture, biology, and language.

For example, the psychoanalyst and philosopher Luce Irigaray has revisited Plato's allegory of the cave (see Chapter 7) in order to highlight its implicit privileging of masculinist logic. In her reading, Irigaray sees the cave allegory as based on birth imagery. Plato dramatizes a prisoner being led away from the cave and toward truth, while Irigaray sees a child being forcibly taken from the womb and thrown into the outside world. Irigaray showed how the specific language of Plato's story does not depict a natural process of moving from shadows to light, but a violent interruption of life in the womb, featuring male "obstetricians" employing technological tools. The goal of this birth/rescue, for Irigaray, is to prohibit the imagistic, prelingual, and female-directed experience of the cave and establish a single reliance on instrumental male knowledge. In this way, Plato's allegory reflects traditional Western philosophy in general, and that the conditions for coming-to-knowledge require the abandonment of the cave and its experiences.

Irigaray argued, however, that true philosophers know they can never completely escape and ignore the "uterine dwelling." Rather than mere silence and illusion, there is a reality to the experiences of the cave and the womb, and these experiences, as Lacan had written of the Ideal-I, follow you throughout life. Plato's story, according to Irigaray, becomes a way to fake an exit and establish an exterior truth based on light and sight that only serves to demonize your earliest and most profound aspects of knowledge—particularly those experiences of touch, imagination, and symbiosis.

Another French feminist, Hélène Cixous (pronounced *seek-SOO*), who is also a professor of English literature, has advocated for what she calls feminine writing, a type of writing that expresses what the Western tradition has repressed. You might recall from Chapter 12 that Virginia Woolf also explored the possibility of moving beyond male sentences. For Cixous, feminine writing does not depend on mastery, or the male ideal of making a clear distinction between subject and object. Like Irigaray, Cixous emphasized the value of human experience before the symbolic order transforms and replaces images with systematic knowledge. This experience, Cixous explained, is not without signification—signification doesn't have to wait for the symbolic order—but it's a different kind of signification. Following the logic of feminine writing leads you to creatively reconfigure and rewrite the language of the symbolic order you generally find yourself in.

IN THEORY

"In the beginning, I adored. What I adored was human. Not persons; not totalities, not defined and named beings. But signs. Flashes of being that glanced off me, kindling me. Lightning-like bursts that came to me: Look! I blazed up. … I *read* it: the face signified." —Hélène Cixous

In contrast to Irigaray, Cixous emphasized that men as well as women can read and compose feminine writing (for her, James Joyce was one case in point). Writing, for Cixous as for Derrida (see Chapter 17), is much more than words on the page. Writing initiates a whole network of intertextuality, and feminine writing seeks to include in that network all of the missing and suppressed elements, especially when these elements contradict, interrupt, and otherwise cause traditional signification to reveal its incompleteness.

Literary critic and psychoanalyst Julia Kristeva (pronounced *kriss-TAY-va*) has also been influential in arguing that what goes on before the mirror stage is an integral part of subjectivity. Kristeva explained that your prelinguistic sense of flow and body rhythms—the life functions associated with the womb and early infancy—stay with you throughout your involvement in the symbolic order. These natal rhythms and flows find ways to emerge and upset the symbolic order, particularly in poetic language. The rhythm of the heart or the lungs, according to Kristeva, finds expression in poetry, song, and any feature of prose that calls attention to the urge for your body to do something with language other than just use it to "rationally signify." In this regard, all kinds of prelinguistic elements, such as baby babbling, cooing, and even rocking, have the potential, according to Kristeva, of becoming literally revolutionary in their overturning of poetic and even political forms.

Who's Pulling the Strings?

So how can these complicated psychological, literary, and philosophical issues relate to politics? Well, Kristeva emphasized Lacan's basic point that all of the intertextuality contributing to the symbolic order inevitably comes from social interactions. In that case, according to Kristeva, intertextuality is always ideological—it always reflects the dominant interests in society. A challenge to the symbolic order with feminine writing or prelinguistic eruptions is therefore a challenge to the dominant social order.

RELATIONS

Frantz Fanon (1925–1961), a French Algerian psychiatrist, attended Lacan's lectures while in medical school. As we'll see in Chapter 21, Fanon brought an enormously influential psychoanalytic dimension to theories of colonization and to political struggles for colonial independence.

Slavoj Žižek (pronounced *SLAH-voy ZHEE-zhek*) has also elaborated on the connection between Lacanian theory and ideology. Following Kristeva as well as the French Marxist critic Louis Althusser (1918–1990, pronounced *ALL-too-ser*), Žižek has explored how politically manipulative the symbolic order is. Consider that if (A) the symbolic order is the primary context for your placement into subject positions, and (B) the symbolic order is ideological and reflects society's dominant interests, then (C) your subject position as well as your psyche are dictated by dominant socioeconomic interests.

Althusser has argued that ideology "calls" you and you willingly answer in order to feel that you belong and have a recognizable identity in society. Althusser called this process interpellation. Žižek has emphasized the psychological power of interpellation by explaining that when ideology calls you, rather like the signs on Lacan's restroom doors, your response is not the result of your identity, but its cause.

The Least You Need to Know

- The development of your psyche begins with a misrecognition of yourself as a reflection of wholeness.
- Your unconscious is structured like a linguistic system.
- Signifiers only lead to other signifiers; the creation of a signified is an illusion that strives to support your Ideal-I.
- Prelinguistic signification can serve as an alternative and a challenge to traditional rational discourse.
- The symbolic order has political interests in your subjectivity.

In the World and Of the World

Part

6

In these chapters, we'll discuss provocative global approaches to important issues that affect all of us. You'll see how literary theory and criticism, which has raised social issues since Plato's time, has consistently been part of popular culture, history, colonialism, and, more recently, environmental issues.

Cultural Studies Tries to Ruin a Good Time

In This Chapter

- Cultural studies expands your reading list
- Cultural standard-bearers
- The Enlightenment contradiction
- Working the cultural system
- The postmodern kaleidoscope

Reading literature is a very cultured thing to do, wouldn't you say? I mean, you could be spending all your time with video games, social media, or reality television.

Oh, I see ….

Well, there's a set of theories and critical approaches that not only addresses reading literature but all those other things you do as well; it's called cultural studies. The first thing to know about cultural studies is that there are two ways of looking at culture. There's culture as I've used it just above—"a very cultured thing to do"— which suggests that culture is made up of "the best" of what society has to offer. As the word suggests, this kind of culture is something that shows cultivation, or careful tending. Then there's culture in terms of *anything* distinctive that a society has to offer. That is, culture describes all those traditions, beliefs, rituals, and shared activities that identify a civilization, nation, or community.

The second thing to keep in mind is that these two definitions do an awful lot of mixing, and they always have. The idea of a "high culture" seems to demand evaluation, discrimination, and, at times, even elitism and resistance to change. And the view of culture as the result of everyday social activities seems to emerge merely by observing any group of people. But just try to keep evaluation out of observation.

People have very strong and sincere opinions about what is good for society and what isn't. With this in mind, cultural studies looks at all products of human society as relevant for debate.

So for your next literary discussion, bring along any book you like. Classic novels, short stories, and poetry are perfectly fine, but so are romance novels, biographies, travel books, cookbooks, comic books, crossword puzzle books, self-help manuals, and that quick-start guide for your new printer. But why stop there? How about those video games, social media, and reality television shows? Sure, no problem. Fashion, music, and architecture? Bring 'em on. Grocery stores, driving habits, and foam packing peanuts? Go for it. Cultural studies will stimulate your thinking about these and any other features of everyday life.

High Fives for High Culture

We'll start, however, with a brief look at three early critics who generally stood by the high-culture idea and saw literature as a defense against the perils of modern society and its deteriorating cultural standards.

Matthew Arnold (1822–1888) was an influential poet and critic of the Victorian era. The title of his 1869 book, *Culture and Anarchy*, gives you a hint about which two forces he saw competing for social dominance. Literature, and poetry in particular, was for Arnold a necessary civilizing force in the modern world. In fact, one of Arnold's most quoted phrases defines literary criticism as the instinct prompting you to know "the best that has been thought and said in the world." Arnold was also responsible for the term *sweetness and light*, which for him did not just mean all things happy and nice, but art that offered pleasure as well as the light of instruction, like enlightenment. In this way, Arnold recalls the classical goal that literature should "delight and instruct" (see Chapters 6 and 8 for this, and Chapter 1 for more on Arnold's views of criticism).

The twentieth-century English critic F. R. Leavis (1895–1978) also wanted to keep everyone on track. Leavis—who along with his wife, Queenie, founded the journal *Scrutiny*—was cheerfully culturally conservative and argued for the superior value of older forms of literature. In his 1948 book, *The Great Tradition*, Leavis zeroed in on the four essential English novelists you should read first—Jane Austen, George Eliot, Henry James, and Joseph Conrad—explaining that these novelists are great because they "not only change the possibilities of the art for practitioners and readers," but they also exhibit an "awareness of the possibilities of life"—an awareness that ordinary writers don't have but that society needs. Leavis and his followers (sometimes called Leavisites) have been called messianic because of their fervent arguments for the salvation that literature could bring to a society struggling against war, mechanization, commercialism, and the diminishing impact of religion.

IN THEORY

"Leavisites fiercely insisted that culture was not simply a leisure activity; reading 'the great tradition' was, rather, a means of forming mature individuals with a concrete and balanced sense of 'life.' And the main threat to this sense of life came from the pleasure offered by so-called 'mass culture.'" —Simon During

Then there's T. S. Eliot (1888–1965). Eliot, of course, is the remarkable American British poet, playwright, editor, and critic without whom there would be no *Cats*, the musical (see Chapter 3 for more on Eliot as a critic). In one of his most widely read essays, "Tradition and the Individual Talent," Eliot argued that literary innovation has its place and value, but only in the context of the existing tradition. Eliot saw tradition, however, not as a static set of preferred texts, but a constantly changing field.

IN THEORY

"No poet, no artist of any art, has his complete meaning alone. His significance, his appreciation is the appreciation of his relation among the dead poets and artists. … What happens when a new work of art is created is something that happens simultaneously to all the works of art that preceded it. … The whole existing order must be, if ever so slightly, altered." —T. S. Eliot

Eliot argued, in fact, that the past is affected by the present just as much as the present is affected by the past. So while your judgment of new work is based on your appreciation of older work, you also look back and see Shakespeare, for example, only through the glasses of what you take to be good literature now. Logically, this means the appearance of new work does not just add more to culture, but it changes your view of an entire tradition. New art changes all art.

The Culture Industry

The "Frankfurt school" is the name given to an approach to cultural studies associated with the Institute for Social Theory, founded in 1923, at the University of

Frankfurt, Germany. Frankfurt school critics were (and still are) interested in pursuing Marxist theories (see Chapter 9), but instead of narrowly focusing on economic issues, these critics explore how culture, as part of society's superstructure, operates.

One big issue at stake, as we saw in Chapter 9's discussion, is reification, or the habit of reducing a whole process of social connections into one object or product that you feel you can take for granted as an independent entity. Frankfurt school critics, and cultural critics in general, tend to see culture as a form of mass deception because of the way culture makes it so easy for you to look at the world and see products instead of processes. High culture, low culture, elite culture, popular culture—they all become fair game for social analysis as critics look for ways to raise your awareness of culture's deep effects on your life.

Enlighten Me—No, Don't

Two of the most important of the early Frankfurt school critics were Theodor W. Adorno (1903–1969) and Max Horkheimer (1895–1973). Their book, *Dialectic of Enlightenment* (1944), is not actually subtitled "And Get Off My Lawn," but it isn't completely unfair to see them as folks from an earlier generation ranting against the new pop-cultural onslaught of Mickey Mouse, Mickey Rooney, and jazz. On the other hand, it's more than fair to recognize the seriousness of such a rant, then and now.

In the 1930s Horkheimer and Adorno, along with many of their colleagues, had to flee Germany in the face of Nazi oppression. Horkheimer and Adorno argued that events in the Western world were part of a bigger pattern having to do with modernity and the promise of progress.

The Enlightenment, since the 1600s, has described the idea that reason and science would lead humanity away from nature, myth, and superstition and toward the rational liberation of the human mind. Scientific progress certainly followed the age of Enlightenment, but, according to many other observers, so did terrible violence and an actual dehumanization of the modern world.

APPLY IT

You may also be interested in a more recent—and widely read—discussion of the dangers of popular culture. Neil Postman's *Amusing Ourselves to Death*, originally published in 1985, takes a critical look at television.

Horkheimer and Adorno described what they called the "dialectic of enlightenment," which, like all processes of dialectic (see Chapter 9), involves an inversion of terms. That is, while science and rational institutions (like modern governments) were supposed to liberate people from primitive views of nature and rule by superstition, the most visible result of such "progress" seemed to be two world wars and an increasing dehumanization of everyday life through an "administered society." According to Horkheimer and Adorno, enlightenment rationality had replaced myth, only to become the new "rational myth" by which people's lives were organized. In their view, "Enlightenment behaves toward things as a dictator toward men."

Cultural studies, therefore, should be based on critical theory (see Chapter 1) as a way of critically investigating all those aspects of modern society that had become mythologized or naturalized but were in fact the result of complex sociopolitical forces. Cultural practices, in other words, had become so reified that their potential for harming people typically went unnoticed. Horkheimer and Adorno compared the situation to a kind of "idiotic drunkenness" in which we all stumble through seemingly innocent activities, leaving disaster in our wake.

Critics of the Frankfurt school were very suspicious, therefore, of culture that seemed neutral or free of sociopolitical importance, particularly popular entertainment. Rather than being a free or neutral escape from modernity's trap, popular entertainment was viewed as just the opposite, a hypnotic force for ensuring the smooth functioning of capitalist society. Popular culture wasn't an alternative to the industrialized world; it was, as Horkheimer and Adorno titled one of their essays, "The Culture Industry: Enlightenment as Mass Deception."

IN THEORY

"Pleasure always means not to think about anything, to forget suffering even where it is shown. Basically it is helplessness. It is flight; not, as it is asserted, flight from a wretched reality, but from the last remaining thought of resistance. The liberation which amusement promises is freedom from thought." —Max Horkheimer and Theodor W. Adorno

Or, as Horkheimer and Adorno bluntly explained, "amusement under late capitalism is the prolongation of work," and "Donald Duck in the cartoons and the unfortunate in real life get their thrashing so that the audience can learn to take their own punishment."

New Forms for New Minds

Adorno, for his part, pointed to newly emerging art forms as a way of avoiding the pop culture trap. If popular forms of art, such as traditional narratives, insidiously supported Enlightenment rationalism, then a real alternative could be found in avant-garde art (see Chapter 9 for the debate between Brecht and Lukács on this topic). Adorno argued that popular art—by design and by definition—had to reflect dominant cultural values. Modernist art, on the other hand, was more distanced and therefore more critical of society.

For example, stream of consciousness narratives allowed the attentive reader (or professional critic) an opportunity to observe details of the modern individual's isolated inner life. Similarly, fragmented and discontinuous stories were reflections of the disconnected and troubled relationship between real people and the surface appearance of modern society.

Adorno's attention to formal developments in art reflect the principle behind the Russian formalists' theory of defamiliarization (see Chapter 4). Adorno was opposed to seeing form as simply a container for content and explored how an artist's methods were intimately related to that artist's message. You can't, that is, just compose any poem or write any novel, as if those forms were empty containers waiting to be filled with your new ideas. For Adorno, many older forms had been ruined by the legacy of modern society—traditional forms of poetry or narrative, for example, had been used to support so much violence in the twentieth century that it was impossible to use them without your own "content" becoming contaminated. The only way for culture to move forward was to create new forms or radically revise the older forms.

In music, for example (and that would be classical music, of course; no Frank Sinatra for Adorno), Adorno championed the work of Arnold Schoenberg (1874–1951). Schoenberg's atonal musical compositions do not follow the traditional Western reliance on central tones and regular structures. Since so much music based on these forms had been commercialized in movies and advertising, Adorno saw any use of the forms as merely contributing to the modern social brainwashing. Avant-garde forms of atonal music, with their fragments and disruptions, served as both a symptom of and a rebellion against the culture industry. Part rational composition and part unconscious cry for help, Schoenberg's work became for Adorno one example of culture struggling to regain a human connection.

Making Copies

Cultural critique has also been pursued specifically in terms of technological change. For instance, the German critic and philosopher Walter Benjamin (1892–1940, pronounced *benya-MEEN*), who was associated with the Frankfurt school (but not a faculty member at the Institute) had some fascinating things to say about photography and cinema in the 1930s that will still make your head spin, in a good way.

For one, Benjamin pointed out that art is different in the "age of mechanical reproduction." In the old days, a painting was a painting. It was a unique object, and if you wanted to see it, you had to go to it. But with the technological development of commercially available photos, posters, and reproductions of paintings, the art comes to you. You can admire a picture of the *Mona Lisa*, for example, without the ritual, as Benjamin put it, of trekking to the so-called original. The result was a shift in how people can appreciate art. The authenticity and history of an original work, what Benjamin called the work's aura, "withered" and became less important in the modern world.

Yet this withering of the aura, for Benjamin, was a good thing because it signaled a democratizing shift in society. As he put it, "mechanical reproduction emancipates the work of art from its parasitical dependence on ritual." Because any mechanically reproduced art, including recorded music, comes to you as part of your own situation, you are free to do what you want with the newly "reactivated" works. In addition, some works of art such as photographs and movies are created without any sense of the original at all. Watching a Charlie Chaplin movie, for Benjamin, was more democratic than viewing a painting by Picasso.

IN THEORY

"Our taverns and our metropolitan streets, our offices and furnished rooms, our railroad stations and our factories appeared to have us locked up hopelessly. Then came the film and burst this prison-world asunder by the dynamite of the tenth of a second, so that now, in the midst of its far-flung ruins and debris, we calmly and adventurously go traveling." —Walter Benjamin

In fact, photography and movies interested Benjamin in particular because of the way their *form*, not simply their content, revolutionized your perceptions. For example, close-ups and slow-motion shots allow you to see what had previously escaped your notice, especially in reified everyday situations such as a hand reaching for a spoon:

"A different nature opens itself to the camera than opens to the naked eye—if only because an unconsciously penetrated space is substituted for a space consciously explored by man." Benjamin linked the political implications with Freudian ones (see Chapter 10) by explaining that "the camera introduces us to unconscious optics, as does psychoanalysis to unconscious impulses."

Material Feelings

One of the most important single figures in the development of cultural studies was the British critic Raymond Williams (1921–1988). Williams did it all: fought in World War II, taught at Oxford and Cambridge, wrote columns and reviews for newspapers on topics ranging from history to television, and published several books that have served as the basis for cultural studies, including *Culture and Society* (1958) and *The Long Revolution* (1961).

Following the work of Italian theorist Antonio Gramsci (1891–1937, pronounced *GRAM-shee*), Williams emphasized the importance of hegemony in social organization. As Williams described it, the Marxist term *hegemony* is defined by the entire "lived system of meanings and values," which "constitutes a sense of reality for most people in society." This entire sense of reality is what Williams considered the proper object of cultural studies.

IN THEORY

Cultural studies as a field is also significantly associated with the development of the "Birmingham school." From 1964 to 2002, the Centre for Contemporary Cultural Studies at Birmingham University in England was led by such influential critics as Richard Hoggart (its founding director) and Stuart Hall.

For example, in his 1961 essay, "Advertising: The Magic System," Williams illustrated his approach by arguing that the point of advertising is not simply to sell a product, but to sell signs of identity as well, particularly signs of gender and class identity. Calling attention to what you probably know already, Williams argued that products like beer and washing machines are strategically associated with lifestyles. What made Williams's approach so productive was his insistence that these associations could and should be interpreted as part of social communication.

For Williams, in other words, a critique of advertising could demystify the contradiction between a product appearing only as a product while actually participating in a system of social, cultural, and even psychological validation.

IN THEORY

The Frankfurt school weighed in on advertising, too: "The most intimate reactions of human beings have been so thoroughly reified that the idea of anything specific to themselves now persists only as an utterly abstract notion: personality scarcely signifies anything more than shining white teeth and freedom from body odor and emotions. The triumph of advertising in the culture industry is that consumers feel compelled to buy and use its products even though they can see through them." —Max Horkheimer and Theodor W. Adorno

But wait, there's more: see Chapter 16 for Roland Barthes's approach to advertising and commodity culture as part of his structuralist analysis of culture.

And that system you inhabit, according to Williams, is not a strictly one-dimensional affair. That is, despite the seeming stubbornness of advertising and other cultural messages, you don't simply deal with one overbearing ideological message. Instead, you're faced with at least three overlapping aspects of ideology—the dominant, residual, and emerging aspects. The dominant and central aspects of culture may be the most evident and manipulative, but they are accompanied by residual ideologies from previous eras as well as emergent ideological features of a culture yet to fully develop. Social hegemony, therefore, is not set in stone but vulnerable to change and reinterpretation, which is exactly what many cultural critics try to point out as well as exploit.

Freaky Styley

Dick Hebdige (pronounced *HEB-didge*), one of the Birmingham school critics, explored how people make use of popular style in order to make their way and make their mark through the layers of social hegemony. Hebdige's 1979 book, *Subculture: The Meaning of Style,* discussed the various ways that nondominant groups, or subcultures, are formed by people reappropriating the signs of culture. If cultural identities are largely based on the sign system of products and consumerism, then reorganizing and reinterpreting those products with new meanings is a form of emergent culture and resistance to the dominant system.

Drawing examples from British punk culture, Jean Genet's scandalous homosexuality, and David Bowie's androgyny, Hebdige surveyed how young people in the late twentieth century created new "social texts" and therefore new identities by redefining ordinary objects, as well as images from magazines, movies, and television, and endowing them with style.

"The most mundane objects—a safety pin, a pointed shoe, a motor cycle," according to Hebdige, "take on a symbolic dimension, becoming a form of stigmata, tokens of a self-imposed exile." Objects integrated into a new style system both warn other people away and "become signs of forbidden identity, sources of value." Style becomes an example of defamiliarizing the dominant culture, of taking what is already there and re-presenting it in new ways. This cultural strategy recalls much of what we have discussed in Chapter 13 regarding gender identity, as well as the Russian formalists' general emphasis on defamiliarization (see Chapter 4).

Behind this approach to social power and cultural change is the work of Michel Foucault (see Chapters 13 and 15), who argued that power is not simply a force that someone wields over someone else, but a system of discourse that we all inhabit. According to Foucault, social change occurs not by directly "fighting the power," but by rearticulating the dominant discourse that you are currently subject to. Hebdige's discussion of style illustrated just this kind of critical rereading of dominant culture's component parts.

Who Are Your References?

The rise of cultural studies as a field has radically changed the way people think of literary studies. What does that have to do with you? Well, the result for most people has been a shift in what the French sociologist Pierre Bourdieu (1930–2002) called cultural capital. Cultural capital, according to Bourdieu, is one aspect of how you acquire or keep your social status. There's money and birth, of course, but society also values your cultural repertoire, or the range of cultural references you can recognize.

While it may have been important in earlier periods to have read all the books in the "Great Tradition" or understand references to so-called elite culture, the last few decades has seen a swing toward a broader (and many people say lower) range of bankable references. Expectations for job interviews or college applications, for example, change over time, and it may be more valuable for an applicant to catch a reference to a television show or an online game than to quote from W. H. Auden. Of course, as you may expect, when it comes to any kind of capital, including cultural capital, "the more, the better" usually works in your favor, too.

At the height of what were called the "culture wars" in the 1980s and '90s, when universities were struggling to figure out which way they would go with all these changes—study Shakespeare or Madonna? Milton or *Buffy the Vampire Slayer?*—the critic Harold Bloom famously foretold that "what are now called 'Departments of

English' will be renamed departments of 'Cultural Studies' where Batman comics, Mormon theme parks, television, movies, and rock will replace Chaucer, Shakespeare, Milton, Wordsworth and Wallace Stevens." Bloom added, darkly, that "this development hardly need be deplored; only a few handfuls of students now enter Yale with an authentic passion for reading. You cannot teach ... such love. How can you teach solitude?" Reading literature, he was pointing out, is different from reading culture-at-large. It's distinctive, solitary, and destined to be an activity limited to fewer and fewer people.

On the other hand, the critic Robert Scholes described the changes that cultural studies had provoked in a more optimistic way: "The exclusivity of literature as a category must be discarded. All kinds of texts, visual as well as verbal, polemical as well as seductive, must be taken as the occasions for further textuality."

What Just Happened?

As we've seen, the driving force behind cultural studies has generally been the changes brought about by modernity. New technologies, the explosion of popular culture, the broken promises of enlightenment progress—these were just some of the instigating factors prompting the search for new ways of thinking about society. Yet time marches on, and many critics feel that modernity was joined—or superseded—by postmodernity.

RELATIONS

See Chapter 21 for a discussion of colonial history and the argument that postmodernity is really the result of Western civilization having to acknowledge the non-Western colonial presence that has always been part of the West's own identity.

A word on terminology first. As we have been discussing it, *modernity* describes technological and political conditions that began to develop as early as the fifteenth century, while *modernism* typically refers to the artistic styles that developed in the late nineteenth and early twentieth centuries in response to modernity. For example, as we saw with Adorno's theories, the threats that modernity posed for the human spirit demanded new modernist forms of art. *Postmodernity* is typically described as the total globalization of the forces of capitalism and modernity, while *postmodernism* describes the cultural and artistic responses to that change. Yet because there's a complicated reciprocal relationship to both of these pairs—(post)modernity prompts (post)modernism which in turn prompts more (post)modernity—things can get a little dizzying.

Postmodernism basically begins with the idea of slapping an old-fashioned hat on a sleek modern skyscraper.

Some of the most relevant early uses of the term *postmodernism* had to do with architecture in the 1940s. Modernist architecture was a matter of form following function, with skyscrapers and other buildings designed with the idea that structure was of primary importance. The clean lines and minimal ornament of the international style of architecture, for example, celebrated structure as an aesthetic end in itself. Just look at how that boxy skyscraper gives you confidence in modernity's promise of technology and order!

Postmodern architecture suggests a playful dismissal of the promise and celebration of structure. Skyscrapers now are topped with fancy pediments or pointed roofs drawn from other eras—and not strictly necessary for function. Buildings might flaunt eclectic combinations of Greek columns and the features of a farmhouse, and Frank Gehry's elaborate creations seem to function without putting any demands on form at all.

> **RELATIONS**
>
> So how is this related to post-structuralism? As we saw in Chapters 16 and 17, structuralism and post-structuralism overlap in ways similar to modernism and postmodernism. Each "ism" seems to morph into its own "post." And in fact, many of the critics associated with post-structuralism, such as Derrida, Butler, Lacan, and Sedgwick, have also been called postmodern critics, since their work offers critiques of modernity. Post-structuralism, strictly speaking, seeks to critique the principles of linguistic and cultural structuralism. But since postmodernism also features a critical view of structures, it's easy to see why some critics fit into multiple categories.

Modernity, in other words, is falling all over itself in postmodern culture. Instead of a stable center, such as the idea of rational enlightenment, for example, postmodernism features multiple centers or no center at all. In fact, postmodern art is not seen as emerging from a source such as an artist's imagination, but from the manipulation of already existing material. Postmodern artists and writers don't *create*, they *appropriate*. In this way art, culture, and society become decentered and lack (or have abandoned) any of the traditional foundations, such as objective knowledge, ethnicity, and gender. Postmodern, anti-foundational art is skeptical of reason and subjectivity, and suspicious of the so-called coherence imposed by earlier models of human interaction.

The French philosopher and critic Jean-François Lyotard (1924–1998, pronounced *LEE-oh-tar*), offered perhaps the most famous definition: "I define *postmodern* as incredulity toward metanarratives." By this Lyotard meant the sociopolitical and philosophical narratives that have shaped much of history, such as the Enlightenment story of human development, the Marxist dialectic of political progress, and any religious narrative of human fate.

For Lyotard, these narratives were running themselves out—or, as he memorably put it, "the narrative function is losing its functors." Like modernity, the big plotlines of history had shown themselves incapable of explaining lived experience and actual social change. Instead, Lyotard looked to micronarratives, or stories we create under local conditions as the best way to understand social interaction. According to Lyotard, the way you make sense of the world is not organized or guaranteed by metanarratives. The knowledge you seem to have about yourself, your relationships, and society doesn't fall into line or follow a single pattern. Instead, your reasons for believing in social justice, science, or a healthy breakfast are based on impermanent, fleeting connections made in "clouds of sociality" and manipulated by politicians, educators, and multinational corporations.

For the French sociologist Jean Baudrillard (1929–2007, pronounced *bo-dree-YAR*), postmodernism is primarily characterized by the complete dominance of simulations. This view takes Benjamin's theories of mechanical reproduction very, very seriously. Baudrillard argued that in a Disneyland-like postmodern world, you can't really perceive actual things and events. Instead of seeing the originals, you have to view the world through the simulations created in the media. Like the situation in the *Matrix* movies, we're living entirely in a "hyperreal" world of symbols, created and controlled by capitalist mass culture.

The Pastiche Prologue

Yet, according to the American critic Fredric Jameson, there is still a narrative at work. Jameson has explored what he calls the "cultural logic of late capitalism" as the defining feature of postmodernity. It isn't simply that modernity has gone completely berserk and shattered into an endless series of network nodes. Instead, "late capitalism"—the reach of capitalism across the globe and deep into almost every aspect of lived experience—affects culture at every level. Where earlier Marxist critics examined the connections between the economic base and the cultural superstructure (see Chapter 9), Jameson argued that the cultural and economic aspects of your life "collapse back into one another," and the result is a world in need of critical approaches to culture as a way of understanding economic structures themselves.

In his work, Jameson "reads" not only literature, but architecture, painting, video, and other aspects of culture in order to raise consciousness about the profoundly mystified situations in which we find ourselves.

For Jameson, one of the most significant features of postmodern art and culture is pastiche, or the technique of copying styles or citing references in a new work. When this is done with an eye to satire, according to Jameson, it's called parody. Parody's imitations of style have a point—you understand what's being made fun of or what's being critiqued. Pastiche, on the other hand, doesn't have a point. Or, put another way, its point is to copy only surface features for their own sake. In either case, for Jameson, pastiche is a "blank parody" that reflects the postmodern dilemma that there is literally nowhere to go to escape the commodification of aesthetics.

The postmodern world, according to Jameson, offers only pastiches and jumbles of earlier styles which create a "glossy mirage" without any depth.

IN THEORY

"It would therefore begin to seem that Adorno's prophetic diagnosis has been realized, albeit in a negative way" because instead of Schoenberg's innovative formal cries for help, "the producers of culture have nowhere to turn but to the past: the imitation of dead styles, speech through all the masks and voices stored up in the imaginary museum of a now global culture." —Fredric Jameson

The mirage and depthlessness of postmodernism is, for Jameson, a lived experience perpetuated by architecture as much as through art and literature. Malls and hotels create worlds within worlds in which space is intentionally disorienting—or rather intentionally orienting toward bringing your subjectivity in line with the building's commercial purposes.

In either case, postmodernism leaves you unable to map yourself. The collapse of culture and economics prevents you from organizing the world that actually supports you, not only because this world is so multiple, mystifying, and adapting to new technologies, but because your own subjectivity is woven into this world. Postmodern subjects are, Jameson argued, caught in a "great global multinational and decentered communications network."

APPLY IT

Novelists associated with postmodernism include Jorge Luis Borges, John Barth, Thomas Pynchon, Kathy Acker, E. L. Doctorow, John Fowles, Salman Rushdie, Ishmael Reed, Italo Calvino, Umberto Eco, Paul Auster, and Dave Eggers.

Postmodernist films include *Blue Velvet* (1986, directed by David Lynch), *Pulp Fiction* (1994, directed by Quentin Tarantino), and *Moulin Rouge* (2001, directed by Baz Luhrmann), as well as the early examples of Alain Resnais's *Last Year at Marianbad* (1961) and Jean-Luc Godard's *Breathless* (1960) and *Alphaville* (1965).

The Canadian literary critic Linda Hutcheon, for her part, argued that the fragmentation and even pastiche of postmodernism is liberating. For her, postmodernism can still be considered parody, particularly when it takes the form of metafiction. For Hutcheon, metafiction, in which a literary work seems aware of its own operation *as* fiction, can serve as a productive subversion of the dominant system. That is, when writers are aware—and make you aware—that purely objective writing is impossible and that writing always draws together various already existing texts, then you're able to stand back from traditional assumptions and critique dominant culture. Similarly, the Egyptian American critic Ihab Hassan explained that postmodern art enables an anti-elitist and anti-authoritarian stand, in which "art becomes communal, optional, anarchic." For Hassan, postmodernism can be seen as a positive critical modification of the assumptions of modernism.

Wait, Let Me Finish

And yet, some folks are not willing to give up on modernity. The German philosopher Jürgen Habermas, who studied with Adorno at the Frankfurt school, has argued that modernity hasn't broken down, it just isn't finished yet. For Habermas, fixating on the local, fragmented, and illusory nature of postmodernity doesn't offer any room for critique, it only reinforces the problem.

The solution is to keep the Enlightenment dream alive by improving public debate. Habermas explained that this wouldn't be easy—you can't just keep talking, you actually need to understand the way people talk to each other in contemporary society. Specifically, he called attention to how conversation isn't just made up of stating facts, but of performative utterances (see Chapter 13 for more on linguistic and cultural performatives). That is, you don't just say things, you say things under certain circumstances that make what you say truthful or not.

If, for example, you mistake what an actor says on stage for a statement of that actor's true feelings, you've misunderstood what Habermas called the validity claim of the actor's line. You might also misunderstand what an actor says in real conversation because, well, maybe he's just acting. In any case, Habermas argued that this kind of thing goes on all the time. What some see as postmodern fragmentation and an inability to communicate with a shared foundation, Habermas sees as the unfinished business of understanding how modern people talk to each other.

But let's take an even quicker way out. In an influential 1985 essay, the American critic Donna Haraway argued that people have become cyborgs. According to Haraway, we are all "theorized and fabricated hybrids of machine and organism; in short, we are cyborgs" and this condition even "gives us our politics." Novelists such as William Gibson, Kathy Acker, Philip K. Dick, and J. G. Ballard have explored this as well. Haraway celebrated the blending of human and machine in the postmodern world, explaining that it offers a release from essentialist definitions of identity, particularly female identity, and acknowledges the reality of daily lives literally lived through technological organs.

So if, as Jameson had suggested, postmodernity keeps you from "mapping yourself" onto a world in which technology, culture, and economics overlap so much that you can't even tell where "you" begin and end, then maybe it's time to grab your GPS, connect to the internet, download that novel you've been dying to read, and accept the inevitable—you're a cyborg.

The Least You Need to Know

- Cultural studies investigates meaning in the social text of everyday life.
- The Frankfurt school critics rejected modernity's promise of the rational liberation of society.
- New artistic forms allow for new social statements.
- Dominant culture tends to run your life, but subversion is possible through the appropriation of cultural signs.
- Postmodernist art and literature reflect the implosion of capitalist modernity.

History Gets Literary

In This Chapter

- New historicism's focus on contexts
- History as literature …
- … And literature as history
- Accounting for cultural details
- One book, many voices

What would happen if Shakespeare could travel through time? It's a trick question, of course, since Shakespeare actually does travel through time. Think about it. "To be or not to be, that is the question," was written hundreds of years ago, yet it still means something today. In fact, all of Shakespeare's plays still mean something. So do *Paradise Lost*, *Pride and Prejudice*, *To Kill a Mockingbird*, and the first *Harry Potter* novel.

It stands to reason that literary works mean different things to different people, as we've seen in so many of the chapters in this book. And it also make sense that historical conditions are an important part of what any work means. Shakespeare's original audiences had their views of his plays, and when you see or read one of the plays you don't re-create that original reaction but instead create your own.

New historicism is a type of literary criticism that can't get enough of the *context* of literature. This includes the context of a work's creation and its original appearance, as well as its consumption by later readers, which is where you come in. The result is that literature gets you thinking a lot about history, and history gets you thinking a lot about literature.

New and Improved

So why "new" historicism? Well, older schools of criticism examined history as well, but typically as a kind of background to literary works. Older historical approaches saw literature as reflecting the spirit of the age or an era defined by relatively broad generalities. History was therefore seen as a kind of prerequisite for literature; history was the supposedly real dimension behind the fictional world of art. In this way, books such as E. M. W. Tillyard's *The Elizabethan World Picture*, *The Miltonic Setting*, and *Poetry and Its Background* were intended to help readers put works of literature in their various contexts.

New historicism emerged in the early 1980s with the goal of moving beyond history-as-background and investigating some of the more challenging and even paradoxical aspects of history. As we've seen in Chapter 19, cultural criticism succeeded in shedding new light on ordinary life as the proper object for investigation. New historicism set out to consider some of the same features, such as everyday events, common cultural practices, customs, domestic life, sexuality, fashions, and all kinds of cultural codes, no matter how minor they may seem. Rather than the top-down view of kings and wars, the new historicists took a bottom-up approach to the interaction between literature and its environment.

Of course, the new historicists were also responding to the New Critics, who had played down the role of literary criticism in considering historical issues. The New Critics, as you'll recall from Chapter 3, said that your goal in reading, first and foremost, is to consider a literary work as a "well-wrought urn" or a timeless artifact. After that, if you like, you could pursue other matters.

New historicism argues that you can't even begin to approach literature without inevitably being involved in historical matters.

Plotting Along in the Past

According to the American historian Hayden White, one pretty convincing reason for seeing literature and history as inherently interrelated is quite simply the literary nature of all historical writing. I mean, you can't spell *history* without *story*, can you? (It's even more clear in French, where *histoire* means both history and story.)

White explained in his groundbreaking 1973 book, *Metahistory*, that historians inevitably have to think through literary forms to compose their accounts of so-called actual events. There's really no other way to write a narrative of history without enlisting all of the usual devices and techniques of literature. Writing history, according to White, is "essentially a literary, that is to say fiction-making operation. And to call it that in no way detracts from the status of historical narratives as providing a kind of knowledge." White insisted that historical narratives definitely produce knowledge, and they transmit facts, but that knowledge and those facts should be understood to follow the same rules of organization as literary works.

Take plot, for example. White very simply reminded us that organizing events and details into a pattern, what he called emplotment, is essential to giving those events and details their meaning. White explained that historical sequences do not have stories on their own—even our own lives don't have stories of their own; instead, we shape them into stories.

IN THEORY

Historical events "are *made* into a story by the suppression of certain of them and the highlighting of others, by characterization, motif repetition, variation of tone and point of view, alternative descriptive strategies, and the like—in short, all of the techniques that we would normally expect to find in the emplotment of a novel or a play." —Hayden White

Think about how important selection and order can be for a narrative. The Russian formalists said that deciding what stays in a story and what gets left out can mean everything to the final product (see Chapter 4). You can take the same story-stuff or events and narrate them in any number of different and even conflicting ways.

Now, White wasn't trying to correct the "mistake" of writing nonfiction like fiction. For him, it was a matter of facing reality. All historians rely on literary forms, whether they acknowledge it or not. It's natural and inevitable, and the only problem with the literary aspect of history is overlooking it or denying it. You might compare this to the idea of scientific paradigms, which are also narratives, since paradigms inevitably give shape to what we mistakenly think of as bare facts. White also recalls Derrida in arguing that histories should not be seen as transparent windows through which you can see what actually happened (see Chapter 17). Instead, historians and readers should see the text of the history as part of history. And finally, for extra points, consider how Lévi-Strauss ultimately created another myth while trying to write an analysis of myth (see Chapter 17 as well). The point here is not that everyone is doing history (or science) wrong, but that reading history or science should acknowledge just that—*reading.*

And then there's metaphor! Metaphors, of course, are used to help you understand something new by comparing it to something familiar. White explained that metaphors also try to make you *feel* a certain way about something, such as when someone compares a long meeting at work to 30 miles of bad road. With metaphors, you're dealing with culturally coded connections, just as in literary works. Making a strict distinction between facts and figurative language, you could worry about the use of metaphors as manipulation, or you could simply accept them as part of historical discourse and consider them critically.

White pointed out, for example, that the French Revolution has been described in history books with metaphors characterizing it as an upheaval, a fall, a rise, an ironic development, an inevitable consequence, a victory, and a defeat. Each characterization is part of a narrative that implicitly (or explicitly) promotes a particular interpretation. For historians, White argued, "the greatest source of strength and renewal" would be closer attention to the literary basis of their work.

For the rest of us, the American critic Louis Montrose leads us back to literary texts and their relation to history by referring to "the historicity of texts and the textuality of histories." Since we have no direct access to what happened in the past, we get to make our way into it by way of new historicist approaches to literature.

There's Culture in My Poetry!

New historicism was actually named by the American critic Stephen Greenblatt in the early 1980s, and while he later tried to change the name of what he was doing to *cultural poetics,* the first name stuck. Still, the term *cultural poetics* is a good reminder that *poetics* refers to a theory of literary form and function, and a *cultural* approach to this means looking at the kinds of social features important to critics of cultural studies (see Chapter 19). So if you like, you can think of cultural poetics whenever you see new historicism and make everybody happy.

Greenblatt's main interest has been in tracking down all kinds of seemingly mundane historical features and integrating them into a reading of a literary text that also becomes a means for exploring history. It isn't necessarily the history of big politics, but the interweaving of important political, legal, and social issues with everyday activities. The point is to see literary texts as integrally woven into the fabric of history, a history that is itself made up of texts of all kinds.

IN THEORY

"The textual traces that have survived from the Renaissance and that are at the center of our literary interest in Shakespeare are the products of extended borrowings, collective exchanges, and mutual enchantments. They were made by moving certain things—principally ordinary language but also metaphors, ceremonies, dances, emblems, items of clothing, well-worn stories, and so forth—from one culturally demarcated zone to another." —Stephen Greenblatt

When you explore literature with regard to what Greenblatt called the "circulation of social energy," or the comings and goings of cultural features, you read differently. You can gain insights into history that "history" cannot offer, and perspectives on the literary work that a more narrow literary reading, such as that suggested by the New Critics, would miss.

As an example, the American critic Brook Thomas has recommended a new historicist reading of John Keats's "Ode on a Grecian Urn," perhaps the most emblematic of the kind of poem the New Critics examined as a self-sufficient artifact (see Chapters 3 and 8).

Keats's poem is generally seen as centering around the idea that truth is beauty, beauty is truth, and both can be protected from the ravages of time through art. Thomas linked this Romantic and abstract theme with Keats's specific historical circumstances involving museums. With this single connection, Thomas makes several fascinating points. First, he points out that the idea of the museum is not just a neutral background to Keats's poem, but runs parallel to its central message, since museums are institutions created for the preservation of beauty. The point here is that instead of simply evoking a timeless image of the survival of beauty, Keats's poem reflects the rise of the modern museum during Keats's own lifetime.

Thomas also explained that the poem's focus on a practical article—the urn—transformed into an aesthetic object is a feature of both the poem's theme and the museum's business. In addition, the images on the urn, as described by Keats, are of nameless ordinary people rather than heroes or famous royalty, perhaps suggesting Keats's own new historicist approach to the common past rather than to notable events. And finally, Thomas argued that for a Grecian urn to end up in a British museum in the first place had to involve a system of global trade, if not outright cultural thievery. The poem itself doesn't bring this up, but a new historicist reading expands the poem into this legitimate context for discussion.

According to Thomas, new historicist readings consider a literary work as "a social text, one that in telling us about the society that produced it also tells us about the society we inhabit today." Why is this so? Because we still feel the effects of the "cultural heritage" expressed or implied in many works. And in the specific case of Keats's poem, we still live in a world where museums both mirror and mask the complex nature of preserving beauty and truth.

Making the Connections

So it's pretty clear that new historicists love everyday stuff, such as letters, fragments of texts, and seemingly unimportant or trivial asides in novels, like a character putting her teacup down a bit too forcefully. Greenblatt in particular likes contextualizing literary works with anecdotes, because they offer a "touch of the real" to an author's work and life.

There's a precedent to this aspect of new historicism, both in cultural studies (as we saw in Chapter 19) and in anthropology. The American anthropologist Clifford Geertz (1926–2006) is known for advocating "thick descriptions" in anthropological reports. That is, instead of standing back and recording only the surface features and events of another culture, anthropologists should really get inside the culture they're studying. They should try to understand it from the inside out. Thick descriptions are reports that reflect not only as many details as possible but also a sense of the system that makes those details meaningful (Sound familiar? It's hard to get far from Saussure; see Chapter 11.)

Thick descriptions are like close readings, in fact, since the anthropological details are related to central controlling ideas. For Geertz, recording the "facts" of anthropological fieldwork were not enough, since you might mistake, as he wrote, a sly wink for a facial tic. Geertz's point, like so many of the culturally oriented critics we've discussed, sees everything that people do as part of socially signifying systems.

IN THEORY

"The culture of a people is an ensemble of texts, themselves ensembles, which the anthropologist strains to read over the shoulders of those to whom they properly belong. … As in more familiar exercises in close reading, one can start anywhere in a culture's repertoire of forms and end up anywhere else." —Clifford Geertz

Knowing Looks

One of the most familiar names in literary theory and criticism also pops up in the context of new historicism's interest in socially coded systems. Michel Foucault (see Chapters 13 and 15) argued that social systems are in control of power, even when power looks like it's in control of social systems. Foucault argued that power emerges only from a network of relations, not just from the single source of a king or a government. This is also reflected in the new historicist interest in "small history" rather than the history of kings and wars.

Foucault's term for the sociohistorical system that enables power at any given time is *episteme* (pronounced *EP-pih-steem*). The word itself is related to epistemology, or the study of how we know things. For Foucault, an episteme describes the field or network of ideas that actually gives meaning to everything you perceive. An episteme is like a paradigm and an ideology combined (see Chapter 9).

An episteme also determines how you talk about what you perceive. It sets out the implicit rules for making sense, which also means it establishes the boundaries of restricted or "nonsense" discourse. For this reason, according to David H. Richter's often cited phrase, an episteme is "a mode of power/knowledge with its own discursive practices: methods of expression that are also methods of oppression."

Power, therefore, resides in the system as a form of knowledge, or a perspective on knowledge, not just in punishment, penalties, or force. For Foucault, modern forms of surveillance and confession, for example, do not simply repress or monitor your true self, but they become integral aspects of your self-identity and even your view of the world. Looking back at any historical period is really a matter of looking into an archive of the various components of its episteme—an archive of lived, ordinary cultural actions as well as texts.

Greenblatt and other new historicists have explained that power works best when it doesn't feel like power, when it provokes the reaction, "Well, that's just the way things are." New historicist readings of literature, for this reason, will often look for instances in which political or social subversion is actively encouraged by those in power, only so that the subversion can be contained, leaving the overall system looking that much stronger and more natural. The idea, particularly as revealed in Renaissance literature, is that keeping a hold on power means showing the durability and even naturalness of your control, not just its force.

Doesn't Know When to Quit

Both Foucault and Roland Barthes (see Chapter 17) have argued that books are not just books. No way. Any literary work is part of the endless network of interconnected social signs. It's as impossible to see meaning in a single literary work as it is to understand the significance of any historical event without its context.

IN THEORY

"The book is not simply the object that one holds in one's hands. ... The frontiers of a book are never clear-cut: beyond the title, the first lines and the last full stop, beyond its internal configuration and its autonomous form, it is caught up in a system of references to other books, other texts, other sentences: it is a node within a network." —Michel Foucault

Yet despite the endless nature of these interconnections, we still tend to settle on what feels like stable ground for meaning most of the time, particularly when we're "just reading a book, darn it."

Tony Bennett (no, not that one), an Australian sociologist, has suggested investigating your reading formation, or the forces that "mediate the relations between text and context." Bennett has combined a Marxist interest in historical determination with Saussure's notions of system and utterance (see Chapter 11). Saussure argued that you are able to make and understand meaningful utterances only because you have unconsciously absorbed a system of grammar. Bennett suggested that your acts of reading are only possible because you have unconsciously assimilated a set of social reading conditions, or "reading formations that concretely and historically structure the interaction between texts and readers."

Each of your readings, therefore, is like a performance that combines a "culturally activated text"; a "culturally activated reader" (that's you); and all the "material, social, ideological, and institutional" aspects that shape your daily life.

APPLY IT

Consider your own cultural activations as a viewer of such transhistorical fantasies as *Romeo + Juliet* (1996, directed by Baz Luhrmann) and *A Knight's Tale* (2001, directed by Brian Helgeland). Movies like these offer entertaining opportunities to consider how the past blends with the present, how you are prompted to view history as an interpretation, and how the present is depicted as historical as well. You might also consider these films as examples of postmodernism (see Chapter 19).

Russian Legacy

One early critic who was very influential for the later development of new historicism was fascinated by what went on "inside" literary works. The Russian literary scholar Mikhail Bakhtin (1895–1975, pronounced *bock-TEEN*) was associated with the Russian formalists (see Chapter 4), but it was really during the explosion of poststructuralist criticism in the 1970s that his writings began attracting wide interest.

I Hear Voices

Bakhtin explored what he called the heteroglossia, or many languages that could be found in literary works. The original Russian term translates as "the word of another," and it calls our attention to the multiplicity of voices that can be heard in a text, such as the voices of the characters, the narrator, and even the author's voice that might be detected behind a narrator.

Heteroglossia opens up a text to interpretations that do not depend on a single view of history or power. Instead, literary works—particularly novels, according to Bakhtin—offer performances of cultural dialogue. And because they are performances, statements in a novel should be read with an awareness of their collaboration or resistance to other statements. Is a narrator, for example, on the same side as the characters? Does a character seem to emerge from the text as the voice of the author? Are characters being sarcastic, or do they indicate something in their speech that only an intimate understanding of the cultural codes would reveal? These last questions recall not only Geertz and his interest in knowing a culture from the inside out, but also Habermas's interest in getting past the "impasse" of postmodernism (see Chapter 19) as well as Gates's discussion of the multivoiced codes of African American Signifyin(g) (see Chapter 14).

IN THEORY

In your ordinary speech, "every conversation is full of transmissions and interpretations of other people's words. At every step one meets a 'quotation' or a 'reference' to something that a particular person said, a reference to 'people say' or 'everyone says,' to the words of the person one is taking with, or to one's own previous words, to a newspaper, an official decree, a document, a book and so forth." —Mikhail Bakhtin

Good novels, according to Bakhtin, are therefore not monological, offering only one authoritative or official point of view, but dialogical and crisscrossed with a variety of attitudes toward dominant culture. Bakhtin himself, for example, argued that Tolstoy's work was more monological and not as socially challenging as Dostoevsky's work, which offered more examples of distinct languages and idioms competing within a single work. One type of literature, which Bakhtin called carnivalesque, even features ordinary voices directly satirizing and challenging authority.

Following Bakhtin's lead, new historicists see history as dialogical, since it is comprised of a variety of voices. Social classes in particular contribute to the dialogical nature of history, as long as your reading of history is not limited to a top-down view and instead includes the everyday actions and activities of ordinary people. In the field of history as such, Howard Zinn's *A People's History of the United States* is an example of an actively dialogical narrative of history.

Step Into My Parlor

History obviously seems to be all about time, but Bakhtin also pointed out how space works to affect our view of literary and historical sequences. He used the term *chronotope* to call attention to the inseparable nature of time and space—chronotope literally means "timespace." It comes down to recognizing that certain spaces presuppose certain views or feelings about time, particularly in literature, but also in daily activities.

For example, the chronotope of the parlor or salon emphasizes the concepts associated with time and space of individual rooms, where characters (such as those found in nineteenth-century novels) meet, discuss, and interact. Such rooms are spaces where people can discuss society and world events, while seeming to be removed from the direct effects (and speed) of events that happen outside. In other words, when two characters turn off a busy street and meet in a parlor, you can expect the scene's time frame to adjust accordingly.

Compare the chronotope of "the room" to the chronotope of "the road." As a space, the road is coupled with an outside time that emphasizes chance, random meetings, and, of course, travel. Strangers meet on "the road," while friends and family meet in "the room."

IN THEORY

With chronotopes, "time, as it were, thickens, takes on flesh, becomes artistically visible." And regarding rooms in particular: "Most important in all this is the weaving of historical and socio-public events together with the personal and even deeply private side of life." —Mikhail Bakhtin

In literary analysis, new historicism urges study of specific chronotopes in order to really understand the significance of events in a novel or play, especially so-called ordinary events. New historicists will investigate, for example how Elizabethans depicted in a specific play thought about rooms, forests, gardens, and even windows, in order to flesh out the cultural significance of a scene.

And remember, the past is anything that isn't "this instant," so you don't have to wait hundreds of years to think historically. History, as a lived construction of experience, is always taking place right on top of the so-called present. This means the chronotope of the internet or the family SUV is just as much a target for new historicism and cultural critique as *Hamlet* may be.

But enough, I'll let you go. I know you're eager to look more deeply into what exactly the timespace of Diagon Alley meant to The Boy Who Lived so long, long ago (remember the 1990s?).

The Least You Need to Know

- History is not a background to literary works, but an integral aspect of them.
- Historians must employ literary techniques to construct narratives of the past.
- Ordinary details and cultural connections should be brought to bear on literary interpretation.
- In shaping sociohistorical circumstances, power and knowledge go hand in hand.
- Rather than being guided by one authoritative narrator, most novels are filled with multiple voices.
- Setting a scene in an interior or an exterior space changes a reader's expectations about time and character.

Postcolonial Criticism Flaunts the Fashions

In This Chapter

- Postcolonial criticism moves the center
- Colonial history's constructions of self and other
- Feminism and postcolonialism
- A writer's choice of language
- Colonial hybridity and mimicry

Isn't it great to settle into a book about imperial conquest, global commerce, socio-economic administration, and colonial psychology? You know, like a Jane Austen novel.

It happens more often than you might think. The history of modern Western imperialism, which began roughly 500 years ago and hasn't completely ended yet, has had an effect on practically every person alive today. It influences how we view the world and its people, and it's definitely left its marks in every type of literature, not just *Heart of Darkness*, *A Passage to India*, or *Out of Africa*.

At its height, for instance, when "the sun never set on the British Empire," the British government controlled the wealth and resources of land that literally spanned the globe. And along with the administrative control of territory and people went the power of British cultural influence. Spain, Portugal, France, and Belgium also controlled significant regions around the world, creating their own busy and complex exchanges of natural resources, commodities, labor, and culture.

While some movements to liberate territory from colonial control, such as the American Revolution, occurred in the eighteenth century, it wasn't until the widespread anti-colonial movements of the middle of the twentieth century—India and

Pakistan became independent from British rule in 1947—that the world map really began to diversify. The United Nations, for example, was formed in 1945 with 51 member states, while today there are nearly 200.

So no matter where you live, and practically no matter what you read, as a twenty-first-century reader of literature you are always dealing with legacies of imperialism and colonial rule that raise questions of history, politics, identity, perspective, and interpretation.

That's where Jane Austen comes in (along with some other folks we'll discuss along the way).

Reading Between the Lands

Postcolonial is a term, like post-structural or postmodern, that serves to critique whatever it was before it was "post" because of the way the original term contained contradictions. That is, the project of structuralism was shown to rely on—but suppress—certain contradictions that only became apparent in post-structuralism (see Chapter 17), and modernity's tensions percolated internally until the more obvious forms of postmodernity brought everything out into the open (see Chapter 19).

DEFINITION

Postcolonialism describes anything involving colonial contact, from its beginnings to independence to the present. And while history has seen colonial projects carried out by nations and empires across the globe, this chapter focuses on Western imperialism. The critics who first began, in the 1970s, to focus on the effects and aftereffects of such imperialism recognized that the issues they were investigating had been stewing in one way or another since the beginning. As the critics Bill Ashcroft, Gareth Griffiths, and Helen Tiffin have stated in their important study, *The Empire Writes Back* (1989), "postcolonial" indicates the "continuity of preoccupations" existing throughout the history of "European imperial aggression."

One of the central goals of postcolonial critics is to get you to shift your emphasis when you read. Specifically, they want you to see how marginal characters or themes rightfully belong at the center of your attention. You've seen this move before. Feminist critics first call attention to male-centered texts that push women's experience to the edges of an interpretation, for example, then advocate a woman-centered approach to interpretation. Postcolonial critics want you to challenge the Eurocentrism of a text by noticing when and how a text that seems to be exclusively centered on European interests actually depends on non-European people, places, and culture. "Reading from the margins" adds to the text those historical and thematic dimensions that have been there all along, but played down or ignored.

In one example of a postcolonial reading, the Palestinian-American critic Edward W. Saïd (1935–2003, pronounced *sah-EED*) turned his attention to Jane Austen's *Mansfield Park*. The novel revolves around the life of an English family, with all the bustle, psychological intrigue, and marriageable daughters and gentlemen that you'd expect in an Austen novel. The wealth that supports the lifestyles at Mansfield Park, however, comes from an estate in Antigua, an island in the Caribbean and a British colony whose value was based on slave labor (slavery would be abolished in British colonies in the 1830s).

Now, the plantation in Antigua is barely mentioned in the novel, but much of the plot is structured around the absence of the head of the household, Sir Thomas Bertram, who has to travel to his foreign plantation to set things in order. When he returns, Sir Thomas has to wrangle all the various love affairs and near-affairs that have sprung up. Saïd's interpretation is not that the novel actively advocates imperialism; his reading brings out a more subtle and even powerful aspect of colonialist culture. Saïd argued that Austen "synchronizes domestic with international authority" by leading her readers to effortlessly connect Sir Thomas's control abroad with his control at home.

Saïd's point is that the values of colonial rule—the rule over slaves in another country—were normalized and validated by the values of British domestic rule. A reader's assumed appreciation, that is, of the perfectly reasonable values of the household story is transferred to the colonial situation, where it implicitly confirms the reasonableness of slavery.

IN THEORY

In much British writing, including *Mansfield Park,* we see "positive ideas of home, of a nation and its language, of proper order, good behavior, moral values. But positive ideas of this sort do more than validate 'our' world. They also tend to devalue other worlds and, perhaps more significantly from a retrospective point of view, they do not prevent or inhibit or give resistance to horrendously unattractive imperialist practices." —Edward W. Saïd

Despite this critique, Saïd really liked Austen. In fact, he argued that "everything we know about Austen and her values is at odds with the cruelty of slavery," and that *Mansfield Park* is a literary masterpiece. The problem is deeper—it's in colonialism itself, which "cannot completely hide" in any work produced in its system. Saïd's very postcolonial argument is that in order to fully appreciate this novel you need, as best you can, to keep in mind its global perspective.

Us and Them

Colonial rule was also enabled by simply dividing up the world into two groups: us and them. One of the founding texts of postcolonialism is Saïd's study, *Orientalism* (1978), which explored how scholars, colleges, and other institutions contributed to an enormously powerful system of defining the world in just this way.

The first thing to know is that Orientalists were and are actual people. Indiana Jones is based on an Orientalist. The term *Orient* refers to the areas of what we now call the Middle East as well as the Far East, and Saïd's study is generally concerned with the Middle East, Islamic cultures, and South Asia (comprised mainly of India and Pakistan, or what they used to call the Indian subcontinent). The changing terms are actually important, since they indicate how these areas—and the people who lived there—have been the subject of continuing scholarship from outside.

Since the eighteenth century, Orientalism has developed as a Western discipline— you could take classes in it and get a degree—diligently studying the languages, cultures, and religions of these regions. Following the theories of Michel Foucault (see Chapters 13 and 20), Saïd explained that as a discipline, Orientalism was both a field of knowledge and a field of power. Western scholars knew all there was to know about Oriental culture, and there wasn't much the actual Orientals (quite a diverse group) could say in response.

IN THEORY

"I have no knowledge of either Sanskrit or Arabic. But ... I am quite ready to take the Oriental learning at the valuation of the Orientalists themselves. I have never found one among them who could deny that a single shelf of a good European library was worth the whole native literature of India and Arabia." —Thomas Babington Macaulay (historian, member of British Parliament, and member of the supreme council of the East India Company, which ruled India's affairs until the country came under direct colonial rule)

According to Saïd, the result of Orientalism, a field of study intimately linked to colonial administration, was to create a very durable sense of us and them, based on qualities that transformed stereotypes into scholarly and historical "facts": "The

Oriental is irrational, depraved (fallen), childlike, 'different'; thus the European is rational, virtuous, mature, 'normal.'" The ancient wonders of Egypt, for example, were admired for their greatness, but it was a fallen, past greatness, and the future belonged to the West. Western scholars were therefore the only ones who could fully appreciate Oriental history and culture.

In this way, Saïd explained, Orientalists created a "projection of the Orient" whose most important function was to make the West look good. Using a term that the new historicists would pick up (see Chapter 20), Saïd showed how Orientalism would "*emplot* Oriental history, character, and destiny" into a Western story line in which colonial rule was inevitable and desirable. Above all, the negative qualities attributed to the Orient assured that the West, as the counterpart, would appear superior.

IN THEORY

"Orientalism was ultimately a political vision of reality whose structure promoted the difference between the familiar (Europe, the West, 'us') and the strange (the Orient, the East, 'them'). This vision in a sense created and then served the two worlds thus conceived." —Edward W. Saïd

The effects of Orientalism, according to Saïd and other postcolonial critics, extend throughout the entire system, affecting not only political and social arrangements, but psychological development as well. Having to live by story lines created under the violence of colonialism creates problems for both colonized and colonizer.

From the 1950s through the 1970s, as formerly colonized countries around the world were achieving their independence (some peacefully, some not), they were faced with creating new versions of what political scientist Benedict Anderson has called the "imagined community" that holds a nation together. After the forced imposition of languages, customs, and even historical memory, how would the new nations define themselves? For that matter, how would the imperial nations, sometimes called the "metropolitan centers," define themselves now that their Orientalist "others" were no longer around to shore up a "superior" Western identity?

The French Algerian psychiatrist Frantz Fanon (1925–1961, pronounced *fah-NO*), elaborated on both the psychological effects of colonialism and the political demands of the expanding colonial independence movement in his books *Black Skin, White Masks* (1952) and *The Wretched of the Earth* (1961). Like W. E. B. Du Bois before him (see Chapter 14), Fanon argued that colonial subjects have two sides to their identities, created through the processes of what Saïd called Orientalism.

According to Fanon, colonialism "turns to the past of the oppressed people, and distorts, disfigures and destroys it." The most profound consequences of colonialism, for Fanon, involved the creation of the colonial subject's own self-image. Rather than seeing colonialism as a benevolent program of well-meaning missionaries setting out to improve the lives of backward natives, Fanon saw an insidious process of character manipulation.

IN THEORY

"On the unconscious plane, colonialism therefore did not seek to be considered by the native as a gentle, loving mother who protects her child from a hostile environment, but rather as a mother who unceasingly restrains her fundamentally perverse offspring from managing to commit suicide and from giving free rein to its evil instincts. The colonial mother protects her child from itself, from its ego, and from its physiology, its biology, and its own unhappiness which is its very essence." —Frantz Fanon

Postcolonial critics, as we've seen with Saïd's *Orientalism*, have shown how this process of character construction helped to reinforce the image of the West as both superior and benevolent. In addition, the whole process is not only reflected in literature but enacted in it as well, calling for interpretations that are actively critical of colonial history. Stepping back even further, critics have also explored how even well-meaning criticism itself may stand in the way of recognizing colonial issues.

Return to Thornfield

Charlotte Brontë's *Jane Eyre*, which we have seen in the context of Russian formalism (see Chapter 4), feminism (see Chapter 12), and queer theory (see Chapter 13), has also been read in the context of colonial identity. In fact, as the critic Gayatri Chakravorty Spivak has explained, the critical history of the novel is particularly interesting because of all the overlapping approaches. Spivak's own uniquely influential criticism often combines aspects of feminism, Marxism, and deconstruction.

Specifically, according to Spivak, while *Jane Eyre* has been considered a "cult text of feminism," the novel shouldn't be limited to a feminist reading, since what drives *Jane Eyre* is really the project of imperial character formation. Seeing Jane as an unproblematic "feminist hero" isn't good enough for Spivak, since Jane's success actually depends on the denigration of another woman.

As we saw in Chapter 12, Gilbert and Gubar interpreted the character of Bertha Mason, the "madwoman in the attic," primarily as an image of suppressed female sexuality. In her reading, Spivak emphasized Bertha's colonial status as a woman from Jamaica and argued that feminist critics have rushed to create a kind of "high feminist norm" that, like colonialism, only serves to set a privileged Western image over the nonhuman colonial other.

IN THEORY

"My readings here do not seek to undermine the excellence of the individual artist." The point is to incite "rage against the imperialist narrativization of history," and "it is crucial that we extend our analysis of this example beyond the minimal diagnosis of 'racism.'" —Gayatri Chakravorty Spivak

Spivak, like Saïd and other postcolonial critics, has emphasized that the text is the proper object of critique, not the author as such. And this isn't to let anyone off the hook, but to point out how systematic, rather than merely personal, the violence and oppression of colonialism is.

Look at It This Way

In fact, Spivak has pointed to another literary text, rather than a theoretical analysis, that serves as an effective critical reading of *Jane Eyre*. The 1966 novel *Wide Sargasso Sea* by Jean Rhys (1890–1979, pronounced *reece*, born on the Caribbean island of Dominica) is a kind of prequel to *Jane Eyre*, in which Bertha's point of view is brought from the margins to the center of the story. (Think *Wicked*, if you weren't already.)

Rhys's novel follows Bertha, whose fictional real name is revealed to be Antoinette, as she is taken from her colonial home and transported to England as Rochester's wife. While *Jane Eyre* limits your understanding of Bertha's character to an animal-like, uncontrollable curse on Rochester's life, Rhys's novel shows you Antoinette's very human side as a colonial female figure trapped in foreign land. *Wide Sargasso Sea* also shows the Rochester character (without a name in this novel) as a victim of the system of patriarchal colonialism as well.

As Spivak explained, Rhys's novel shifts the point of view, but it cannot change the tragic direction of the original novel's depiction of colonial "othering." Antoinette's role, like so many colonial subjects, is to serve as a foil or contrast to the Western figures—in this case, Jane. Bertha's presence as an uncivilizable animal-like figure makes Jane's rise possible.

IN THEORY

"In this fictive England, she [Bertha] must play out her role, act out the transformation of her 'self' into that fictive Other, set fire to the house and kill herself, so that Jane Eyre can become the feminist individualist heroine of British fiction." —Gayatri Chakravorty Spivak

Other Others

Then there's *Frankenstein*. Spivak's approach to this novel has focused on the education that the creature receives while eavesdropping on a non-Western "Other"—the character Safie (best pronounced *SAH-fee-uh*).

Safie is the daughter of a Christian mother and a Muslim father, and the novel makes a point of painting the father pretty much as an Orientalist caricature: he's untrustworthy, devious, oppressive, opposed to learning, violent, ungrateful, and traitorous. The novel tells us that Safie's mother, on the other hand, bore qualities "beyond the scope" of Islam, and had taught Safie not only Christianity, but "to aspire to higher powers of intellect, and an independence of spirit." According to Spivak, Safie is the perfect illustration of the non-Western Other just waiting for the liberating and civilizing mission of the West. And as Felix teaches Safie to read (French, by the way), this is exactly what the novel depicts.

The creature, on the other hand, while obtaining the same education as Safie by listening through a wall in the cottage, must serve as the novel's figure of the "Other's other," like Bertha is for Jane. The creature cannot be admitted to any Western family in the novel but must literally drift off and out of the pages. Spivak and other critics have pointed out that the same logic is at work in Shakespeare's *The Tempest*, in which the "colonial figures" illustrate the two types of non-Western Other: Ariel, who can be trained and useful, and Caliban, who remains "absolutely Other."

You can see, again, how moving what might be thought of as marginal figures and events into the center of your reading will open new avenues for interpretation and appreciation of the entire literary work. Even the creature's language skills, which we discussed in terms of Russian formalism (see Chapter 4) and deconstruction (see Chapter 17), can be viewed from a postcolonial perspective. Fanon, for example, following Lacan's theory of how language provides us with our subjectivities (see Chapter 18), would argue that the creature's imperial education produces a self-divided, even self-hating identity.

Choosing Your Words Carefully

The next question is actually a simple one, even if the answers are not. Which language should a postcolonial writer use? Is the native language best, or should literature be written in the master's language?

Compelling cases have been made for each option. On the side of writing in a native language is the Kenyan writer and critic, Ngugi wa Thiong'o (pronounced *n'googgie wa tee-ONG-goh*). Ngugi (his surname) has emphasized the importance of "decolonizing the mind," since the most dangerous aspect of colonialism and rule by a foreign power is not the immediate physical force, but the lingering cultural and psychological destruction. Imperialism teaches children, in particular, to turn away from their native languages and embrace the "superior" language of the invader.

IN THEORY

"The night of the sword and the bullet was followed by the morning of the chalk and the blackboard. The physical violence of the battlefield was followed by the psychological violence of the classroom." —Ngugi wa Thiong'o

Language for Ngugi is much more than a tool for communication, it's also "a carrier of culture." After writing in English during the early years of his career, Ngugi decided to switch to Gikuyu, his native Kenyan language, as the carrier of his culture and experience. Of course, Ngugi's work is translated into other languages, including English, but he composes in Gikuyu and in that way contributes to the continued survival and development of that language. As Ngugi has written, "I believe that my writing in Gikuyu, a Kenyan language, an African language, is part and parcel of the anti-imperialist struggles of Kenya and African peoples."

APPLY IT

Check out Ngugi wa Thiong'o's novel, *Matigari* (1987), and Chinua Achebe's *Things Fall Apart* (1958).

On the other hand, the Nigerian writer Chinua Achebe (pronounced *chinwa ah-CHEH-bay*) has argued that writing in English (or French, or any of the imperial languages) is not simply a matter of caving in to colonial indoctrination. There are other factors to consider.

For one, according to Achebe, English offers Africans who read different languages a single shared language. Even in his native Nigeria, Achebe has cited "half a dozen or so" languages he would have to learn in order to appreciate all of the literature produced there. Perhaps the more important point, however, is that by writing in English Achebe is changing the very nature of that language. English, as a language and as a literature, is only defined by its products and its use. Whatever is added to the cumulative national or linguistic library will inevitably change the character of that library (as T. S. Eliot noted; see Chapter 19).

IN THEORY

"What I do see is a new voice coming out of Africa, speaking of African experience in a world-wide language. So my answer to the question *Can an African ever learn English well enough to be able to use it effectively in creative writing?* is certainly yes. If on the other hand you ask: Can he ever learn to use it like a native speaker? I should say, I hope not. … The price a world language must be prepared to pay is submission to many different kinds of use." —Chinua Achebe

In fact, Achebe has noted the parallels between postcolonial writers and African American writers operating in a "white English" literary tradition. Achebe explained, for example, that James Baldwin was concerned about using a language that did not seem his own until he stopped trying to imitate it and started *using* it. Achebe took from that lesson the principle that "the English language will be able to carry the weight of my African experience. But it will have to be a new English."

Taking a phrase from the author Salman Rushdie, postcolonial critics have pointed out that the literature of formerly colonized people illustrates how "the empire writes back" to the Western world. That is, formerly marginalized figures are no longer simply the recipients of discourse and instruction, but the sources of new narratives and identities.

Are You Lookin' at *Me?*

The critic Homi K. Bhabha has highlighted the connections between new forms of postcolonial writing and older forms of hybridity and "colonial mimicry." Mimicry is what Bhabha sees as the result of the colonizer's mission of "educating and civilizing" the colonial subject. That is, while the goal of a missionary (such as the character of St. John Rivers in *Jane Eyre*) is to help "raise up" the native to be like the English, the result, according to Bhabha, is the creation of a subject that is "almost the same but not quite," or even "not quite/not white."

IN THEORY

"If the effect of colonial power is seen to be the *production* of hybridization rather than the noisy command of colonialist authority or the silent repression of native traditions, then an important change of perspective occurs. The ambivalence at the source of traditional discourses on authority enables a form of subversion."
—Homi K. Bhabha

Colonial mimicry, in fact, confronts the colonizer with something between flattery and mockery. The artificial, forced, and even violent nature of colonial education is reflected in the gaze of the hybrid colonized subject. And according to Bhabha, this turns the tables on the colonizer since "the observer becomes the observed."

Colonial subjects act like reflecting doubles for the colonizer—they may be wearing the right clothes, speaking the right language, and even gesturing correctly, yet they reflect with a difference. Bhabha has said that mimicry doesn't "re-present" the colonial ideal, it ironically "repeats" that ideal. Like Gates's theory of African American Signifyin(g) (see Chapter 14), which emphasizes "repeating with a difference," colonial mimicry takes advantage of the ambiguity of language and any sign system, such as clothing and gestures.

APPLY IT

You may be interested in these influential and bestselling works that reflect postcolonial issues: Naguib Mahfouz's *The Beggar* (1965); V. S. Naipaul's *The Mimic Men* (1967); Nadine Gordimer's *The Conservationist* (1974); Wole Soyinka's play, *Death and the King's Horseman* (1975); Salman Rushdie's *Midnight's Children* (1980) and *Haroun and the Sea of Stories* (1990); J. M. Coetzee's reimagining of the Robinson Crusoe story, *Foe* (1986); Michelle Cliff's *No Telephone to Heaven* (1987); and any collection of Derek Walcott's poetry.

Bhabha's argument also reflects Jacques Derrida's notion of writing, in which any utterance resists staying within its "intended limits" and will inevitably work its way into other, possibly subversive modes. And while you're at it, you can relate colonial mimicry to Barbara Johnson's reminder of the "materiality of the text," Barthes's designation of a text whose writing refuses to stop at borders but continues on across endless fields of intertextuality, and Bakhtin's notion of dialogic discourse (see Chapters 17 and 20).

Without erasing or generalizing the important distinctions between these theories, it's fair to say they all indicate how restless, shrewd, and gifted writers—and readers—can be when it comes to addressing the complexities of human interaction. The postcolonial opportunity, which some critics also call postmodern (see Chapter 19), lies in the creation of new spaces and identities between borders and in the gaps between existing subject positions, no matter how oppressive those positions have been in the past.

The Least You Need to Know

- Many literary works should be read with attention to the history of imperialism.
- Scholarly publications and institutions enabled the violence of imperialism by reinforcing negative views of non-Western people.
- Literary criticism should be aware of overlapping and alternative views prompted by any single work.
- Some postcolonial writers advocate writing in indigenous languages, while other writers see composing in the colonial language as genuine, progressive creativity.
- Colonial indoctrination can lead to ironic, creative, and subversive mimicry.

Ecocriticism Offers a Word from Our Sponsor

In This Chapter

- Ecocriticism as activist literary criticism
- Beyond anthropomorphism
- The construction and control of landscapes
- Native American perspectives
- Theoretical exchanges

Read locally, think globally. *Really* globally. Not just about the people in the world, but all living things in the world and all the elements necessary to keep them alive. That's what ecocritics want you to have in mind whenever you read. And they mean it.

Hit the Ground Running

Ecocriticism, which blends ecological awareness and activism with literary theory and criticism, also raises the question, "But what does literature really have to do with the environment, except maybe for all those trees that get turned into books or the energy needed to power my e-reader?"

Ecocritics begin by arguing that in the context of the ongoing global environmental crisis, everything you do has some effect, good or bad, on the situation. Cultural attitudes and literary representations serve either to perpetuate the behavior that damages the earth's ecosystem or to help change the direction of exploitative and dangerous activities. And yes, especially if you're a cyborg (see Chapter 19), you'll need to work out your relationship to the environment.

As we've seen throughout this book, literary theory has been instrumental in calling attention to issues of power, inequality, and oppression. Ecocritics raise awareness of these issues as they bear on the most comprehensive relationship of all, that between human beings and the world we live in. As Cheryll Glotfelty, one of the key figures in ecocriticism has explained, literature is connected to the world in ways that go beyond discussing the world of merely human society. According to Glotfelty, literature "plays a part in an immensely complex global system, in which energy, matter, *and ideas* interact."

IN THEORY

"Ecocriticism is the study of the relationship between literature and the physical environment. Just as feminist criticism examines language and literature from a gender-conscious perspective, and Marxist criticism brings an awareness of modes of production and economic class to its reading of texts, ecocriticism takes an earth-centered approach to literary studies." —Cheryll Glotfelty

The approach that ecocriticism takes also helps illuminate the reciprocal relationship that always exists between theory and criticism. Glotfelty has noted that as theory, ecocriticism "negotiates between the human and the nonhuman," which means trying to discover previously unknown or ignored principles that unite humans with other aspects of the natural world. On the other hand, ecocriticism's critical stance "has one foot in literature and the other on land." This indicates the position ecocritics take when they read—a position that requires close reading of texts as well as an intimate understanding of nature. Ecocritical *theory*, therefore, as it uncovers new ways of seeing relationships in the natural world, leads to new ways of *reading*. And vice versa: ecocriticism's critical reading of both texts and nature helps enable new theories.

Another founding critic of the field, Lawrence Buell (rhymes with *mule*) has explained that ecocriticism is not a unified movement or critical school, but instead, like feminism's multiple perspectives, "ecocriticism gathers itself around a commitment to environmentality from whatever critical vantage point." Ecocritics are driven by issues and questions rather than guided by a single method or paradigm.

What kind of questions? As we'll see, the questions range from asking about themes to looking deeply into literary form and even scientific and theological issues. Some questions you can ask right away of anything you're currently reading: How does this literary work represent nature? How do its metaphors and symbolism suggest an opinion about the land? Does the work seem to value the human world over the natural world, or does the work seem to subvert the valorization of technology?

In Chapter 2, you'll recall that critics want you to see natural imagery as more than mere scenery. In *Frankenstein*, for example, any given description of nature typically reflects a character's personality or even an important theme in the novel. Ecocritics suggest you also consider how Shelley's descriptions of European nature contribute to the novel's environmental orientation. Some critics have pointed out in particular that Victor's journey from Switzerland to Ireland is filled with travelogue-like passages emphasizing the interplay between uninhabited nature and the towns that define human history.

While any work can be interpreted with regard to ecological issues and the questions mentioned earlier, Buell has suggested that works with a specifically environmental orientation—what is sometimes called "green literature"—will include the following qualities:

- Nature is not just background for the work, but an active presence, illustrating the necessary interaction between the human and the nonhuman.

- The work is not exclusively focused on human interests and fates.

- Humans should be shown as accountable to the environment.

- Nature should be seen as a process, not simply as a static or timeless element in the world.

APPLY IT

Check out some of the most popular and iconic books with environmental themes: Aldo Leopold's *A Sand County Almanac* (1949), Edward Abbey's *Desert Solitaire* (1968), Annie Dillard's *Pilgrim at Tinker Creek* (1974), and Gary Snyder's *Practice of the Wild* (1990).

As you can tell from the suggestions of what to look for in literature, ecocriticism is a form of critical advocacy. Like so many of the critics represented in this book who feel that the point of understanding the world is to change it, ecocritics actively look for ways to contribute to the health of the planet.

Ecocriticism can range, therefore, from environmental concerns focused on how the world can be made a better place for humans, to the complete abandonment of the anthropomorphism of seeing humans as the center of the ecosystem. In the case of "deep ecology," what matters most is the health of the entire ecosystem, regardless of what happens to humans. The earth, according to some critics, should be considered "Gaia," an organism unto itself, with regulating processes geared toward its own survival no matter who lives in it or on it. When humans or any of the other inhabitants provoke an unacceptable level of imbalance, they are eliminated from the system.

IN THEORY

"The most important function of literature today is to redirect human consciousness to a full consideration of its place in a threatened natural world."
—Glen A. Love

But hang on. We're still here, at least for now. And keeping in mind that the word *ecology* itself comes from the Greek word *oikos,* or house, let's consider how several foundational texts have helped define ecocriticism's approach to keeping our house in order.

Coming from the scientific side of things, Rachel Carson's *Silent Spring* alerted people in 1962 to the dangers of pesticides and air pollution. Carson's book was an instant popular success and helped to initiate the modern environmental movement in the United States and abroad.

In literary criticism, Leo Marx's *The Machine in the Garden: Technology and the Pastoral Ideal in America* (1964) explored the inherent tension between America's love affair with myths of the pastoral, or natural, world, and ever-increasing industrialization. Similarly, in *The Country and the City* (1973), the British cultural critic Raymond Williams (see Chapter 19) examined how nature is transformed by human commerce and culture, often operating as a mythical counterpart to the modern psyche.

Both the United States and Britain, of course, already had a long history of exploring environmental issues in and through literature.

It's Writing, Naturally

According to some ecocritics, the first instance of nature writing in the Western tradition—and one that actually set a bad precedent—was the statement in the Bible that man was to have "dominion over the fish of the sea, and over the fowl of the air, and over the cattle, and over all the earth, and over every creeping thing that creepeth upon the earth." Other early examples include ancient Greek pastoral poems, which sang the praises of nature, and Renaissance poetry and drama, which often contrasted busy city life with the repose and magical quality of the country, such as in Shakespeare's *A Midsummer Night's Dream.*

Ecocritics, however, have generally pointed to nineteenth-century traditions in the United States and Great Britain for the most influential examples of writing that really takes nature seriously. Such writing offers detailed descriptions of the environment, particularly as it appeared to the author and affected the author's life.

In this regard, the American transcendentalist movement is significant. Transcendentalists such as Ralph Waldo Emerson (1803–1882), Margaret Fuller (1810–1850), and Henry David Thoreau (1817–1862) saw nature and humanity as inherently good, and there was no need for organized religion or moral institutions to lead people to live better lives. All you need, according to the transcendentalists, is self-reliance, optimism, and a heightened sense of natural details.

For Emerson, the human mind was naturally inclined to the divine, if only you could live simply and clearly in sympathy with the natural forces that surround you: "See this divinity of daisies around us. Can we not be level to them? What need is there of miracles?" Writing and thinking should therefore be organic extensions of nature and not dictated by strict forms. Writers should write so that their minds ensure "an order of expression which is the order of nature itself."

Perhaps the most prominent work of nature writing for early ecocriticism was Thoreau's *Walden; or, Life in the Woods* (1854). In this book, Thoreau recorded his two-year stay in a tiny hut near Walden Pond in Massachusetts. The book describes details of the surrounding environment as well as Thoreau's own activities as he kept up his simple housekeeping.

IN THEORY

"Perhaps the commonest attraction of environmental writing is that it increases our feel for both places previously unknown and places known but never so deeply felt. The activation of place-sense that comes with this vicarious insidership is apt to subside quickly, however, unless it is repeatedly jogged … we tend to lapse into comfortable inattentiveness toward the details of our surroundings as we go about our daily business." —Lawrence Buell

And while Thoreau stayed at Walden Pond in order to experience the kind of primal immediacy that Emerson advocated, all you aspiring nature writers should take note that Thoreau spent five years writing and revising the story of his two-year experiment. As the editors of *The Harper Single Volume American Literature* have wryly put it, "with extreme consciousness of effort," Thoreau "mastered a language of spontaneity."

However it was achieved, Thoreau's effective prose has continued to inspire. Buell, for example, explained that Thoreau's nature writing "keeps environmental perceptiveness activated by shuttling back and forth" between reporting what sound like objective facts and throwing in "whimsical twists" that defamiliarize those facts, such as describing muskrats as people and people as muskrats.

APPLY IT

If you're looking for an alternative or complement to Thoreau's *Walden,* consider the 1850 nature diary, *Rural Hours,* written by Susan Fenimore Cooper (1813–1894, daughter of James Fenimore Cooper, author of *The Last of the Mohicans*).

In Britain, as we've seen in Chapter 8, the Romantic poet-critics spent a lot of time and ink exploring nature and its importance to human beings. The British critic Jonathan Bate has pointed out, however, that literary criticism has often overlooked or downplayed the actual environmental emphasis of the Romantics' writing. Critics, according to Bate, have rushed to transform the natural images of poetry by Wordsworth, Coleridge, and Keats into metaphors for everything except nature. For example, Bates argued that while Marxist critics have viewed the personification of nature in Wordsworth's *Prelude* as a device for talking about politics, Bate sees nature in Wordsworth's poem representing, well, nature.

Ecocritics have generally pointed out, in fact, how often nature is seen only as a metaphor for something else in literature. *Walden,* for example, has been read as a political critique, and Mark Twain's Mississippi river has been interpreted politically as well. Nathaniel Hawthorne's *The Scarlet Letter* and "Young Goodman Brown" prominently feature images of the forest, yet critics tend to focus only on the allegorical significance of the forest as a place to face your demons rather than, as the ecocritics would prefer, exploring the forest imagery in greater and more literal detail.

On the other hand, as Buell has argued, the natural settings of some literary works manage to bring nature to you as an active force, and with an ecologically responsible sense of the reciprocal relationship between the human and the nonhuman. In Thomas Hardy's *Return of the Native* (1878), for example, Buell says the famous setting of Egdon Heath is given "an aboriginal personhood" that clearly acts as a "potent force" in the novel, influencing character development and not simply serving as background. Nevertheless, Buell has noted that despite the active role given to nature in the novel, "Hardy barely scratched the surface" when it came to really discussing the setting's actual ecosystem, which, while fictional in name, was based on an actual place.

Portrait of the Land as a Young Woman

Speaking of settings, just check out that landscape. Which one? Just look anywhere, because what you'll see is a landscape, if that's what you're looking for. According to ecocriticism, nature is nature, but a landscape, like a weed, is really in the eye of the beholder.

As Alison Byerly has explained, Western civilization has a long tradition of turning natural entities into aesthetic objects for consumption. The picturesque movement in late-eighteenth-century European art, for example, featured carefully balanced compositions of natural scenes, and tourists would even travel (long before cameras) with curved, tinted mirrors that produced the proper look of a natural scene in a single "shot."

Recalling Raymond Williams (see Chapter 19), Byerly explained that while nature has been exploited for its material resources, it's also been exploited for its aesthetic value and treated as a commodity, such as treating the Grand Canyon as art and exploiting it as a tourist destination. Regarding the U.S. National Park Service in general, Byerly argued that "the aestheticization of landscape permits the viewer to define and control the scene, yet fosters the illusion that the scene is part of self-regulating nature."

IN THEORY

"Naturally the question suggests itself, Why did these people want the river now when nobody had wanted it in the five preceding generations? Apparently it was because at this late day they thought they had discovered a way to make it useful." —Mark Twain, *Life on the Mississippi*

Blending ecocriticism with feminist approaches, ecofeminists have argued that one of the most prevalent of all metaphors that transform the natural environment into an object for observation, consumption, and control is the idea of the wilderness as a refuge for men.

In wilderness romances, for example, it's the men (or even more often the adolescent boys) who must strike out into the wilderness in order to prove themselves and escape the feminizing influence of civilization. Think of Twain's *The Adventures of Huckleberry Finn*, James Feminore Cooper's *Leatherstocking* tales, or Melville's *Moby Dick*.

Meanwhile, argue ecofeminists, another metaphor has been just as prominent, which is the view that mastering nature means mastering women. Judith Fetterley (see

Chapter 12) has argued that the American wilderness is often depicted as a female to be tamed. From this perspective, it's culture and rational, masculinist knowledge that prevails over nature's irrational femininity, and as the ecocritic William Howarth has written, "The dogma that culture will always master nature has long directed Western progress."

Critic Annette Kolodny went even further by highlighting the sexual subtext for much male-authored American literature. Her 1975 book, *The Lay of the Land* (yes, the pun is intended), explores how images of American domination, exploitation, and control are gendered. In her work, Kolodny also refers to the influential *Eros and Civilization* (1955), written by Herbert Marcuse, one of the key members of the Frankfurt school (see Chapter 19).

IN THEORY

"America's oldest and most cherished fantasy: a daily reality of harmony between man and nature based on an experience of the land as essentially feminine— that is, not simply the land as mother, but the land as woman, the total female principle of gratification—enclosing the individual in an environment of receptivity, repose, and painless and integral satisfaction." —Annette Kolodny

Ecocritic Vera L. Norwood has summarized Kolodny's views, as well as those of historian Richard Slotkin, by explaining that "masculine culture in America characteristically sees wilderness as a place for defining virility, for playing out aggressive, adventure-seeking, sometimes violent impulses," and, in fact, "women were thought to be more comfortable in rural, cultivated nature—in civilized gardens." Norwood has also pointed out, however, that women writers such as Isabella Bird, Mary Austin, Rachel Carson, and Annie Dillard complicate the equation by showing how "women have acted as heroines in preserving the natural environment so central to American culture."

Varieties of Ecocritical Experience

Appropriately enough, one set of questions that ecocritics consider involves their relationship with other approaches in the environment of literary theory itself. The Canadian ecocritic Anne Milne has explained that contemporary theory, despite its emphasis on the textuality of all experience, is not entirely at odds with ecocriticism's insistence on the real. Specifically, theory's critical view of master narratives, binary oppositions, and other skeptical approaches to the human construction of reality speak directly to social constructions of nature as well. By investigating what Milne calls the "ecological imagination," ecocriticism invites collaboration with new historicism, cultural studies, ethnic studies, psychoanalysis, deconstruction, and postcoloniality.

Seeing But Not Scene

Since its inception, ecocriticism has been significantly influenced by Native American studies. Take the issue of landscapes as just one example of productive comparative critique.

The Native American writer Leslie Marmon Silko has shown, in fiction as well as criticism, that for Native American culture there exists no break between the land and any inhabitant of that land. The European idea of standing back to observe a landscape—and, as we've seen, the impulse to take ownership of and control that landscape—simply does not follow from a Native American approach to the land. According to this view, observer and observed fuse together when you understand the true nature of reality.

IN THEORY

"So long as the human consciousness remains *within* the hills, canyons, cliffs, and the plants, clouds, and sky, the term landscape, as it has entered the English language, is misleading. … Viewers are as much a part of the landscape as the boulders they stand on." —Leslie Marmon Silko

In addition, the symbolic value of "woman as land" is disrupted by a Native American ecology as well. In an essay appearing in a volume pointedly titled *The Desert is No Lady*, Patricia Clark Smith (1943–2010) and Paula Gunn Allen (1939–2008) have explained that "for natives the land encompasses butterfly and ant, man and woman, adobe wall and gourd vine, trout beneath the river water, rattler deep in his winter den," and all of this is "beyond human domination." Women, therefore, are viewed as an affirming part of nature, not an image of nature available for appropriation and manipulation.

Collective Energies

The critic William Rueckert (the guy responsible, in fact, for coining the term *ecocriticism* in 1978), vigorously advocated seeing poetry and all literature as a source of power. Literary works, according to Rueckert, are like "renewable fossil fuels," since they release stored energy and yet never become depleted.

IN THEORY

"Reading, teaching, and critical discourse all release the energy and power stored in poetry so that it may flow through the human community." —William Rueckert

Rueckert's own recommendations for getting the most out of this literary energy include checking out the poetry of Adrienne Rich's *Diving into the Wreck*, W. S. Merwin's *The Lice*, and Walt Whitman's *Song of Myself*, as well as the prose of William Faulkner's *Absalom, Absalom!* and, of course, Thoreau's *Walden*.

Other ecocritics who have explored theoretical intersections include SueEllen Campbell, who linked post-structuralism with ecocriticism by showing how both approaches see identity only in relations (hard to get away from Saussure, isn't it? See Chapter 11 for more). Campbell has also linked ecocriticism with the Lacanian principle of fundamental loss as the basis of desire (see Chapter 18), since "ecologists also see an experience of lost unity and a desire to regain it as central to our human nature."

Michael J. McDowell has argued that Bakhtin's theories (see Chapter 20) reflect many of the central concerns of ecocriticism. For example, the multivoiced and dialectic form of literature that Bakhtin valued seems perfectly suited for the ecocritics' view of a world in which no single species dominates.

IN THEORY

"The ideal form to represent reality, according to Bakhtin, is a dialogical form, one in which multiple voices or points of view interact. … Beginning with the idea that all entities in the great web of nature deserve recognition and a voice, an ecological literary criticism might explore how authors have represented the interaction of both the human and nonhuman voices in the landscape." —Michael J. McDowell

McDowell has also explained how Bakhtin's notion of the chronotope (see Chapter 20 again) offers a valuable theoretical tool for analyzing the essential unity of time and place in nature writing. You can have your chronotopes of rooms and SUVs and the specific atmospheres they create; ecocritics will run with the chronotope of the river, the hill, the tree limb, or that spot at the end of the leaf where a butterfly stands, looking, I might say, like a tiny open book.

The Least You Need to Know

- Ecocriticism advocates reading as a means of raising your consciousness of the global environmental crisis.
- Nature writing has a long history of exploring the relationship between the human and the nonhuman.
- A landscape is an aesthetic creation of the human observer.
- Nature and images of the wilderness have been associated with femininity in negative as well as positive ways.
- Native American perspectives on the natural world emphasize symbiosis and unity rather than separation and dominance.
- Ecocritical interpretations of literature can incorporate a wide variety of critical approaches and literary theories.

Glossary

aestheticism   The idea that art, beauty, and your artistic responses offer ways of knowing that differ from rational knowledge.

aesthetics   The study of beauty and artistic taste.

affect   An emotional response.

antagonist   The character or force of opposition in a story.

anti-foundationalism   The view that truth is not grounded in any kind of absolute essence but is contingent or conditional.

approach   The perspective you take or interests you have in mind when considering a literary work.

audism   The prejudicial idea that hearing and vocal communication are necessary for a full life.

binary opposition   A contrast between two mutually exclusive terms. Deconstructionists argue that the contrast is never neutral because one term is always privileged over the other.

canon   The set of literary or other artistic works deemed by any particular group as particularly worthy of merit and study.

catachresis   For deconstructionists, the use of a metaphor (such as table *leg*) for which there seems no alternative. Also generally defined as a forced or contradictory metaphor (such as *blind mouths*).

catharsis   (1) The purging or release of emotion you feel while experiencing a fictional narrative. (2) The purification of your emotions as a fiction leads you to fear and pity the "correct" things. (3) The clarification that occurs when fiction reveals the logic behind tragic events.

character   In a literary work, any figure or personage, whether human or not.

collective unconscious   Psychiatrist Carl Jung's term for humanity's shared psychic memories and deep primordial images.

conflict   Any struggle or confrontation between characters or forces.

constructionism   The view that identity (particularly gender identity) is not essential or biologically determined, but is a product of social forces.

critical theory   A term originally coined by the Frankfurt school critics to refer to their Marxist approach to cultural analysis. Now it is often used to refer to literary and cultural critique in general.

critique   An act of critical analysis or judgment.

Deaf   When spelled with a capital letter, this refers to people who identify as part of the Deaf community, shaped by shared culture and the linguistic difference of sign language.

decentering   Advocated by post-structuralists, the undermining of a traditional center that stabilizes the logic of a system. Freud, for example, decentered traditional views of identity by calling into question the exclusive power of the conscious mind.

deconstruction   A critical approach to philosophical assumptions and a method of revealing internal contradictions in literary and cultural texts.

demystification   The act of exposing the hidden steps, stages, or processes in cultural exchanges.

device   Any specific literary technique, such as parallelism.

dialectic   (1) The conversational nature of Socrates' teaching. (2) A process of transformation involving thesis, antithesis, and synthesis, often featured in Marxist criticism.

diegesis   A narrative, rather than an imitative (or mimetic) account of something. An instance of telling rather than showing.

discourse   In general, any use of speech and writing. In cultural studies and post-structuralism (following Foucault), discourse refers to the rules and conventions that reveal communication to be always caught up in social power relations.

emplotment   Organizing things into a narrative or story line.

Enlightenment   The late-seventeenth- and early-eighteenth-century intellectual movement emphasizing the power of reason.

essentialism   The view that identity and human differences are biologically or spiritually determined and fixed.

exposition   The setting out of background or other explanatory information in a narrative.

fallacy   A false belief or an error in reasoning.

figurative language   Speech, such as metaphors, not used to convey literal meaning.

focalization   In fiction and film, the focusing of point of view through (not on) a particular character.

form   (1) The general type or genre of literary works, such as the form of the sonnet. (2) That aspect of a literary work involving its structure, technique, and component parts.

gender   The social construction of sexual identity.

hegemony   The power projected by dominant economic, cultural, and ideological systems.

heteroglossia   Bakhtin's term for the multiple voices that can be discerned in a single narrative.

idealism   In Plato's philosophy, the view that truth is present only in abstract ideas or concepts. For the Romantics, the view that the imagination can get you closer to truth than reason alone can.

ideology   (1) Consciously held political beliefs. (2) The false system of beliefs that arises to obscure real political and economic exploitation.

imagery   The use of language to evoke visual images as well as feelings, thoughts, and any aspect of the senses.

imaginary order   Lacan's term for the dimension of the human psyche that relies on an image of the self.

inform   To influence or shape the development of something, such as a theory informing a particular interpretation.

internalize   To make any philosophy, ideology, or viewpoint part of your "natural" way of seeing things.

interpellation   Althusser's term for being absorbed into an ideological system.

intertextuality   Any instance of an intersecting relationship or series of relationships among and between literary and cultural texts.

irony   The contrast between an intended meaning or situation and an opposite or unexpected result.

MacGuffin   In movies and fiction, anything (typically unimportant for its own sake) that serves as a central object of desire and prompts the development of plot.

materialism   The view that truth is present only in material objects and actions, as opposed to idealism.

metafiction   Fiction about fiction, or any narrative that emphasizes self-consciousness regarding its fictional nature.

metaphysics   The kind of philosophy that investigates "first principles" or the truths that underlie existence.

mimesis   Imitation or representation in art and literature.

motif   Any repeated element, such as a recurring image, that establishes a pattern.

mystification   As used by Marxist critics, the process of obscuring actual economic and political motivations to make the results seem natural.

neo-Aristotelian   Loosely describes critics who advocate developing theories organically out of actual literary examples.

neoclassicism   The idea that literature, art, and criticism should follow models set by ancient Greek and Roman (or "classical") writers.

paradox   A self-contradictory statement or situation.

parallelism   Any instance of similar phrasing or imagery that forms a balanced pattern.

parody   An imitation intended to mock or ridicule.

pastiche   An imitation or aggregation of past styles, texts, or images.

patriarchy   A social structure privileging men or paternal authority.

plot   The arrangement of events in a narrative.

poetics   A set of principles describing the features and functioning of any form of literature.

positive meaning   Self-sufficient meaning, in contrast to *relational meaning*.

post-structuralism   A critical response to the structuralist project of objective, scientific analysis, resulting in a rejection of universalist foundations. Often associated with deconstruction.

postcolonial   As a general term, this describes anything involving colonial contact, from its beginnings to independence to the present.

protagonist   Often, the main character in a story, or the character that readers most likely identify with.

queer   A term that spent a lot of time as a derogatory label for homosexuals, but which has been redirected by cultural critics to describe the socially constructed nature of all forms of sexuality.

real   Lacan's term for the dimension of existence that forever escapes human subjectivity.

reification   The ideological and mystifying process of reducing a whole series of social connections into one object or product.

relational meaning   Meaning that emerges only when one thing is seen in relation to another, such as a color in the spectrum.

resolution   The wrapping up of a plot, but also a text's concluding statement or position regarding any central theme.

Romanticism   Very broad term that generally describes a view of art emphasizing the imaginative and expressive aspects of the artist.

semiology   Saussure's term for the study of sign systems.

semiotic   Kristeva's term for the state of consciousness in humans before language takes over.

semiotics   Peirce's term for the study of sign systems.

sign   Saussure's term for a linguistic entity (including but not limited to words) that links signifiers (sound images) with signifieds (concepts) and serves as the basis of language and thought.

Signifyin(g)   Gates's term for an African American literary tradition that emphasizes the figurative rather than literal use of language.

socialist realism   An early-twentieth-century movement expressly designed by Communist Party leaders to bring revolutionary messages to the masses by highlighting optimistic and heroic depictions of socialist society.

structuralism   A project of the objective, scientific analysis of structures and systems in language and literature.

subject   Used to describe a person seen to be under the control of or abiding by a particular philosophical, political, or theological system, such as the "fully conscious Cartesian subject" or the "Freudian subject."

sublime   A feeling or reaction beyond rational thought and even beyond "normal" imagination. Can be used as a noun or an adjective.

symbolic order   Lacan's term for the dimension of the human psyche dependent on and controlled by language.

text   Used generally as a term for any literary work. Also, a specialized term, used in deconstruction, to highlight the endless intertextuality of any work of literature.

theme   A literary work's main issue or statement.

theory of mind   The ability of people to infer and interpret other people's internal states of mind.

transcendentalism   A movement most closely associated with nineteenth-century American writers featuring a belief in the close relationship between humans, nature, and the divine, and a skepticism toward organized religious doctrine.

trope   Any figure of speech.

universal   Used to describe any principle or philosophy that is assumed to be true in all cases. Universality is opposed by much literary theory that sees truth as dependent on cultural factors.

writing   Derrida's specialized term describing the endless intertextuality and ambiguity at work in language and thought.

Index

C

N